What people are saying about …

# 30 Ways in 30 Days to Strengthen Your Family

"I have great appreciation and respect for Rebecca Hagelin. She is a bestselling author and speaker, a passionate defender of the institution of the family, and a committed conservative leader. Rebecca is the former vice president of the Heritage Foundation and a passionate defender of life from conception to the grave. Rebecca is also a valuable member of the board of directors at Family Talk. It is an honor to call Rebecca Hagelin my friend."

**James C. Dobson, PhD,** founder
and president of Family Talk

"One of the biggest concerns parents express to me as a pediatrician is fear that their children will be swallowed whole by a hypersexualized, violent, and twisted culture. The brilliance of Rebecca Hagelin's book is that it gives effective tools to parents from a sound world-view and this blend serves to assuage their fears beautifully."

**Meg Meeker, MD,** bestselling author
of *Strong Fathers, Strong Daughters*

"Parents need help, and not the sort of help that comes from books and speeches that are long on meditation and reflection. They need practical ideas to do real things to protect and serve their children, and that's Rebecca Hagelin's specialty. This is a book that will change how you parent your children—for the better and immediately."

**Hugh Hewitt,** *New York Times* bestselling
author and nationally syndicated talk-show host

"Rebecca Hagelin's book provides a series of bold, radical, and refreshingly practical recommendations for bringing parents closer to their children. This world's popular culture seems perversely determined to divide the generations, and Rebecca shows a way to protect your family and win your children's hearts in the process."

**Michael Medved,** national talk-radio host and
bestselling author of *The 10 Big Lies about America*

# 30 ways *in* 30 days *to* strengthen your family

# 30 ways *in* 30 days *to* strengthen your family

## rebecca hagelin

David C Cook®
*transforming lives together*

30 WAYS IN 30 DAYS TO STRENGTHEN YOUR FAMILY
Published by David C Cook
4050 Lee Vance View
Colorado Springs, CO 80918 U.S.A.

David C Cook Distribution Canada
55 Woodslee Avenue, Paris, Ontario, Canada N3L 3E5

David C Cook U.K., Kingsway Communications
Eastbourne, East Sussex BN23 6NT, England

The graphic circle C logo is a registered trademark of David C Cook.

LCCN 2016931546
ISBN 978-1-4347-1037-6
eISBN 978-0-7814-1477-7

© 2016 Rebecca Hagelin
Published in association with the literary agency of Wolgemuth & Associates, Inc.
First edition published by Regnery Publishing in 2009 © Rebecca Hagelin,
ISBN 978-0-5969-8568-1, *30 Ways in 30 Days to Save Your Family*

The Team: Ingrid Beck, Alice Crider, Amy Konyndyk, Tiffany Thomas, Susan Murdock
Cover Design: Nick Lee

Printed in the United States of America
Second Edition 2016

1 2 3 4 5 6 7 8 9 10

022916

# CONTENTS

# Foreword

Remember when you first laid eyes on your newborn baby? Remember how tiny and vulnerable he seemed or how determined you were to always protect her? Most parents pray their children will grow up to be strong, productive, and patriotic, with a robust moral sense.

But as soon as you bring your children into the world, others try to pry them from you. Crass marketers try to lure them into commercialism. "Experts," from doctors to teachers, try to replace your good values with theirs. When we in the media talk about the culture wars, what we're really talking about is the battle for our kids' hearts and minds.

When my friend Rebecca Hagelin first released *30 Ways in 30 Days to Save Your Family*, it brought the ammunition that all of us, as parents, long needed. Now her updated version—with a slightly changed title—includes current research, updates on technology, and the latest contact information for organizations and resources to help you raise children of character. And the best part about this new edition is that it contains reflections from Rebecca's daughter, Kristin Carey. Kristin is a beautiful young woman in her early twenties who provides insight from a young person's perspective on each of the issues covered in the book. Kristin's words will further inspire you to be true to your calling as a mom or dad, to fight for your children, and to love them well. The book also contains a bonus chapter on marriage, jointly authored by Rebecca, who has been married to Andy for thirty years, and by Kristin, who is newly wed to Randy. The chapter provides encouragement and hope for all generations, regardless of where you are in your journey through marriage.

Rebecca and Kristin have given us the perfect guide, the perfect handbook, to keep a toxic culture at bay while forging a closer, deeper, more meaningful relationship with our spouses and children.

I've known Rebecca for many years, and her knowledge about cultural issues, the media, and the pressures on today's families and kids is vast. She's also a loving, committed wife and mother and a marketing wizard. Her writings and speeches have encouraged many parents and families over the years, including mine. But what marks her most is her undying faith in God, forgiveness, and the hope that each new day brings. Even though her message is a somber one, Rebecca's spirit is lighthearted and optimistic—and her book provides practical solutions that, if put into practice, will strengthen each member of your family as well as the unit as a whole.

*30 Ways in 30 Days to Strengthen Your Family* breaks down common parenting problems into manageable pieces and provides practical solutions that any frazzled parent can easily put to use. It is designed for today's parents combatting today's problems; I'm sure it will speak to you as it spoke to me.

This is the handbook I wish America had years ago. Reading this book gave me hope—both as a father and as a concerned citizen. Read and use Rebecca's strategies, and you can become the parent you always wanted to be.

—*Sean Hannity*

# Introduction

I came very close to not writing this book.

How could I, an imperfect mother with an imperfect record, have the moral authority to even suggest to other parents how to raise their kids? Shortly after my first book, *Home Invasion: Protecting Your Family in a Culture That's Gone Stark Raving Mad*, hit the bookstores, a very high-profile writer for whom I have great respect said, "Rebecca, I saw your book in the window of the bookstore. Wow. You have a lot of guts—you have kids who can still embarrass you. You're very brave—or very foolish—to write a book on parenting."

Her words stung more than she realized. Yes, I do have three children who are living testaments to all the great successes—and great mistakes—I've made as a parent. And, yes, I have made many, many blunders. But I let that comment play over in my head one too many times, and soon I began to doubt whether I had any right to try to help any parent do anything. Despite the many moving letters from parents thanking me for the tips, in spite of the warm embraces I received from moms, dads, and even teens who attended speeches I made across the country, the fear that I would be shamed as a flawed parent started building in my heart and mind. Why on earth would I write a second book?

Please understand, I have great kids. My doubts were not about them. Drew, Nick, and Kristin are precious blessings. I so admire the young men and young lady they have become. When this book was first released, they were twenty-one, nineteen, and sixteen—all old enough to know the difference between right and wrong, yet still young enough to make serious mistakes that could affect the rest of their lives. Now they are twenty-eight, twenty-six, and twenty-three, and I still pray every day that they will make the right decisions, but I have to keep front and center in my mind that it's totally up to them to make all their own choices.

However, I can tell you this one thing for certain: they have been taught what is right and what is wrong. They left our home and entered adulthood with a strong moral compass—one that can clearly help them find their way—but it is up to them to decide to use it or not. My husband and I did our very best to pass on our understanding of truth as God gave us the ability to see it. While by no means did we impart the messages perfectly or always wisely, we always, always did so with hearts completely captivated by immense love for each of them. I pray every day that our love and efforts to do right by our kids were enough to send them on their way well equipped to live fulfilled lives marked by kindness, generosity, happiness, and a passion for Christ. I also constantly pray that where I failed, God's grace will be sufficient to wash away any lingering effects of my errors and leave behind only cherished memories and sound advice that each of them can call on for a lifetime.

Truth is a powerful tool. As parents, we have the obligation to step up to the plate and share what we know to be true with our kids. Too many moms and dads seem to be so concerned with image or political correctness that they fail to teach their kids what is noble, just, pure, and true. And I believe we have an obligation to help each other out too. We parents aren't looking for the "perfect mom" or "perfect dad" to emulate. We are looking for help, validation, and formulas that have worked for others. I have been blessed with a unique opportunity to share what I have learned with moms and dads who don't want to miss the obvious or make mistakes just because they didn't know any better. I now believe that to be silent about what I have learned, about what I know to be true, would be immoral—something akin to a pediatrician withholding a medicine that he knows will help someone else's child just because his own kids still get sick too.

I know there are plenty of parents who have wisdom to share, so in my column, now jointly authored by Kristin, that is carried by the *Washington Times*, Townhall.com, *The Patriot Post*, and other sites and papers across the country, I invited moms and dads to send in their own insights and tips on the thirty subjects I chose to write about. The emails came flooding in, and what you now hold in your hands is a work to which many of them contributed. In order to protect the privacy of people whose stories I share, I used only first names and in some cases even changed those. I also edited some of the comments for clarity and brevity.

In addition to advice from other parents, I wanted input from my children—some assurance that what I wrote is authentic and actually works. So I involved Drew, Nick, and Kristin in the process. However, I will say up front that the inmates did not take over the asylum! And because they have never been parents—especially not parents of *themselves*—I didn't incorporate *all* their changes or suggestions. I did, however, listen carefully, cry a few tears at the mistakes I made in raising them, and incorporate lessons learned from the school of hard knocks.

Drew and Nick gave pretty blunt feedback—and I thank them with all my heart for it. We've always had a very close relationship, and I've loved every minute of being the mom of my two boys. Drew and Nick, I'm so proud of the young men you have become and so very thankful that you have followed your passions and are pursuing the unique talents God has given each of you. Thanks for letting me hug on you endlessly throughout your childhood, and thank you for the ways you have shown your love to me.

When asked for specific points I should highlight, Drew, a pensive guy who is also blessed with a keen sense of humor and tons of creative talent, thought it was important for me to emphasize age-appropriateness in media consumption. In other words, to remind parents that movies or television shows that might be unsuitable for seven-year-olds might be perfectly fine for fifteen-year-olds. He also said he always believed my husband, Andy, and I didn't let him watch most R-rated flicks because we thought they would turn him into a bad person. My goodness! I discovered I had failed miserably in explaining to our children that the main reason we were selective in our media choices is that much of the content is just plain raunchy. Andy and I decided long ago that media content that violates our consciences and what we understand to be right would not be viewed in our household. It was heartbreaking to realize I had never adequately made the point that content can be wrong on its face. I suddenly remembered a saying my mother often used that illustrates the point: "I don't know why they call X-rated movies 'adult movies'—they aren't right for adults either!"

Drew also underscored something else—a critical insight that I hope you will take note of: the importance of being consistent in upholding the rules you have set. He said, "When a parent isn't consistent, their 'rules' don't appear to have any meaning behind them. They also aren't even useful in trying to teach anything. When standards are inconsistently applied to some situations and not others, it also makes the parents look like they are discriminating against specific individuals."

Of course, he's right. Consistency is probably the toughest skill to master as a parent—and one of the most important. We can't disregard our own values and standards just because we are tired, aren't in the mood to fight, or lose our courage. And we can't bend the rules for some people when there is a value or principle at stake. When we do, it confuses the tender hearts and minds that have been put in our care.

Nick has a spunky, argumentative streak and an entrepreneurial spirit, and he excels in design. As a child, he was always thinking past my next answer. He shared that it is important for parents to show a unified front on sensitive issues with their children. When my husband and I were firmly in agreement, even Nick would give up trying to outwit us. Nick also wanted me to give parents a warning: your kids will get annoyed with you when you make and enforce rules that others don't. However, he also said, "Now that I'm older I realize the importance of the standards and limits you set when we were kids." Wow. As a parent, that was very encouraging! Still, he also emphasized the importance of not having a lot of unnecessary and trivial rules.

Both boys reflected on the tremendous impact it had on their behavior when we trusted them. For instance, my husband and I have never been huge believers in arbitrary curfews. We always insisted on knowing where and with whom our kids were and on being able to contact them via their cell phones whenever we wanted to. (By the way, as far as I'm concerned, the purpose of giving a child or teen a cell phone is so that Mom and Dad can call when they want to. That's always been a hard and fast rule with me: when I call, you best answer the phone—or no more cell phone for you!) But we've never believed there was a magic bewitching hour they had to be home by. As long as they kept our trust and faith in them, they actually had more freedom than many of their peers. Drew summed up the impact that our faith in him had: "The fact that you and Dad thought we could handle ourselves and that I had your respect made me want to keep that respect. I definitely didn't want to violate the trust and do anything stupid. Knowing you trusted me helped me keep that trust. It's a much better system than having a bunch of meaningless rules."

Kristin was sixteen when this book first came out. At the time, she helped me edit much of the book and encouraged me to redraft several sections. A gifted writer and thoughtful young woman, Kristin was invaluable in keeping me motivated through very long days or when I was having difficulty expressing myself. She was inspiring and insightful throughout the process, and I incorporated many of her ideas and stories into the book. Since she was still living under our roof when I was working hard to pull this together, she got called on a lot for instant feedback, editing help, and assistance! She also graciously wrote her own brief introduction—I was very moved (and amused) upon reading it. I hope you enjoy it too.

*Having your mom write a book about parenting is absolutely terrifying.*

*When my mom started working on her second book, I knew I wanted to be involved. I think she assumed I was helping her because writing is one of my passions and because, for me, getting my hands a little messy in the production of a book is tasting a little bit of bliss. Or maybe she thought I wanted to make sure the ideas she was going to provide would make sense in the eyes of a teenager.*

*What I really wanted to do was save my name.*

*Sure, Mom said she wouldn't write anything that would embarrass me ... but this just might be the one thing I will never fully trust her on. This was coming from the woman who thinks it's okay to tell my friends naked baby stories.*

*I was going to be sneaky. I had a plan. I told her I was going to check for typos and make little suggestions about the wording of things. And I did. But, secretly, I was also making sure nothing got said that I didn't want said.*

*I think she caught on. She has a way of doing that. It's like moms can read minds sometimes. I can't wait until I'm a mom and I can read minds ... but that's beside the point.*

*The point is that as I was scanning the pages of her book, I realized why my mom is a superhero. (You can't blame me for being cheesy and saying things like that. She says cheesy things too, and I am her daughter. Besides, even when we say cheesy things, we mean them.) My mom is a superhero because her heart is in the right place and because when she finds things that make her come alive, she goes and does them. The way I see it, the world has two problems. The first problem is that we all let our hearts get wrapped up in the wrong places and, when we do, we forget about the things that really matter. The second problem is our fear, or timidity, or whatever it is that keeps us from chasing after the calling of our hearts once they are in the right place. My mom decided that the value of a strong family really matters to her, and she does everything in her power to preserve that value.*

*My world is a better place because she and my father dedicated themselves to providing my brothers and me with the best they could. They gave us everything we needed as kids, as maturing teenagers and young adults, as part of humanity, and as unique individuals. I believe the most important thing my parents gave us is their example. They showed us how to live, how to love, and what it means to have faith. I'm not sure if I could put into words why I believe their strong example has been so influential in my life, but one of my all-time favorite quotations does an amazing job of it. In his book* Blue Like Jazz *Donald Miller wrote, "I was outside the Bagdad Theater in Portland one night when I saw a man playing the saxophone. I stood there for fifteen minutes, and he never opened his eyes. After that I liked jazz music. Sometimes you have to watch somebody love something before you can love it yourself." I have grown up witnessing undying love and persistent belief. They come easy for me because I have seen them at work. My parents would never have had to tell me what the words love and faith mean, but they did that too.*

*Art comes from the soul of the artist. It doesn't shy away from challenging culture, and it doesn't try to match the standards of society. Art represents what the artist is trying to convey, but it never reaches perfection. Parenting is a strange and beautiful art form. I admire all parents who take up the role of the artist, who eagerly pursue their own potential and try to set an example for their children. I hope you will read this book and find inspiration, encouragement, technique, and an appreciation for the power of your own influence in the lives of your children.*

*Chances are that, even though I tried to prevent it, I'll turn a page in this book after it's published and blush. But I'm guessing I'll get over it pretty fast because it's really not that bad being embarrassed by a superhero.*

*And, Mom, that's not an invitation.*

Thanks, girlfriend! You're a treasure.

In updating this book for rerelease in 2016, I again called on Kristin to help. Now that she's a young married woman on her own (married to the best son-in-law in the world, Randy), I thought it would add an entirely new dimension to the book for her to write her reflections at the end of each chapter. Her words offer moms and dads an added bit of encouragement from a responsible young adult who lived through the processes outlined in the book. She also often presents a humorous "reality check" and gives a unique perspective on how she translated what Andy and I were trying to do in raising children of character. In addition, Kristin and I coauthored a brand-new chapter for this book—on marriage. We are two different women, from two different generations and perspectives, but we share an undying commitment to biblical principles. We seek to offer hope for every generation.

I also called for help from outside my family when writing the original text of this book. Two great writers in very different life stages helped me draft sections of the book and offered tremendous insights. The first, Ashley Samelson McGuire, then a young single woman, provided her perspective on the many pressures put on teens these days. Ashley is an amazing researcher and writer and has a brilliant future in whatever area she chooses. She is now married and is a terrific wife and mom in her own right! The second, Paul Gallagher, is a seasoned father of six and also an incredibly talented writer and editor. Paul and his wonderful wife, Cindy, have loads of insights to share on parenting—and their precious and respectful children prove just how wise their parenting is.

A very special thank-you from the depths of my heart goes out to Rebekah Coons. Bekah kept me organized and on schedule and helped me keep my sanity through many difficult days. She gave me the treasured gift of inspiration—one thing an author desperately needs when facing a looming deadline. She also shared a couple of very personal and moving stories about how her parents influenced and shaped her life. I know you will enjoy them.

Tori Ueltschi Barnett—then just Tori Ueltschi—was a super friend and helper during my book tour the first time around and a true source of inspiration throughout a very busy time in my life. She continues to be a great friend, and I absolutely love hearing of her joy as a wife and her adventures as a mother of three little ones!

I also owe a huge debt of gratitude to my "small group"—the folks Andy and I meet with nearly every Tuesday for Bible study and prayer. These dear friends prayed me through a lot of difficult times while I was writing the original book, and I will always be thankful to them for their friendship, spiritual guidance, and encouragement.

And finally, to my dear hubby, Andy—thank you from the depths of my soul for being such an honorable father to our children. You will always be my knight in shining armor and my "help meet."

You were critical in helping Kristin understand how to recognize the type of man who would make an excellent lifelong, loving spouse, which she found in Randy. I pray that all our children will one day have a marriage like ours, and I thank you—oh, thank you so very much—for your undying loyalty, love, and friendship.

*Chapter 1*
# Commit to the Daily Battle

## The Challenge

Fighting the modern culture on a daily basis is tough. Today's families are busier than ever, and it's so easy when you're tired or just plain worn out to throw in the towel and set your values aside. I know. I've been guilty of doing it myself sometimes. As a mother of three, I've had plenty of battles and challenges along the way. And I'm the first to admit that far too many times I've failed to uphold the standards I've said I believe in.

As parents, too many of us are so fearful of losing our battles that we never even try to win. Others give in or give up along the way. Many parents don't seem to realize that in today's world you must fight to protect your children's innocence, their childhood, their character, and their best futures. But it's a battle that's well worth fighting.

According to research done by the Motherhood Project of the Institute for American Values, "Ninety-five percent of mothers agreed they wish American culture made it easier to instill positive values in children." Over 80 percent of mothers "expressed concern about the influence of advertisements on children and, more generally, the influence of media." Over 85 percent of mothers also "agree with the statement 'money has too much control over our lives' and agree that childhood should be a time when children are protected from large parts of the adult world." So the question is, why aren't these same moms doing more to protect their own sons and daughters?

Of course, such concern over the pop culture's negative influence on our kids is nothing new. One of the main reasons I wrote *Home Invasion* and this book in the first place was the thousands of emails I have received over the years from parents who read my column. They express frustration, anger, and often helplessness—all powerful emotions in response to the continuous onslaughts from a culture that has gone stark raving mad.

We can't waste a single day. We have a very, very short time to mold our children's hearts and to develop their minds and thinking. Each day we fail to take the opportunities to forgive, discipline, and teach valuable life lessons is a day we will regret. Somewhere down the line our children will learn about consequences, some of which might cause quite severe and needless suffering, if we don't teach them about the results of their actions when we have the chance.

For those of you who are struggling to live up to your own standards, I offer a word of truth and encouragement. You can start today—and you can still win.

If you have only recently come to the realization that your kids need you in the battle with them, please don't despair over the days lost. You must remember that despair is not an option. Beating yourself up endlessly over past mistakes can rob you of the incredible beauty and opportunity of today. Yes, your challenges might be greater, but each new day offers a chance to start over again. I've heard it said that "parenthood is not a dress rehearsal. You get one chance to do it right." Although I believe that fully, it is equally important to remember that each morning offers a brand-new chance to reclaim your home, to touch your child's heart in a deep and meaningful way, and to teach lessons that will always guide them.

You might not be able to save the world, although it is a noble and worthwhile effort to try your best to influence the overall culture for the better. But you can—you must—work hard to protect your family. It doesn't take an act of Congress to make your home the nurturing environment it was intended to be. It does take developing a loving relationship with your children, making a commitment to the daily battle, and upholding a pledge to become more involved in your kids' daily lives.

We've got to teach our children sound values at home so that when they are confronted with damaging messages outside the home they can recognize them as such and know how to reject them. It's also imperative that we teach our children that our battle is not with them; it is with other adults who have a different worldview and care nothing about their futures.

Let's be clear: adults create and operate the hard-core porn sites; adults own the music companies that produce sexist, racist, and violent music; adults are the ones spamming your child's email account with porn; adults are the ones who allow the popular sites that kids visit, such as YouTube, to be filled with obscene material; and adults are spending billions of dollars on oversexualized marketing campaigns aimed at your kids.

As I've said before, the problem isn't with "kids today"; the problem is with adults today.

We must teach our kids character and values, principles of courage, how to say no, and how to rise above the pop culture that seeks to do them harm. Moms and dads, if you don't stand in the gap for your kids, nobody will.

I'm not talking about building walls around your children to shut them off from the rest of the world. I'm talking about building strength of character within your children so they will know how to make the right decisions when they go out the door every day into a world filled with chaos.

Days build upon days. They become weeks, months, and years. And before you know it, your child is walking down the graduation aisle and out your door. When that time comes, you will be grateful for every moment you spent with your sons and daughters. As a mom of three grown children, I can absolutely testify that one day you will relish every second you spent with them. And you will be so very thankful for every day that you awoke with a heart purposed toward your children and their upbringing. You will never, ever regret the time you spend with your children, but you will mourn the days you missed. Vow to be engaged every day with your children. It is a vow that will serve you and them well.

# In Your Shoes

When our children were under my care, I woke up nearly every morning with a prayer to my Lord asking for the strength and commitment to uphold the values that my husband and I had set for our household. My prayer went something like this: "Dear God, please help me today—on this one day—to be the mom you have called me to be. To be brave for my children, to be discerning, loving, gentle, and firm. And to always remember that you are only a prayer away."

It seems that just when I started to get discouraged or give up, God sent me a little reminder that I was doing okay. One of my children, or their friends, would say or do something that reminded me they appreciated and even valued the tone we tried to establish in our household.

One night, quite a few years ago, we had about six or seven teenage boys hanging out at our home, as we usually did. My husband and I made a point of creating an atmosphere that reflected our belief that every child is special and welcome, and we came to truly love and value the children around us. We often stayed up very late with them on weekends, just talking. At around two a.m. (yes, that's two in the morning), one of the guys, Richard, said out of the blue, "Hey, guys, I feel so at home here. Isn't it wonderful how we can go to each other's houses and all feel like we are with our own families?"

I share this story with you because committing to the daily battle isn't about being confrontational all the time. It's about upholding standards and morality in such a way that all the children who come into your home feel as if they are truly loved—as if they are part of a family that cares about them enough to challenge the status quo. If you have the right demeanor and attitude about enforcing rules of civility and respect and morality in your home, the tone of your home will be one of comfort. The environment of your home will be safe. And your kids and their friends will want to hang out there.

# From My Home to Yours

Since I've asked you to fight the culture war every single day, it would probably be decent of me to offer a few practical tools for your arsenal.

- Physically love your children every day. (Read more about this in chapter 19, "Teach Your Children Every Day That They Have God-Given Value.")
- When you take something away, replace it with something better.
- Respect your children's maturity. In other words, understand and consider what age-appropriate material is. A movie that should be forbidden for your ten-year-old might be perfectly acceptable for your sixteen-year-old.
- Never expect that you have to "go it alone." But at the same time, be prepared to do so. Look for allies in the battle, but don't stop doing the right thing when you find you are the only one who feels something is not right for your children.
- Set time as well as content limits on media. Remember, both the quantity of media our kids consume and the poor quality of the material can hurt them.
- Spend as much time as possible actually engaging your children in conversation.
- Laugh. A lot. Default to laughter when possible.

- When tears flow from the eyes of your children, always wipe them away. Do so with a tender touch and humility.

- Never, ever storm from the room in anger. Remember, you are the adult. It is your responsibility to act like one.

- If your teenager storms from your presence into her bedroom, give her awhile to calm down. Then gently knock on the door and insist on talking. But never, ever let the sun go down on her, or your, wrath. And never let an angry teen leave the home—especially if he is driving.

- When you mess up, miss the mark, or make an error in judgment, always apologize to your kids and ask their forgiveness.

- When your kids mess up and say they are sorry, never withhold your forgiveness and grace. Remember, they are learning about God's grace and mercy by watching you.

- Set content standards for your home and stick with them—no matter how tired you are.

- Watch television and movies with your children. When objectionable material comes up, discuss it with them. Remember, you don't need to shield them from everything. Your goal should be to help them develop discernment and judgment in gradual increments so they can go out on their own and make moral and healthy decisions.

You'll find plenty of other tips to help you in the daily battle in chapter 5, "Make Your Home Inviting, Warm, and … Fun!"

# Reflections from a Daughter

Thomas Merton wrote in his book *Seeds of Contemplation* that "every moment and every event of every man's life on earth plants something in his soul. For just as the wind carries thousands of invisible and visible winged seeds, so the stream of time brings with it germs of spiritual vitality that come to rest imperceptibly in the minds and wills of men."

When I think back to my childhood, I am often surprised at the things I remember. On the surface level, they are seemingly random scenes stitched together by a general sense of how my childhood felt. But as I dig deeper, I uncover attitudes, beliefs, judgments, and abilities that originated from the impressions those experiences left upon my mind and soul.

For example, I have a very faint memory of riding in the bucket seat on the back of my dad's bicycle, and another of him teaching me to ride my own bike. Later, I remember sitting in his lap in his Mazda with my hands on the steering wheel as we drove down our quiet neighborhood road. When I was in middle school, we took a trip out West, and he let me drive the car through the desert.

The general feeling those memories give me is a calm sense of adventure: the excitement of something dangerous combined with the comfort of my dad's strong presence. And when I look closer, I see the lasting influence of these memories. Throughout it all, my dad was building my confidence, teaching me not to be afraid of things, even if they were activities typically reserved for older kids.

Everything about the way my parents raised me—educationally, behaviorally, morally, and so forth—showed me that they believed I could excel and instilled in me the sentiment expressed in 1 Timothy 4:12: "Don't let anyone think less of you because you are young. Be an example to all believers in what you say, in the way you live, in your love, your faith, and your purity" (NLT).

The little memories you create for your children add up to become a great shaping force in their lives.

# Act Now

Date _____

Today I pledged that every day from now on I will fight for my children and their futures. I will not back down. I will not grow so weary that I give up. And I will remember that, above all else, my goal is to show my children that I love them enough to dare to challenge the status quo.

Signature _____

# More Help

At the fantastic site **Grow Together (growtogether.org)**, Jeff Myers, president of Summit Ministries, offers a plan and real help in the battle for our children's lives, their very souls. Jeff helps parents and churches reconcile generations, teaching them how to break down generational barriers and develop meaningful lifelong relationships.

The resources available at his site include a discussion-starter film and book called *Grow Together: The Forgotten Story of How Uniting the Generations Unleashes Epic Spiritual Potential.* The content is deeply compelling and divided into simple, manageable steps.

Sean Hannity's great book ***Let Freedom Ring: Winning the War of Liberty over Liberalism*** will help prepare you to teach your children the fundamental principles and values that make our country great, in light of the unique challenges we currently face.

Ryan Dobson, cohost of *Family Talk* and noted speaker on issues of the family, has a fantastic book every parent should read: ***Wanting to Believe: Faith, Family, and Finding an Exceptional Life***. Ryan shares poignant stories from his childhood and words of wisdom from his father, Dr. James Dobson. It is an inspiring book that will help you become a better parent every day.

## Chapter 2

# Envision the Childhood You Want for Your Children, and the Adults You Want Them to Become

## The Challenge

As I travel the country speaking to civic, religious, and parenting organizations about the joys and challenges of parenting, I'm met with nearly universal desperation from parents who are sick and tired of always having to battle for their kids' hearts, minds, and very souls.

When I was mothering our three children, I admit that I sometimes fell back in my own war with the culture. It's tough, tiresome, and tedious. I sometimes forgot exactly what it was I was trying to achieve. The trouble is, when caught up in the "tyranny of the urgent" and with the numerous struggles of each day, losing sight of the big picture is very easy.

The Good Book says, "Where there is no vision, the people perish" (Prov. 29:18). I submit to you that perhaps the biggest reason so many of our families and children seem to have lost their way is that we, as a culture and as individuals, have lost sight of the vision of the lives we want for our children.

Some parents have been so overwhelmed since the day that tiny bundle was placed in their arms that they have never really stopped to consider the childhood they want their offspring to have or the adult that child should become.

But I'm convinced that all decent parents, whether liberal, conservative, or somewhere in between, want pretty much the same thing for their kids. We want them to be happy and safe, and we want them to develop into adults of character. Taking the time to picture what childhood should be like helps us protect it. And creating a vision of our children's best future reminds us of the prize. It's not enough for us to be against things, We must be for something too. We must know what we believe and be purposeful about making it a reality. It helps to actually write it down. Here's what I wrote:

*I believe that childhood should occur within a protected space of innocence. I believe our children should be able to daydream and play in their make-believe worlds, far from adult concerns and issues. I believe our daughters should be free from the fear of pregnancy and our sons should not have to worry about sexually transmitted diseases. I believe our children should also be free from teenage sexual activity and the complexities and guilt that come when their innocence is compromised. I believe our kids should know there is a Creator who loves them and has a unique purpose for their lives. I believe they should understand that we are here for them—that Mom and Dad are committed to answering their questions and challenging their intellect, and that they can depend on us to guide them. I believe our children should feel confident enough in our gentleness to come to us with their own hopes, dreams, and fears.*

*I believe the teenage years should be filled with conversations, laughter, and a warm and secure place called home. I also want my children to grow up and have happy families of their own. I want them to be marked by good character and generosity; to be responsible, honest, healthy, and courageous; to be respected and respectful; to live their dreams free of encumbrances from mistakes made in their youth; to know what it's like to be committed to someone fully; and to understand the value and honor in being loyal, true, and just.*

Have you ever deliberately thought about the type of adults you want your children to become? What do you believe childhood and the teen years should look like? I'm not asking what they do look like but what they should look like. Now write it down. (It doesn't have to be deeply profound or complicated. Feel free to borrow from my vision statement or from your own childhood experiences growing up. What did you long for? What did your parents do right?)

There's not one parent reading this book who wants his son to grow up to be a lazy bum. There's not one dad who wants his daughter to be known for being "easy," not one mother who is hoping her child will go through multiple marriages that end in painful divorces. None of us want our children to get sexually transmitted diseases, have abortions, or end up addicted to drugs.

What are we doing now to prepare our children to become the adults we envision? We must constantly remember the beautiful, lovely, fulfilling lives we want our kids to enjoy and start understanding that the decisions we make today about how we raise them will have a direct impact on how they choose to live their lives when they are on their own.

# In Your Shoes

I think one of the greatest visionaries of our time was Martin Luther King Jr. He ignited an entire nation and helped bring liberty to an oppressed people while changing the course of history—all by being committed to a vision. He is an example of how articulating a dream can help make it a reality. His incredibly moving speech on the steps of the Lincoln Memorial said, in part:

> I have a dream that one day this nation will rise up, live out the true meaning of its creed: "We hold these truths to be self-evident, that all men are created equal."
>
> I have a dream that one day on the red hills of Georgia sons of former slaves and the sons of former slave-owners will be able to sit down together at the table of brotherhood.
>
> I have a dream that one day even the state of Mississippi, a state sweltering with the heat of injustice, sweltering with the heat of oppression, will be transformed into an oasis of freedom and justice.
>
> I have a dream that my four little children will one day live in a nation where they will not be judged by the color of their skin but by the content of their character.

Dr. King's dream was for his children and all the children that would follow after them. He held on to his vision and never let go.

Because he could visualize it, he could articulate it, which he did time and time again. And because he could articulate it, he was able to inspire others to visualize the dream and to work against all odds to achieve it.

I believe that we, as parents, can do that too.

Our personal battle may not be against racism or sexism or the oppression of a people. But it is a battle all the same. It is a battle against the forces that would oppress traditional values, decency, and honor. It is a battle against a world that treats our children as something less than human. Dr. King spoke not just of ending racial inequality but of creating a world where children would be judged only by the "content of their character." Do we not also have that dream for our children?

## From My Home to Yours

The idea of having a specific vision and constantly keeping it in the front of your mind is timeless and has been proved over and over again to work. One of the bestselling books of the modern age is Norman Vincent Peale's *The Power of Positive Thinking*, in which he described how our thinking shapes who we become. But long before Dr. Peale, there was the wisdom of the Bible. One of the most powerful Scripture verses is Proverbs 23:7: "As [a man] thinketh in his heart, so is he" (KJV). Children and teens usually end up being exactly who they think they will be, which often comes from who the adults around them think they will be. It's not enough for us to have a vision for our children; we must teach them to have one too and to think about it every day.

We must teach them to understand that, regardless of their circumstances, they have total control over their character and actions toward others. Talk about personal power! We have to remind them (and ourselves) that although they might not be able to control what happens to them, they are in complete control of how they react to the events of their daily lives.

Giving our children the gift of positive thinking is priceless and will serve to actually help them shape their behavior into a positive force. If they start off every morning thinking about the things they are thankful for, the things they wish to be, and how they can advance what is good, the chances are very high that their actions will flow out of these constructive thoughts.

One of the very best resources I know to help us and our children focus on the way things should be, rather than getting bogged down in the negative, is Tommy Newberry's *New York Times* bestseller *The 4:8 Principle*. The focus of Newberry's book is Philippians 4:8, which reminds us how to add a bounce to our step and honor to our lives. The verse teaches us to think about truth, honor, justice, purity, loveliness, and good news. It tells us that if we train ourselves to think about these positive things, we will actually feel better and our lives and actions will begin to reflect those virtues. The verse says, "Finally, brethren, whatsoever things are true, whatsoever things are honest, whatsoever things are just, whatsoever things are pure, whatsoever things are lovely, whatsoever things are of good report; if there be any virtue, and if there be any praise, think on these things" (KJV).

As Newberry explained, "Research indicates that the average person thinks approximately fifty thousand thoughts per day." Each thought moves us toward our full potential or away from it. Unfortunately, we live in a society bent on nursing old wounds and highlighting what is wrong with just about everything and everyone. As a result, we have grown accustomed to viewing the world, our lives, and ourselves through a lens of negativity—and that negativity stands in direct contrast to the positive, passionate, and purpose-filled people God wants us to be.

I often wonder how different our world would be if the precious minds of all of America's teens were filled with thoughts of truth, honor, justice, purity, beauty, and good news. I'm guessing that would transform our culture overnight! Teaching your children to think this way could make their teen years far more beautiful than what the pop culture can give them. And teaching them to think positively now will help them carry those thoughts with them for the rest of their lives.

Years ago I had the amazing opportunity to hear Tommy Newberry speak—and my very special guest at the event was my then-fifteen-year-old daughter, Kristin. She sat in such rapt attention to his message that it surprised even me. Her heart seemed to absorb every word like a sponge. She made sure we picked up a copy of his book, and I later found it in her room with passages marked by her own hand. It wasn't until then that I fully realized just how hungry our kids are for positive messages and just how much negative garbage is forced into their brains by the pop culture. Even in my home, my own daughter was starving for solid advice on how to fight the clutter of negative messages being forced upon her by our culture.

I'm also thankful to report that Kristin's captivation by such a life-giving message was not short lived. I recall one evening after experiencing a particularly bad day at work, I was griping and complaining in short bursts over dinner and throughout our precious family time. My comments weren't directed at anyone in particular, but it was apparently pretty obvious that I was in a very negative state of mind. I just couldn't let go of the injustices of the day, thus allowing the bad day to create a less than joyful atmosphere for my family. After a while, Kristin had had enough. She very gently, and very respectfully, said, "Mom, do you remember the 4:8 principle?"

Such an abrupt reminder of truth from my teen daughter was just what I needed. I laughed, told her she was right, and in that very moment decided to forbid my brain from replaying the "horrors" of the day. I determined that I would instead think about all the wonderful blessings in my life. That doesn't mean I didn't continue to create a plan for how to correct the mistakes and deal with the consequences of the day, but it does mean that I decided to enjoy what was good and came up with a positive plan to move the bad in a better direction. Rather than dwelling on the injustices, I switched to a mode of focusing on how I could create justice; instead of reliving wrongs done to me, I started focusing on forgiveness and thanking God for all the times I had experienced grace and mercy; instead of worrying about the consequences I would suffer from the results of someone else's error, I started coming up with solutions. In that moment, as never before, I realized how critical it is not to let someone else steal our happiness. And I learned that when we take the time to teach our children the value of holding on to a vision of loveliness, it just might circle back to help us hold on to our own dreams too.

## Reflections from a Daughter

God made every single individual uniquely in his image. That means each of us was designed to show and tell the world something specific and wonderful about his character in a way no one else can. Determining God's purpose for you and for your family isn't easy, but perhaps it isn't as hard as it seems.

In his book *See You at the House*, Bob Benson wrote, "If God can take a tiny seed and, in the process of giving it his life, endow it with a knowledge of what it is supposed to be; if he can give it the purpose and strength and fruitfulness to not only accomplish it all, but to perpetuate itself as well; and if he can give it an inner calendar to tell it when all of this is supposed to be done, why is it so hard to believe he has done the same for our hearts?"

If you prayerfully develop a vision that is grounded in scriptural truths and built around the values and desires that are important to you, you simply can't go wrong. As you truly seek God, he will align your life to his will. We may not know exactly what it is we or our families are becoming when we live according to the visions we develop, but we can be fully confident that we will become exactly what we were made to be.

# Act Now

Date _____

Today I wrote down the vision I have for my children and for their futures. I also sat down and shared that vision with them and listened to their feedback.

Signature _____

# More Help

Reading these books will help you maintain a more positive outlook, which will definitely rub off on your children!

- *The Power of Positive Thinking* by Norman Vincent Peale
- *The 4:8 Principle: The Secret to a Joy-Filled Life* by Tommy Newberry (tommynewberry.com)
- *The 10 Habits of Happy Mothers: Reclaiming Our Passion, Purpose, and Sanity.* This wonderful book by Dr. Meg Meeker, noted pediatrician and cohost of *Family Talk*, will help even the busiest of moms find new joy in parenting! I just can't recommend this book enough.

## Chapter 3
# Assess Your Home

## The Challenge

Most parents just don't know the content of the media their children are consuming on a daily basis. But once you have determined the vision you have for your children and their future, you must take inventory of their daily lives to determine if the messages they are consuming support or work against that vision. According to a 2010 Kaiser Family Foundation report, today's teens consume seven and a half hours of media each day. And if you factor in multitasking (for example, listening to music while they surf the Internet or playing a video game while they watch television), that number rises to ten and a half hours each day. Most parents don't know that the number one cable channel teen girls choose is the racy MTV, that the number one music genre choice for kids of all races and socioeconomic levels is the often-foul rap and hip hop, or that 90 percent of kids who go online stumble across hard-core porn simply because their parents have never taken the time to install a filter.

It's time for a little opposition research. As parents we must spend some time in the media's world to find out which messages are being pumped into our children's still-developing brains and how much pressure they are under from manipulative marketers trying to get a piece of the more than two hundred billion dollars that America's youth spend each year. Today's children have more disposable income than any other generation of kids in history. And greedy companies know it. They will do anything to get your kids hooked on the adrenaline high that comes with viewing sexualized and violent media—and spending money to pursue it.

The mass marketers are after your children 24-7. They slam your kids' email inboxes with pornography. They prominently display a lifestyle of betrayal, moral relativism, and sex, sex, sex in television programs. They are never too busy or too tired from a long day's work to pay attention to your children. They know how to get your teens to spend money: feed their raging hormones and take advantage of their emotional roller coasters with nonstop adrenaline-pumping messages of sex, violence, and rebellion. (More on this in the next chapter, "Understand How Marketers Target Your Children.")

The reality is that most parents don't want to look into or listen too closely to what their kids are doing. Why? Because if we find objectionable media habits, then we're faced with either having to do something about them or having to confront the fact that we're turning our backs on the problem and our kids. For many parents, it's just easier to remain ignorant. We often choose peace over principle. We value a quiet home with uneasy smiles more than we value developing our children's character, risking possible conflict along the way.

The ugly truth is that in many cases the American home has become a septic tank for the culture's toxic sewage. After all, teens at school may share the web addresses for pornographic sites, dish about the wildest sex scenes on television, or recommend the latest

violent video game, but it's often in the privacy of their own bedrooms that our sons and daughters consume hour upon hour of the
sludge that is perverting their views of sexuality, relationships, and
life in general. It's time for us moms and dads to pay attention to
what's going on in our daughters' and sons' bedrooms and in our own
family rooms. Children are like blank slates when they are handed to
us as newborn babies. Their minds are ready to be filled with good
things or with bad things, and it's up to moms and dads to provide
a healthy mental diet. I've heard it said, "Garbage in; garbage out."
Our children will largely become what they consume. It's up to us
to provide them with the materials that will build courage, fortitude,
fidelity, sound judgment, and strong character. If you have no idea
what others are pumping into your children's developing minds, how
on earth are you going to protect them? How are you going to select
age-appropriate materials and teach them how to decipher negative
images if you don't even know what they're seeing? Moms and dads,
if you don't stand in the gap for your kids, nobody will.

## From My Home to Yours

As I mentioned, the number one television viewing choice of teenage girls is MTV. The Medical Institute for Sexual Health in Austin,
Texas, has analyzed music videos and found that 60 to 70 percent
of them contain highly sexualized material. And of that, a full 81
percent connect violence to sex every single time.

According to the Kaiser Family Foundation's report on media
usage, "Children's bedrooms have increasingly become multi-media
centers, raising important issues about supervision and exposure

to unlimited content. Outside of their bedrooms, in many young people's homes, the TV is a constant companion: nearly half say the TV is on 'most' of the time, even if no one is watching."

Even while many polls show that parents are concerned about what their children watch and learn from the media, according to the Kaiser report, over two-thirds of all eight- to eighteen-year-olds say their families have no rules about how much television they're allowed to watch. The same goes for time spent playing video games and time spent on the computer. Studies indicate that parents who impose rules and enforce them do influence the amount of time their children devote to media. Kids with television rules that are enforced most of the time report much less daily media exposure than those from homes without rules.

In order to understand their world, walk one week in your children's tennis shoes. What are they listening to, watching, and reading? Take a trip to the mall and look at the posters that scream out to them from the music and clothing stores. What do the images portray? Anorexic-looking teen girls and young women in skimpy underwear adorn the windows of many clothing stores. When my daughter and I pass by such windows in lingerie stores, I don't ignore them. I take the time to point out how sad it is that young women would lower themselves to appearing shamelessly in their underwear in order to gain fame and fortune.

Music has long been the language of romance. Some of the most moving and inspirational songs of all time are about love and the mystery of the male–female attraction. But what the modern culture has done to this romance language in many cases is distort and cheapen it. Listen to your kids' iPods. Make a point to scroll through their menu of songs and take inventory of the often foul and disrespectful lyrics that stream directly into their brains. Put the earplugs into your head as your son does, feel the emotional beat and sensuality of the music as your daughter feels it, and listen to the words and messages. My guess is that your heart will break over what you have discovered. It may be a rude awakening, and you may want to hang your head in despair over the lost innocence of your children.

Have you ever actually sat down and played one of your children's video or online games? You might be more than shocked to find out the content of bestselling games such as the *Grand Theft Auto* series. As the title suggests, the goal is to steal cars. If that's all there was to it, it would be bad enough, but it gets worse: in the game, the way to acquire and hold on to the cars is to kill the police officers who try to stop you. And the sick minds behind the game give you plenty of choices—shooting them with a rifle, cutting them up with a chain saw, setting them on fire, or decapitating them. If you shoot an officer, you get extra points for shooting him in the head. In another game that was popular a few years ago, the player could stuff dollar bills into the panties of dancing showgirls. Is that really what you want your son to be doing "virtually" in the privacy of your own home? Thousands of kids engage their imaginations, eyes, and minds with these and other violent and sexual activities via the big screen while good moms and dads are just a room or two away—blissful in their ignorance.

Video games simply aren't in the same class as movies and television when it comes to making an impression on young minds. Most forms of media offer a passive experience; you watch other people doing things. But with video games your child becomes a participant. Your son actually becomes the character who rapes the girl, decapitates the police officer, and beats the prostitute. Your son decides who lives—and who dies. He alone pulls the trigger with the click of the controller he holds in his hand.

According to Dr. Elizabeth Carll of the American Psychological Association, this active participation enhances the "learning" experience. And, unlike a movie or a television show that might be viewed once or twice, the games are played repeatedly, often for hours on end.

## In Your Shoes

I received an email from Debbie, who shared these thoughts:

> Watch TV with your kids! I don't necessarily approve of all the shows, but my daughter's peer group does, and by watching them I learn the perspective of their age group and can point out the fallacies of these programs. The Internet is another tough one. The computer geeks at work gave me a program link that allowed me to spy on my daughter's web usage. I was pleasantly surprised. She listed me and her nine-year-old brother among her heroes (her dad got strokes too). Other parents have not had such pleasant experiences. But you have to know what your kids are doing, and that's one way to do it. My daughter gave me the password to her email accounts. I read some tortured and profane

emails from her friends and I saw her replies, and I was proud of her. She was a role model to her peer group. But that didn't happen by accident. She knew I was looking over her shoulder, and I think maybe she was more careful about her replies because somebody might read them.

What kind of influence are you having on your kids at home? Has your home merely become the pit stop where people sleep, keep their clothes, bathe, and have the occasional meal together? Or is it something more? How you view your home is essential to how effective and nurturing your home will or will not be for your children. Have you ever really thought about it?

## Reflections from a Daughter

It's always easier to go with the flow. The things that are popular, whether music, television shows, or a clothing style, are popular for a reason. They look and sound good, they're entertaining, and they're exciting.

They're also convenient. When something is popular, it's easy to find.

But as Christians, we're called to think a little deeper about the choices we make—to choose for reasons beyond pleasure or convenience.

Romans 12:2 says, "Don't become so well-adjusted to your culture that you fit into it without even thinking. Instead, fix your attention on God. You'll be changed from the inside out. Readily recognize what he wants from you, and quickly respond to it. Unlike the culture around you, always dragging you down to its level of immaturity, God brings the best out of you, develops well-formed maturity in you" (THE MESSAGE).

We grow stronger not by finding a comfortable place within the status quo but by searching out and reaching for things that are higher.

# Act Now

Date _____

Today I started taking inventory of my home. I told my kids that I care enough about them to start watching, listening to, and reading what other adults are telling them. I vow to go through my home and analyze the content of what I find in light of the vision I have set for my children. And I vow to never again be ignorant of the pressures placed on my kids by the mass media.

Signature _____

I evaluated _____'s

- video games: _____ (list of games) on: _____ (date).

- TV shows: _____ (list of shows) on: _____ (date).

- email/Facebook/Twitter/Instagram/Pinterest/
  Tumblr/Yik Yak/YouTube/Reddit/Snapchat
  accounts: _____ (list of accounts)
  on: _____ (date).

*Chapter 4*

# Understand How Marketers Target Your Children

## The Challenge

As I mentioned in the previous chapter, today's kids are more targeted by marketers than any generation in history. This generation spends an estimated two hundred billion dollars a year of their own money, so they are very profitable targets for exploitation and manipulation. You can see why marketers compete as never before for the attention of these sophomoric spenders.

So fierce is the competition for cash that modern marketing techniques have become, in many cases, insidiously evil. Selling to tweens isn't just about finding out what they want; it's about figuring out how to manipulate their minds.

Sex sells, and it is a staple of today's marketing campaigns. Worse is that many of the highly sexualized campaigns today are targeted at children. Both ads and entertainment programming sell empty promises of sexual power, every kind of sexual perversion, and a crude incivility. MTV (with its tawdry Spring Break specials) and prime-time shows such as *Glee*, *Pretty Little Liars*, and many others have become expert at feeding the raging hormones, edginess, and roller-coaster emotions of our youth, producing highly titillating material that ignites their adrenaline and leaves them begging for more. Instead of helping our sons and daughters positively approach and channel their sexuality and develop an understanding of decency and civility, the entertainment world pours gasoline on youthful passion and confusion.

Plainly put, our kids are being used.

To understand why and how marketers target them, consider these facts, courtesy of the Campaign for a Commercial-Free Childhood:

- Children under twelve influence five hundred billion dollars in purchases per year.
- This generation of children is the most brand conscious ever. Research reveals that teens between thirteen and seventeen have about twice as many conversations about brands each week as adults do.
- Companies spend about seventeen billion dollars annually marketing to children, a staggering increase from the one hundred million spent in 1983.
- Children ages two to eleven see more than twenty-five thousand advertisements a year on television alone, a figure that does not include product placement (showing a character drinking a Coke, for example). They are also targeted by advertising on the Internet, cell phones, MP3 players, video games, school buses—and in school.

- Almost every major media program for children has a line of licensed merchandise including food, toys, clothing, and accessories.
- In their effort to establish cradle-to-grave brand loyalty and get children to beg their parents for things, marketers even target babies through licensed toys and accessories featuring media characters.
- Viral marketing techniques take advantage of children's friendships by encouraging them to promote products to their peers.

As the National Institute on Media and the Family notes, when it comes to marketing to kids, the old equation has been turned on its head. Years ago marketers would reach out to parents to get the kids. Today they can go directly to the kids—who will then want their parents to make the purchase. That makes the sales job easier because children are certainly less discriminating and skeptical than adults and therefore easier to persuade. As the cliché goes, "Follow the money." That's exactly what marketers have done, and the easiest path is the one through your child's pocket.

What makes this all the more disturbing is the content of the messages. At best, marketers breed a highly materialistic view of life, leading kids to believe that happiness can be found in a line of stylish new clothes, the latest "hot" music, or an exciting new toy. But as the luster fades with the most recent acquisition, the desire for another new thrill takes its place. The temptation to be up to date with friends and classmates induces many kids (and many willing

parents) to live beyond their means, trapping themselves in a spiritually empty cycle of "buy now, pay later" as they frantically try to keep
up with the latest and greatest.

Even worse is the trashy content in many ads and television
shows. To appear to be cutting edge, companies apparently see no
choice but to lower standards and feed us crass images of sexuality and rebellion. As an executive from The WB network told PBS,
"Teens are consumed with sex. It's all around them. If you're going
to reach them, you have to talk about it."

This is so lazy. Take it from the mother of two sons: boys aren't
consumed with sex. Excited about girls? Sure. But being crazy about
girls and consumed with sex are different things. Maybe if images of
sex weren't "all around them," thanks to The WB and its ilk, more
boys would think about girls as human beings instead of just sex
objects. But that would be hard, and selling sex is easy.

These companies do work hard at one thing, though: marketing their tasteless products. They conduct focus groups, stop kids
on the street, grill them about their interests, and photograph them.
MTV executives even visit the homes of typical teen viewers to better understand their targets. And what's the result of all this? The
creation of characters that MTV uses across their programming who
feed the egos and worst instincts in our kids. Why? So they will keep
tuning in to the programming and be exposed to the commercials
their advertisers pay for.

As the PBS special *The Merchants of Cool* explains, MTV has
created caricatures of teen boys and girls known as "Mooks" and
"Midriffs." The Mook is "wilder and bolder and ruder and cruder
than the average boy; they are pro wrestlers, the stars of the *Jackass*

TV show, and the guys on MTV's Spring Break specials dancing crazily with scantily clad women they met 10 minutes earlier." The Midriff is consumed with her sexual power. She uses her body and an attitude of superiority to control those around her. The marketing geniuses that make MTV the number one viewing choice for teenage girls know exactly what they are doing—manipulating girls to become manipulators themselves.

Today's media have built an industry on studying your kids. It's time to learn what they know about your sons and daughters and then teach your kids how not to become pawns of their greed.

Learn about the forces arrayed against you and arm your kids with the truth. Read *The Marketing of Evil: How Radicals, Elitists, and Pseudo-Experts Sell Us Corruption Disguised as Freedom* by David Kupelian, the managing editor of WND.com. Today's youth are under tremendous pressure to conform to the value system of those who are selling them short of the best they can become, but we can't protect them if we don't know how it's being done.

And we've got to do more than just understand it. We've got to teach our children about marketing techniques and instill sound values in their hearts, along with the will to stand up against those who would use them. If we take the time and energy to equip our sons and daughters, then when they are confronted with clever, damaging marketing messages, they will recognize them and know how to reject them.

One way to counteract the effect of advertising is to help your kids dissect it. That's the advice of Bob Smithouser, an editor with Focus on the Family's Plugged In (pluggedin.com). Smithouser supplies a list of questions for you to ask the teenagers in your family:

- What is the sponsor really selling, the product itself or just an image connected with the product?
- Is this ad trying to exploit a human weakness such as vanity, lust, greed, pride, envy, or a desperate need to be accepted by others?
- What's the catch? Is there fine print or a hidden disclaimer that exposes this as an offer that really is too good to be true?
- Why do some ads want customers to "buy now, pay later"? What will that cost in the long run?
- Do I really need this product, or is the sponsor just trying to create a need for this product?
- What information is conveniently left out of this commercial message? For example, beyond the sticker price, certain vehicles cost more to insure and maintain than basic transportation.
- What is the sponsor really selling, the product itself or just an image connected with the product?

Teach your teens to look for ads trying "to exploit a human weakness such as vanity, lust, greed, pride, envy, or a desperate need to be accepted by others." And encourage them to ask, "What's the catch?" Warn them to look for the fine print, and to watch out for deals that are "really too good to be true," for "buy now, pay later" offers that hide the total cost to them, and for information "conveniently left out of" ads.

Another good question from Plugged In: "Do I really need this product, or is the sponsor just trying to create a need for this product?" Advertising cultivates insecurity on a host of subjects: "Bad breath, impending baldness, or the devastation of a dropped cell phone call. And for every manufactured fear, there's a product or service waiting to restore calm."

As Smithouser notes, "Cursing advertising or blaming it for leading us into temptation is pointless. Rather, we must arm ourselves and our teens with the tools to deconstruct ads and expose those with questionable agendas. Manipulative advertisers prey on people's insecurities. They encourage comparison ('Be like—or better than—the guy next door'), which destroys contentment."

Let's give our teens the perspective to see beyond commercial messages that get in the way of what's really important.

The good news is that, as the Kaiser Family Foundation has reported, kids say their parents have tremendous influence on them. When children and teens face problems or questions, they are more likely to go to Mom or Dad first for advice and help if the parents have previously taken the initiative to talk to and teach their children about difficult issues.

The question is, what kind of influence are you having on your children?

When you ignore or pretend that you don't see unhealthy, immoral, or just plain tacky and cheap messages, your children interpret your silence as an endorsement of the material. When you mindlessly plunk down sixty bucks for the latest video game or give your ten-year-old the cash to buy clothes that make her look like a streetwalker, you're part of the problem. Don't walk silently past that Victoria's Secret display at your local mall. Tell your kids why it's wrong. Ask your children pointed questions about the television shows and movies that interest them. Find out what they think so you can spark discussions that will give you a chance to tell them what you think and why.

# In Your Shoes

I asked the readers of my regular column how they deal with advertising. Here is how one mom responded:

> One of the best ways to fight materialism, sexualization, and lack of respect is … to limit the amount of time on the television. My husband and I work at this two ways. First of all, we established when they were young that the TV goes on only after they have been given permission, and we establish how long it's going to be on (each child got to choose one half-hour show a day—subject to our approval). We pushed PBS shows, even if we had to occasionally point out some things the people were saying that were mistaken, just because then we didn't have to deal with commercials.
>
> When they got old enough to see commercial TV, I used a technique I learned from my mother— I would watch with them and point out, derisively if it seemed right, the sales pitch of the commercial. So when the commercial showed someone doing something awkwardly so that the "Peel-o-Matic" could then be hawked, I could say, "Boy, that lady

doesn't know how to peel carrots, does she? You're
better at peeling than she is." After a while, the children start noticing the assumptions and tactics and
commenting on them—and for a while, you'll have
to live with their preaching back to you. But they
become wary of commercials.

Another mom wrote:

> I explain to my kids that advertising is paid space
> that companies, politicians, and others buy in order
> to get people to do something. Most of the adver-
> tising that my kids see is to get them to spend their
> money, or to bug me to spend mine! I am careful
> to explain that part of what makes a powerful ad is
> to build desire in someone—to make them want
> something so badly that they will pick up the phone
> and spend money at that moment to buy it. We
> discuss commercials as they come on television and
> I ask, "What is the company selling? How did the
> commercial make you feel?" And, "Did you feel that
> way before you saw or heard the ad?" I'm also very
> deliberate about explaining that television shows
> and movies try to sell things too—mostly ideas
> about how people should behave. They often tell
> stories in an emotional way so that the viewer (my
> son or daughter) will feel a connection and want to
> keep watching. Then I explain that the greater the

number of people that watch the show, the more
money the stations can charge for advertising—so
it all comes back to how much money can be made.
But I also point out there is nothing wrong with
wholesome entertainment, commercials, or good
storytelling—as long as you know that the person
doing it has an agenda.

# Reflections from a Daughter

Mom never failed to express her thoughts about strange, manipulative, or racy advertisements when they came on TV or when we
walked past them in the mall. Every time we approached a Victoria's
Secret display, I knew to expect one of two things from her. Most
days, she would verbally share her disappointment. But every now
and then, when she was feeling particularly energetic, she would
hurry to position herself on the opposite side of the store from us as
we walked by and start performing some ridiculous song and dance
so we would look at her (or run as far away as possible) instead of
toward the display. It was her way of objecting to the store's marketing strategy through a little humor (much to our embarrassment).

    I appreciate that she cared enough to do something when mar-
keters pushed messages contrary to the best she wanted for us. I'm
also thankful that she kept a positive demeanor as often as possible
while she expressed her objections, rather than getting angry about it
or setting a negative tone for the day.

    If you allow marketers to make you angry or upset, you don't
really win, any more than you do if you allow them to silently and

freely influence your children. Sometimes humor is the best weapon against marketers with negative messages.

# Act Now

Date _____

Today I determined I would not allow marketers to manipulate my children and undermine my values. I started asking my children specific questions to help them dissect the messages in media and advertising.

Signature _____

# More Help

Here are four great websites that will help you figure out what marketers are trying to sell to your kids:

**Parents Television Council (parentstv.org):** This great organization's mission is "to protect children and families from graphic sex, violence and profanity in the media, because of their proven long-term harmful effects." ParentsTV.org is a wonderful source for the latest information and actions you can take to have an impact on what ends up being broadcast across the nation's airwaves. You can be involved in one of their local chapters or campaigns to directly contact advertisers who should not be financially supporting programs that promote irresponsible or immoral behavior. The Parents

Television Council should be one of the first groups you count on. If you're looking to become involved in the battle, they will equip you well.

**Campaign for a Commercial-Free Childhood (commercialfreechildhood.org):** Their mission is "to support parents' efforts to raise healthy families by limiting commercial access to children and ending the exploitive practice of child-targeted marketing. In working for the rights of children to grow up—and the freedom for parents to raise them—without being undermined by corporate interests, CCFC promotes a more democratic and sustainable world." That's exactly what our goal as parents has to be, and the CCFC works to make it a reality. They emphasize concrete action, as their "CCFC Highlights" page on their website makes clear: it lists information about their successful campaigns, including their drive to get Scholastic Inc. to stop hawking its dreadful, oversexualized Bratz dolls in schools and to get companies to stop marketing violent PG-13 movies to kids.

**Parent Further (parentfurther.com):** You'll find lots of good information on this site. For example, it contains guides to help you make sense of the various types of ratings that are out there for everything from video games to television shows.

**Salvo (salvomag.com):** It's the best magazine out there on the insidious effects of marketing and the media. *Salvo* is "dedicated to debunking the cultural myths that have undercut human dignity, all but destroyed the notions of virtue and morality, and slowly eroded our appetite for transcendence." (I so appreciate the mission of *Salvo* that I volunteer my time as a senior editor.) It's perfect for young adults raised on the attention-grabbing graphics of today's Internet. And *Salvo* doesn't shy away from tough topics—including cloning, euthanasia, evolution, eugenics, and all aspects of human sexuality, just to name a few. You can find out more, and order a sample copy, at SalvoMag.com.

## Chapter 5

# Make Your Home Inviting, Warm, and … Fun!

## The Challenge

When parents become aware of the cultural challenges, a common mistake is to go overboard and shut down all opportunities for fun. Although you must never compromise your values and principles, sticking to them doesn't mean turning your home into a lifeless, cold environment where your personal list of "Thou shalt nots!" is overwhelming. If you have an uninviting home, neither your kids nor their friends will want to spend time there.

Children and teens are drawn to warmth, love, and excitement. But they also want to be in an environment where they feel safe and have boundaries. Your challenge is to create a nurturing home that provides all these things.

In a lecture at the Heritage Foundation, noted historian David Patterson encouraged people to think of the home as the highest calling:

Russell Kirk noted that "cultural restoration, like charity, begins at home." And he was quite right.

For cultural restoration entails the restoration of what is most high, most dear, most enduring. And the ground for all such things is the home. The home is the place where our names are first uttered with love and therefore where we first discover that we mean something…. It is the center from which we define and understand the nature of everything we encounter in the world…. Without the home, everything else in the world or in a culture is meaningless.

Patterson pointed out that home isn't just "a place or a thing" but "an event in the life of the holy," and thus a mother isn't just somebody "who gives birth, but one who emanates light, love, and compassion. Through her humanity receives a revelation of the light created upon the first utterance of Creation, the light that sanctifies all Creation."

It's pretty sobering to think about the fact that I, as a mother, am called to "emanate light, love, and compassion." I love my children completely and unconditionally. I would take a bullet for each of them. But the harsh reality is that my intense love does not always come across as, well, loving. I know that although I am moved with compassion for my children when they hurt, make mistakes, or have to suffer consequences, they often don't see or feel my compassion. Sometimes they see only my anger, disappointment, and fear. And if these emotions manifest themselves in a mere list of dos and don'ts, then I—and my children—have missed the point of this special place called home.

It's time to understand the difference between a house and a home, and vow to make yours one to come home to every day.

A house is a place where there are walls, floors, and rooms. It is a physical structure of function and utility. It is cement and pipes and wood and wiring, all void of human understanding, emotion, and creativity. It is governed by the parameters of the physical world— the water comes out here, you can access electricity there, paint peels, wood rots, and weeds eventually take over.

A home, on the other hand, is a place of belonging, acceptance, and comfort. It is a place where family members can make mistakes, be challenged to be their best, and experience the warmth that comes with grace, forgiveness, and redemption. It is where our life stories are molded, where verses and chapters are added as the years pass. It is a space for the development of the soul, the shaping of the spirit, and the expansion of the mind. A home is a place for reflection and quiet and solitude—a respite from the pressures of the world. And I believe that a home should also be a place of laughter, warm memories, and zany fun.

There is much in this book on the importance of establishing rules and boundaries for your home. Right now, I would like to focus on how to make it inviting.

## From My Home to Yours

**Don't make your house a "NO!" Zone.** I've done thousands of radio interviews around the country on the issue of protecting our homes and families from an ever-invading crude culture. Invariably, at least one well-meaning caller will say something like, "I agree that the culture is evil—so I've ripped out the TVs, don't allow the Internet in my house, and don't let my kids have cell phones." Sadly, these parents have mistaken technology and hardware for the problem. The problem isn't the technology—it's the way we use it and the way we allow others to misuse it in our homes. Instead of banning everything, we should harness the good and filter out the bad. We should set limits but not shut down access.

You can and should relax, but you can't let down your guard. You must have hard-and-fast rules without turning your house into a boot camp. How you describe and teach your standards is just as important in protecting your children as what rules and safeguards you adopt for your family. Take this advice from Shannon, who shares how to say yes and no to younger children:

> I try to say yes as often as possible—even when it's "Yes, we can do that tomorrow" (rather than right this minute). Or, "Yes, you may have five raisins" (rather than the three hundred they want). Or, "Yes, you can watch a movie after we pick up the toys together." And when I have to say no, I try to keep my voice cheerful and my face loving. After all, the refusal is about the stuff rather than about the child. "No, you can't have another Popsicle now. Nope. Nope. Nope." And my little ones will usually smile back. And when they continue to ask, I try to stay cheerful and say, "Nope! But we can read a story, and if you are hungry you can have _____ or _____." And if they are still asking, I'll say, "What's the answer to that question?" I

try to save the mean face for when there is defiance of me or meanness to each other or dangerous behavior.

And when I give directions and parameters, I phrase them positively as often as possible, as in, "Clean up the spill." (Telling them not to spill is just a ludicrous idea.) "Talk, please." (Instead of "Don't whine!")

Shannon's advice can be broadened to apply to teenagers too. "Yes, you can have friends over, but you have to do your homework first." "Yes, you can go to the movies after you help me clean up."

**It's all about your attitude.** Sometimes we let our teenagers' attitude control the mood of our home. What a mistake! With their developing emotions, raging hormones, and fluctuating biological moods, they need Mom and Dad to be the calm, steady force of reason. You've probably heard the saying "If Mama ain't happy, ain't nobody happy." Truer words were never spoken! The mom sets the tone for the home. You can be the mean principal or the sweet, inspirational teacher. You can be the one your kids fear or the one they come to for advice. Of course this applies to fathers too. The bottom line is that if we allow our kids to set the tone of the home, it will be an emotional cyclone. And if we operate with frustration or weariness, our entire home and everyone in it will become miserable in minutes, regardless of how carefree they were when they walked in the door. But if we set a tone of joy and hope, the home will be a more inviting place for everyone.

Jim shared an important point on demeanor in his email: "I am reminded of something John Cleese said: 'People often confuse being serious with being somber.' I'm always a serious dad. I'm also seriously very happy with my girls. I am often seriously playful out at the park or in the pool. I can be and often am somber too, as the situation warrants. But that's up to the situation, not a 'Sarge' state of mind."

**Make your home fun!** When my kids were little, my husband and I made a decision to create an atmosphere where they and their friends would want to play. We called our house "The Popsicle House," meaning that in the steamy days of summer, the little kids in the neighborhood knew there was always a cold, delicious Popsicle or two awaiting them at the Hagelins'. We took great delight in watching their little eyes light up and their faces beam as they took the colorful melting pop from our hands. It was a glorious pleasure to hear them smack their lips and giggle with delight with every slurp. And, of course, there was the cleanup: I must have helped wash a thousand little sticky hands and wiped down just as many stained and smiling cheeks.

Our door was always open to the neighborhood children, and it must have slammed shut a million times a day. We often had dirty fingerprints and footprints adorning the walls and floors. But there was also a lot of laughter, running, and creativity blooming within our walls. How I cherish those memories!

We've also always stocked our home and yard with plenty of gadgets, art supplies, and costumes. Over the years we've kept a stock of bikes (many purchased at yard sales), skateboards, and just about every other kind of kid-powered transportation you can imagine. When our kids were little, we had Big Wheels, little red wagons, and trikes. Although we've never been blessed with a swimming pool, that hasn't kept our kids (and us) from getting wet. Summertime saw our yard marked with snaking hoses and sprinklers and the blur of water balloons flying in midair or splashing on some squealing child's back. Summer nights often found our kids and their friends gathered around campfires in the backyard—complete with marsh-mallows, hot dogs, and soda. The sounds of crickets and the gentle breezes were often punctuated by the war cries and hysterical laughter associated with shaving cream fights or mischievous games of Ring and Run, a game of ringing the doorbell of a friendly neighbor and running away or hiding around the corner. (Little did my kids know I usually called my friends first to warn them that the fun was about to begin.) We've had tree houses, wooden bridges hanging between huge trees, playhouses, and forts in which epic battles took place.

As our children grew into teens, we were always very careful to change the environment with their ever-developing and changing interests. The basements and garages of our various homes have been transformed from garage band practice rooms to silk-screening and art studios to photography darkrooms. We have purchased foosball tables from Craigslist, art equipment from eBay, and countless video games, guitars, and other fun stuff from pawnshops. We've "invested" in a movie library, VCR and DVD players, and classic board games.

And as they grew older, the kids kept on coming. Some of my happiest moments came when my home was filled with the banter of teenagers—whether it was in the middle of the night during a sleepover of chatty girls or on a Saturday afternoon when the guys gathered for another delightfully noisy band practice. I was truly blessed to have the opportunity to get to know my children's friends and to know that they enjoyed hanging out in our home. All through the college years, many of those friends continued to descend on our home during holidays. And today, now that they are all grown and many of them are starting families of their own, they still come to see us. What a joy. What a blessing to still be part of their lives!

**Feed them, and they will come.** I've already mentioned the Popsicles and campfire foods, but honestly, I can't make this point enough times: kids and teenagers love food. It is an important part of their social gatherings, and if your home isn't known for having it, you will have a lonely life indeed. On the other hand, if your home is filled with what kids crave, they will come.

Years ago, my husband and I dedicated a substantial part of our budget to the feeding of the masses—specifically, the masses of kids we hoped would fill our home. We still save pizza coupons; cram our freezers and pantry with two-for-one sales on ice cream, sodas, and chips; and always have jars of colorful candy in more than one room at a time.

Okay, so at this point you're probably wondering about the eating habits we encourage. I've got to admit, since we fed our children healthy meals the vast majority of the time, I was never one of those to worry too much about weekend grazing! We bake cookies, brownies, and cakes. We have hosted make-your-own-ice-cream-sundae bars and purchased every kind of chip you can imagine. I am a "supplier" of junk food, and I'm proud of it!

Weight has never been a problem for our children because we also made sure they got plenty of exercise in organized sports, bicycling, and running around the neighborhood. They were never allowed to just sit around and watch hours upon hours of television. There are just too many fun experiences awaiting the child whose imagination is not stifled by canned television programming. Food isn't the enemy.

It's the consumption of too much of the wrong kind, accompanied by physical inactivity, that robs our kids of their best health.

**Create opportunities to interact.** Of course, when your home is filled with children or teenagers, adult supervision is imperative. But just being there isn't enough. It's far more effective and enjoyable for everyone if you become a natural part of the activity than if you are the "secret police" slipping around every corner. Be bold about your presence—but not intrusive. Let visitors know what rooms are off-limits and, of course, what behavior is and isn't acceptable. And, most important, look for opportunities to interact and get to know the kids in your home. Engage them in conversation and let them know that you are truly interested in them and their lives. You just never know when you might make a lifelong friend, help shape a destiny, or even learn something from the younger generation.

# Reflections from a Daughter

One night shortly after we moved into our first house, my husband and I went out for dinner. As we sat there talking about what the year ahead of us would hold and going over everything we needed to do to get settled, a thought suddenly hit me and I blurted out, "I can't wait to see what the new towels feel like when they come out of the dryer!" When I saw the bewildered expression creep across Randy's face, I realized how incredibly lame it was that I could be so excited about towels, and we both burst out laughing. But I wasn't any less excited, nor was I sorry about it, because the towels were ours, and the house was ours, and we were making it into our home.

We have a vision for what we want our home to be like for ourselves and for our future children: comfortably clean, filled with books, and heavily trafficked by friends and new acquaintances. We want company around a big table, breaking bread and forming a tight-knit community. A true home is where walls come down and souls come out because people know there is love there, and that makes it safe. When you create an atmosphere that is inviting, warm, and fun, then kids, teenagers, and adults will come, and they will be blessed by it. We believe that because we experienced it firsthand. Both sets of our parents created homes where there was lots of activity and lots of food and where lifelong friendships were forged.

A home has the potential to be a foretaste of heaven. Our earthly homes will never be perfect, but if we keep our eyes on the perfecter of our faith, our homes can be places where family and visitors alike see frequent glimpses into eternity. After all, heaven is coming home.

# Act Now

Date _____

Today I decided to adopt a tone—and a style—for my home that would make it a warm, inviting place for my children and their friends.

Signature _____

Some ideas for making my home more inviting are:

_____

_____

# More Help

**Happy Housewives Club (happyhousewivesclub.com):** Darla Shine created the Happy Housewives Club after deciding to trade her briefcase for a diaper bag and discovering a lack of respect for the hard work of stay-at-home parenting. It is an invaluable resource for every parent. She covers topics from fitness and working from home to crafts for kids and healthy meals. I highly recommend checking out her creative ideas.

*Chapter 6*
# Create Family Time

## The Challenge

Do you know your family?

You may think that's a silly question. "Of course we know each other," many parents would reply. "We live under the same roof. We see each other daily. We go on vacations together. How could we not know each other?"

Some research, however, suggests that many parents and their children are, in an important sense, almost strangers.

One major study, sponsored by the Alfred P. Sloan Foundation, comes from the UCLA Center on the Everyday Lives of Families, and it paints a portrait of family life in crisis. It reports that the time many families spend together is crammed with wall-to-wall activities. Mothers and fathers ferry their kids feverishly about—a playdate here, a practice there, not a moment to spare—tethered by cell phones and sustained by meals on the run. You can't really know your children if all your time with them is spent running to and fro in a frenetic whirlwind. Genuine intimacy is impossible under such conditions.

Of course, there's nothing wrong with activities per se. Nobody's saying kids should just sit at home. Involvement in sports, for example, is incredibly beneficial for children, especially teens. Take it from a mother who has cheered her sons at track meets and baseball games. I counted it a blessing that my son spent many of his high school Friday nights at five-hour track meets, with no time or energy left over for mischief.

But it's critical to stop and reflect on what might be missing in their lives—the most important physical part of their development: you.

This isn't mere sentiment talking. It's a matter of social science. Newsmax.com reported that a study conducted by the Associated Press and (believe it or not) MTV found that kids between thirteen and twenty-four listed spending time with family as the number one activity that makes them happy. It makes a huge difference.

Take something as simple as the family dinner. Sure, it's nice, but who on earth has time? The bottom line is this: if you want to help your children avoid a host of problems, you will make time.

In our household, especially when three teenagers were living at home, we designated nights when we would eat together and told our kids, "Your friends are welcome to join us." This firm but inclusive directive made for many now-treasured evenings when we bonded with our children and their friends. I know in my mother's heart that the time, laughs, and discussions had a powerful impact on all of them. And the data support my hunch: one study from the National Center on Addiction and Substance Abuse at Columbia University found a connection between frequent family dinners and lower rates of teen smoking, drinking, and drug use: "Compared with teens who frequently had dinner five nights or more per week with their families, those who had dinner with their families only two nights per week or less were twice as likely to be involved in substance abuse. They were 2.5 times as likely to smoke cigarettes, more than 1.5 times as likely to drink alcohol, and nearly three times as likely to try marijuana."

Just being there with your children also helps them. A comprehensive study, drawing on data from the National Longitudinal Study of Adolescent Health and published in the *Journal of the American Medical Association*, notes that "teenagers were less likely to experience emotional distress if their parents were in the home when they awoke, when they came home from school, at dinnertime, and when they went to bed, if they engaged in activities with their parents, and if their parents had high expectations regarding their academic performance."

When you think about it, it makes sense. After all, if you are available for and nearby your children, even if you don't do anything in the conventional sense of the word, your presence sends the undeniable message, "I care about you enough to be here."

But what about single parents? Your job is harder. But it is not impossible. You must find allies in the battle—other adults who share your values and will support you and help you raise your children to be all they were meant to be. I've dedicated an entire chapter to the importance of joining hearts and hands with other adults in this adventure we call parenthood. It's chapter 14, "Secure Allies in the Battle." Please read it. Being a single parent doesn't mean you have to go it alone. Don't give up, give in, or become discouraged. You can raise wonderful, happy children.

Another study, published in the journal *Family Relations*, certainly caught my maternal eye. It noted that children who succeed in school tend to have mothers "who frequently talk and listen to them." Fathers, too, make quite a difference. Here's how FamilyFacts.org sums up a study on the impact of dads reported in the *Journal of Marriage and Family*: "Compared to peers with less paternal attention, children whose fathers spent leisure time, shared meals, helped with homework or reading, and engaged in other home activities with them have significantly higher levels of academic performance."

The pop culture frequently portrays dads as disposable, doltish, or dangerous. The reality, of course, is that dads play a vital role in their children's development and well-being. A study published in *Child Development* reveals that "father absence was associated with the likelihood that adolescent girls will be sexually active and become pregnant as teenagers." Many other studies reveal the essential person Dad is in the lives of his children.

And what about Mom? It has been said that the most powerful word in any language is *mother*. Yet our society increasingly belittles the role and seems to place higher value on the mom who hires others to care for her children than the mom who sacrifices to raise them herself. One study published in *Family Relations* found that the children "who were most successful in first grade (in terms of test scores and teachers' ratings) had mothers who spent a great deal of time in positive interactions with them." It also found that their academic success "correlated with their mothers' involvement in talking with them, listening to them and answering their questions."

We know the importance of maintaining a balanced diet for good physical health. The UCLA study shows that it's just as crucial, for the sake of our mental and emotional health, to lead a balanced life.

And how do we restore balance to our frantic family lives? Make a point of injecting some downtime into it—heck, schedule it. Go for a walk—not a power walk but a slow one. Play a game together, preferably a board or card game with everyone sitting around the table interacting.

Realize, too, that not every activity must involve the whole group. Take that walk or play that game with one son or one daughter. Give everybody a turn. In time, you'll find yourself having real conversations with the people who matter most. And don't neglect your spouse! A regular date can really help strengthen your marriage.

It's impossible to overemphasize the importance of having dinner together—sitting down, away from the television, as a group—as often as possible. The potential a family dinner affords to impart lessons in courtesy, hash out problems, or just have a good laugh is unmatched.

Reviving this balance is also crucial to one's spiritual health. It's all too easy, when every minute of our day is jam-packed, to neglect church and daily prayer. Big mistake. Only by slowing down can we hope to really hear the voice of God. Taking a formal retreat occasionally is a fine idea, but we also need the mini-retreats that God uses to recharge our batteries when we take time to talk with and visit him.

If you're feeling overscheduled, look at your family's time and how it's spent. Get together and discuss ways to pare down outside activities and make more time for each other. One fair way to take more control of family time is to set the number of activities each child can do in a school year. Instead of track, drama, tennis, football, soccer, and horseback riding for each child, leaving you the frazzled chauffeur struggling to fit everything in, let each child choose two or three activities for the year when school starts. And stick to it when the new seasons begin. In addition to lightening up your schedule, this method will help teach your children about priorities and time management.

It's crucial that we make time for what is truly important, not merely so that we can fashion some pleasant memories, but so that we can raise our kids to soar above the toxic culture and to become the men and women God intends for them to be.

Mom and Dad, you are vital. The culture won't tell you that, but the facts, your gut, and your kids' lives testify to your power. Your opportunity to enjoy them when they're small and to shape them when they become teens will disappear before your eyes.

Don't just give your family things. Give yourself. You'll get far more back than you can possibly imagine.

# In Your Shoes

You can even try things that seem drastic. One parent shared with me what she did:

> Several years ago one cold winter month my family's frantically busy life came to a screeching halt: we became quitters. Okay, so not really quitters—but we did cancel every scheduled event for two weeks. What a beautiful two weeks that turned out to be! Instead of rushing from piano to ballet to Scouts to … whatever, we abruptly stopped in the middle

of the mayhem and did something radical—spent evenings together. After schoolwork was done, we gathered around the fireplace and drank hot chocolate and just talked to each other. Some evenings found us lounging on the couch and floor, with each person quietly reading a book or magazine, or simply sketching. There was no clock watching, no exhaustion, and no tension—we were the masters of our universe. After our brief family sabbatical we were more deliberate about the activities we picked up again, and our entrance back into the social scene found us well rested and more reflective. Those two weeks changed my life as a mother, and I emerged with a greater sense of purpose in using both my and my children's time more wisely.

When my son Nick left for college in the fall of 2007, I wrote about it as a sobering moment that left me very thankful for all the time we had spent together:

My husband and I held each other and cried more than I think we had in years of marriage. We left our son Nick alone in his dorm room, far from home, after nurturing and loving him for eighteen years. Our little boy is now a tall, responsible young man facing life on his own. Yes, it's what good parents everywhere dream of and want for their kids—to become independent adults who fly from our arms into a world where they can make their own mark. But still, the tears come—for me, mainly because I now know from painful personal experience that there is a certain brevity to childhood. Those wild and wonderful days have vanished forever.

I thank God for the five years we homeschooled, for the opportunity I had to work from a home office, and for the fact that my husband has always put family ahead of work. I'm grateful for the nights I said prayers with Nick and tucked him into bed and for the hours spent helping with homework, listening to teenage rants, attending endless track meets, and watching him learn from his mistakes. Basically, I'm thankful for every second I spent with my boy. It's still difficult to see him go.

It doesn't help a bit that we went through this just one year ago when we left our first son, Drew, at college. In fact, this time is worse—there are now two empty beds and two sons whose laughter I won't hear around the house anymore. Nick's and Drew's childish antics and boyhood ways are gone. What remains are the memories.

When I first began writing this chapter, I had to come to a very hard realization about my own life: I had allowed great causes and great opportunities to creep into my family life and crowd out time I should have been spending with my own teens. As the years went on and the causes I believed in grew more urgent, it was too easy to go to "one more" meeting in the late afternoon or attend just "one more" event in the evening. My BlackBerry was my constant companion, and many times when I was with my family, my mind was actually somewhere else.

There it was: I, the one who gave up career advances, home-schooled, and deliberately moved away from the big city to raise my children in a real neighborhood with a slower pace when they were small, had somehow managed to overcommit myself outside the home when they became teenagers. Writing this book caused me to stop and evaluate my own life, and I'm so glad I did. I decided to step aside as a vice president of the Heritage Foundation and take on a new role that would allow me to work from home, with the vast majority of my work tasks complete by the time my daughter walked in the door from school. In the world's eyes, it was probably a foolish decision—one doesn't just walk away from being a vice president of the Heritage Foundation—especially in the uncertain economic times in which we lived. But my husband and I decided it was what we must do. And so we did. When I told our daughter, who was sixteen years old at the time, the plan, she jumped off the bed and threw her arms around my neck. What confirmation! Good causes and careers will always be waiting for us after our children have gone. But childhood and the teenage years wait for no one.

I'm not saying every mom or dad should change or quit their jobs! I am saying you should constantly evaluate and reevaluate how you are spending your time when you are not with your family. Is it worth it? Have you become a victim of "mission creep," either in your career or in your volunteer activities? Can you afford to slow down? Can your kids afford for you not to? Is this the time your children need you more than you need the extra income? These are not questions society teaches us to ask, but if we don't, when our children grow up and leave our homes we could be left with a lifetime of regret for not having asked those difficult questions.

## Reflections from a Daughter

At many family dinners my poor mom was the victim of two little boys (and sometimes a husband) who made it their mission to try to gross her out—by talking about the process of tanning an animal hide using the animal's brains or describing their doctor's visit to have their ingrown toenails removed, for example. She would play along, often running away from the table with her fingers in her ears and laughing all the way, even though there was a little truth to her performance.

Family dinners and family vacations were important parts of our lives. Now that I am grown, I am incredibly thankful that Mom and Dad insisted on them. They have become some of my proudest, sweetest memories. Relationships within families, though they can sometimes be draining, have the potential to be the most life-giving relationships in the world.

In his book *Theirs Is the Kingdom*, Robert D. Lupton said,

> The fundamental building blocks of the kingdom
> are relationships. Not programs, systems, or pro-
> ductivity.  But  inconvenient,  time-consuming,

intrusive relationships. The kingdom is built on personal involvements that disrupt schedules and drain energy. When I enter into redemptive relationships with others, I lose much of my "capacity to produce desired results with a minimum expenditure of energy, time, money, or materials." In short, relationships sabotage my efficiency. A part of me dies. Is this perhaps what our Lord meant when He said we must lay down our lives for each other?

It's in our messy, imperfect relationships that we learn the biggest life lessons. It's in the midst of noise and activity that we often have the most meaningful conversations. And perhaps it's in the seasons when our families are hardest to be around (when teenagers are restless or after a stressful move) that the most kingdom work is accomplished by simply spending time together.

# Act Now

Date _____

Today I started looking for ways to increase the amount of time I spend with my children. I pledge to make that time as meaningful and enjoyable as I can and to show my children, by my very presence, that they mean more to me than anyone else in the world.

Signature _____

# More Help

**FamilyFacts.org:** Looking for scientific data about families? You'll find a solid resource in this free website at the Heritage Foundation. FamilyFacts.org is a clearinghouse of useful, reliable information distilled from numerous studies and academic journals worldwide. The findings from lengthy reports are boiled down into bite-sized blocks that are easy to understand.

You can also find many websites suggesting ways to expand and improve your time together, but here are five to get you started:

**FamilyTime (familytime.com):** This website is filled with cooking ideas, fun family activities, helpful reminders, moneysaving offers, and more. You can try the recipe of the day, follow tips for decorating or organizing your home, or get some pointers for creating a family garden.

**Families with Purpose (familieswithpurpose.com):** You'll find loads of tips on this website. "Family activities don't have to be elaborate, expensive planned out ideas," the group notes. "Sometimes, simple is better. Kids are looking for your time and attention, so don't forget the simple things in life." Here are a few ideas from a list on the site:

- Read a book together
- Fly a kite
- Bake cookies

- Go fishing
- Plant flowers
- Build a tent and eat lunch inside
- Go for a walk
- Shoot hoops or play catch
- Play hide-and-seek
- Catch fireflies

**Make Mealtime Family Time (makemealtimefamilytime.com):** As you might guess, this website focuses on the benefits of eating together. It even allows you to download a free set of mealtime conversation cards.

**FamilyLife (familylife.com):** This site contains tons of free resources on how to improve both the quality and quantity of your family life together. You can also sign up to receive emails filled with helpful tips on family living.

**Family Talk (drjamesdobson.org):** The go-to resource for all things related to faith and family, this site by Dr. James Dobson is your one-stop shop for videos, tools, books, free research, and counseling. It is a must-visit-often site if you are serious about making your family the strongest it can be.

*Chapter 7*

# Discuss the Modern Challenges of Friendship with Your Teens and Evaluate Your Own Friendships

## The Challenge

This isn't rocket science: teenagers are social creatures who want to be respected by their peers, surrounded by friends, and invited to all the right parties. The need for acceptance is tremendously high in the preteen and teenage years, and peer pressure is omnipresent. Finding true and loyal friends who share high values can be extremely difficult.

The pressures and subject matter your child may have to deal with are far greater than what you and I—or any generation before us—had to face. Here are just three of the difficult issues involving friendship that are unique to this generation of children:

**Absentee Parents:** With so many households run by overstressed single parents or two parents who work long hours, there is often a serious lack of adult supervision and interaction. These days, instead of parents teaching values, it's often the sexualized media that are teaching our kids' friends what is and isn't acceptable. The resulting

onslaught of sexual promiscuity and teen pregnancy and the prolif-
eration of porn mean the chances are very high that the kids your
sons and daughters are hanging out with may have serious personal
problems. Others may come from homes where the parents simply
haven't yet had their eyes opened to the dangers of the culture.

**Brokenness:** The breakdown of the family in the last thirty years
is stunning. For every hundred children born in the United States,
more than sixty are born into a broken home. That means they are
born either to a single parent or into a family that will suffer from
divorce. So many children come from fractured families that it might
be difficult for your child to find friends who haven't been deeply
wounded by the tragedy of divorce. Many teens today have no one
at home modeling what basic married commitment and fidelity
are—let alone friendship. In broken homes, often no one circles
back around to the children to provide counseling and therapy. Our
society still hasn't quite figured out how to help children through
this pain. Social science researcher Pat Fagan says ours has become a
"culture of rejection." What a sad environment in which to grow up.
The result is an entire generation of young people who are searching
for help and meaning through their loneliness and heartache. And
since even the most wonderful families and adults in the world are
incredibly busy, it might just be that your children find themselves
counseling their friends through great heartaches. But our kids were
not intended—nor are they qualified—to bear such burdens.

**"Me, Me, Me":** Society is fighting against us as parents and
pushing our children into a "me first" world. The "me, me, me"

mentality teaches our kids that people are rarely good for anything more than what they can give us. Our children are told to look out for themselves and get what they can, even if it is at the expense of others. They are fed an almost constant message that tells them to obtain whatever makes them happy, whether it's money, cool clothes, popularity, or a relationship—the list goes on and on. And they're shown that treating anyone who gets in their way with contempt or rudeness is not only okay but even funny.

There are two critical steps parents must take in helping our pre-teens and teens navigate these uncharted waters of friendship. The first is to spend a lot of time talking with your kids about the challenges they face with their peers. The second is to model friendship ourselves. The easiest way for your children to understand the meaning of true friendship is to see it modeled firsthand by you. With the typical challenges that teens face in forming friendships being compounded by the issues just mentioned, it's more important than ever for us as parents to take an active role in teaching our children about friendship and to watch how we provide for and select friendships in our own lives. If we don't model friendship for them, how will they ever learn what true friendship looks like? From television and the movies they watch?

## From My Home to Yours

The following tips are designed to help you discuss and handle the many challenges your teens face.

**Should your son or daughter suddenly abandon a friend who begins to suffer from depression over his deadbeat dad**

**or missing mom?** No, but your child needs to know that he is not expected to handle the situation by himself. Make sure you know the family situations that your children's friends come from (see chapter 14, "Secure Allies in the Battle"). For those kids who come from single-parent homes, make sure you've spent time talking to the parent to see what the needs are. Don't ever put your children in a situation where they have to be the counselor. Make sure they know they are to always respond in love but that if they sense depression, extreme loneliness, or heartache in their friend, they are to let you know right away. You should then circle back to the parent and provide support or even recommend professional counseling.

**There's a verse in the Bible that says, "Walk with the wise and become wise, for a companion of fools suffers harm" (Prov. 13:20).** Another one states, "Bad company corrupts good character" (1 Cor. 15:33). Even those without faith can testify to the truth of these statements. You must be very deliberate in teaching your kids how to choose friends wisely and how to surround themselves with good company instead of bad. Teach them the character qualities they should be seeking in their friends: loyalty, kindness, honesty, and respect toward their parents and others in authority, to name a few. Be actively involved in knowing whom your kids hang out with at school, at the mall, and at church. Get to know the parents of their friends and build relationships with those families. It's up to us to protect our kids from fools and teach them how to walk among those who are wise.

**What do you do when your teen's friend has become involved in sexual activity, drinking, or other harmful behavior?** First, step in right away and protect your child. Second, connect with an adult in that child's life. I know of one mother who found out that her daughter's best friend was sneaking out at night to sleep with her boyfriend. This woman was obviously troubled by the situation but didn't know what she should do. I simply said, "If it were Sarah slipping out at night, wouldn't you want someone to tell you?" She got my point and then faced the difficult step of having to call the girl's mother to discuss the rumor. The mother was devastated, but not as much as she would have been if the daughter had gotten pregnant or hurt in her late-night jaunts.

It's critical in these circumstances to let your son or daughter know there are times when friendships must be cut off. Your first priority is your child's well-being, and we all know that even the best of kids can be pulled down by their friends. Author Lindy Keffer wrote an article about friendship for *Brio & Beyond* magazine called "We're All Broken," in which she talked directly to teenagers and offered great advice. You may want to use it as a guide when talking to your son or daughter about the difference between simply being kind and opening your heart to be a friend:

> If you're hanging out with someone who makes excuses for her failures or who promises to change but never acts on it, chances are you've got bad company. Either way, you're still called to love that person. But loving someone who's a bad influence doesn't mean sharing the intimate parts of your life with her. It means being kind when you pass in the halls. It means not gossiping. Those are loving

things you can do without getting pulled down by
a bad influence.

**Set the example of what true friendships look like.** Mom and
Dad, this might be a little tough for you, but maybe it's time to evaluate who you spend time with. Are your friends good examples for
your children of what a friend should be? Do they provide strength,
encouragement, comfort, and peace? Or are they more prone to
complain, drain you, and criticize others? Maybe it's time to spend
less time with those whose values you don't really share and seek out
those whose values you do.

And be extra sensitive about how you behave with your friends.
Given the number of marital problems today, a popular activity
among women is to meet at Starbucks and complain about their
husbands. Refuse to do this. Absolutely refuse—whether your children are with you or not. You should spend time with women who
help strengthen your marriage, not feed anxiety or trouble.

Another key point for moms to examine is how we talk about
our friends when they aren't around. If you are constantly dissing
your friends in front of your children, your kids will wonder just
what kind of person you really are. The silent thoughts that will go
through their minds are, "If she's so bad, why is Mom hanging out
with her?" and "I didn't know my mom could be so critical of people
she says are her friends."

**Dads, a special word to you: be a strong enough father that
you are willing to maintain only those friendships that make you
a better person.** Your role as a good husband and father is critical in

today's world. If you have friends who compromise your integrity in your children's eyes, you will be less effective in forming those hearts entrusted to your care. Teen guys and girls especially need to see men of character in action. So don't spend guys' nights out whooping it up with your friends. Don't use foul language with your buddies when you're shooting the breeze. Do find other men who can help build your faith.

You might want to consider joining an organization such as Promise Keepers (promisekeepers.org) that is designed to help men be loyal, true, and the primary influencers on their families. Make sure the guys you hang out with are men you would be proud for your sons and daughters to know as you know them.

## In Your Shoes

Kristin was blessed with many great friends who hung out en masse at our home over the years. But you know how catty preteen and teenage girls can be. As they started entering their teen years, I established a hard-and-fast rule in our home: you are not permitted to trash and criticize girls who aren't around. Period. No talking about your friends behind their backs. I always explained to Kristin that if she refused to engage in such banter, then all her friends would soon figure out that she would never say ugly things about them when they weren't around either.

When my best childhood friend, Suzanne (Harper) Ebel, and I turned forty, we decided to meet in a fun city and celebrate our birthdays together. We took a long weekend trip to Chicago and included our preteen daughters in the festivities. The four of us spent seventy-two hours doing girlie stuff like shopping and lunching and laughing. All three nights found us up into the wee hours talking about warm memories of our moms and our friendship as children and giggling like crazy over distant teen crushes on boys. We spoke freely of our faith as young women and how we made it a point to encourage each other. We spoke about how much we valued and counted on our loyalty to each other and how important that bond was when we often faced those who made fun of our strong Christian values. Our girls sat in rapt attention in their pajamas and listened to every word. The weekend was a blast and a great way to celebrate our birthdays, but, more important, Suzanne and I were able to show our girls the priceless treasure of a true and lasting friendship. Suz and I are now over fifty (please say it ain't so!), and we still live far away from each other. Kristin is married, and Suzanne's daughter, Adrianna, is in college. But Suz and I are still very conscious of how important it is for our daughters to see how true friendships and bonds will go the distance and the years.

My high school best buddy, Carmen (Morejon) Bauxauli, and I have also stayed close through the years and miles. Our daughters (hers is Amanda) do not even know each other, but they both understand that Carmen and I are girlfriends for life! Our husbands are now great friends too. Even though Carm and I went through long periods of time when we didn't talk (blame it on life getting in the way), every time we did call or email we easily picked up where we left off—as if hardly a day had gone by. That is the type of friendship our daughters need! As my mom used to say, "When it's true friendship, you don't have to work at it." Wiser words were never spoken. I recall the impact it had on me when I first heard her say that. It immediately helped me determine which relationships were draining or only surface level and which ones were healthy and true. It's critical that our children learn to distinguish the difference and have the courage to make the necessary changes.

# Reflections from a Daughter

The morning of my wedding, my bridesmaids, my mom, and I sat down at a long wooden table for brunch. I felt so very at home sitting there with the women who knew me best, those faith-filled women I've grown up with and am still growing with who would be standing up front with me later that day when I said, "I do."

There was plenty of happy laughter around the table as we shared stories. And the tears of bittersweet joy came too, especially when my mom got to talking about lifelong friendship, the kind of friendship that doesn't end when life changes and many miles separate and faces aren't seen for far too long.

She told us how she and her closest friends would sometimes go years without hearing from each other, times when the day-to-day aspects of life got in the way for a while. But then the phone would ring because one of them was hurting or something wonderful had happened or they had simply decided it was time to catch up. And when the phone rang she'd answer, and they'd pick up right where they'd left off.

That kind of friendship can't be forced, but it doesn't just happen either. It's a gift that can't be earned, but it also requires intentionality. For true and lasting friendship to develop, you have to be purposeful about opening up, about being vulnerable, about drawing the surface-level conversation deeper in order to share each other's joys and shoulder each other's burdens.

My friends and I weren't entirely focused on faith when we met. But we all now recognize that the qualities that characterized our friendship—honesty, an active desire for deep joy, and loyalty to one another—caused us to grow together toward Christ. And even though we're scattered all over now, we're fully confident that we will keep growing closer in friendship as we each grow closer to Christ.

## Act Now

Date _____


Today I began talking to my kids about the unique challenges they face in the world of friendship, and I started evaluating how I model friendship for them.


Signature _____

*Chapter 8*
# Know the Difference between Your Principles and Your Preferences

## The Challenge

In our world, right is often declared "wrong" and wrong is declared "right"; materialism and position are valued more highly than character and commitment; and styles, music, and what is deemed socially acceptable change faster than the speed of sound. It's no wonder our preferences are often front and center in our lives, blinding us to the fact that adhering to a solid code of principles is the compass that will guide us through the ever-shifting winds of trends.

That's why it's so important to know the difference between what you believe in and what you prefer in a given moment.

Principles are the foundation upon which you stand. They are the standards by which you live. They are the things worth sacrificing, fighting, and sometimes even dying for. Principles are the beliefs on which you will not compromise, no matter what. Principles are the foundation for achieving the vision you have for your children. (Remember that vision you wrote down back in chapter 2?)

Preferences, on the other hand, are things you can—and should—give up if the cost of having them is greater than the cost of setting them aside. They are the items you forsake for the sake of another. They are the styles and trends that often confuse us about what is truly important. Preferences are the first "me" in "me, me, me." There is nothing wrong with having preferences or in getting them. But when securing what we want becomes more important than practicing what we believe, then we've got problems.

When I was a teenager, a woman named Joyce Strader often reminded me to "never sacrifice the permanent on the altar of the temporary." I've thought about her wise admonishment many times during my life, and I am so grateful she cared enough to remind me that the choices and compromises we make today based on selfishness or mere desire can damage things that are lasting, such as our conscience, our character, and our reputation.

# From My Home to Yours

Take the time to write down a list of principles that should guide your life and then compare each one to a preference that might relate to it. For example:

My preference is that my daughter will make all As in high school.
But …
*My principle is that she will always do her best.*

My preference is that my son will have a haircut that my friends like.
But …
*My principle is that he will be clean.*

My preference is that my daughter will be popular among her peers.
But …
*My principle is that she will always stand for virtue, honesty, and truth.*

My preference is that we will be efficient and tactical in the way we run our home.
But …
*My principle is to create an environment that fosters the belief that mistakes can be redeemed.*

My preference is to get along with everyone.
But …
*My principle is to stand up for what I believe in.*

My preference is to be a cool mom.
But …
*My principle is to challenge my children to tower above the toxic culture.*

Sit down with each of your children and help them make a list too. Then go over what might be missing. At the end of the exercise, you'll have a pretty good road map filled with warning signals about what circumstances might be difficult for you or them. Discuss what those situations might be and then develop a plan with your child on how to avoid them. You should also be aware that your children might find themselves in situations they haven't planned on that just might cause them to forgo a principle because of temptation. You should discuss the likelihood of falling into one of these temptation traps and talk about how they can avoid the temptation in the first place. For instance, if you have a teenage son, one of his preferences when he is on a date with a girl might be to make out with her, even though his principle is to remain sexually pure and be respectful of women. When faced with such a choice in the heat of passion, how likely do you think it is that he will choose to uphold his principle? Um ... probably not very likely. But if you've taken the initiative to discuss it with him in advance, when there is no "hot temptation" cuddled up next to him in a dark car, you can help him avoid making a huge mistake. Teach him to avoid placing himself in the situation at all. He should decide well in advance to be involved in group dates and to avoid being alone with his heartthrob in a secluded area. This is where curfews are helpful too. In other words, help your son understand that boundaries and decisions made early in the evening can help him uphold his core principles later on.

Train yourself—and your children—to think about principles when you find yourself in a quandary or when you feel confused about what you should do. The idea is to think first about the principle involved. Then ask yourself, "If I get my preference (or my desire), will it do harm to the life principle I want to uphold?"

# In Your Shoes

I heard this powerful story from a father about how he will never regret standing for one of his principles in the midst of a dire situation:

> One of the biggest principles I have tried to practice
> with my son, Ken, is that I will always trust him

unless he has shown that he cannot be trusted. When he was sixteen years old, he was involved in what I thought was a minor lapse of judgment during school hours with several other boys. During lunch, when they have off-campus privileges, the boys went into a dilapidated vacant house, despite the obvious No Trespassing signs plastered all over the walls. A curious neighbor called the county and soon the house was swarming with police. Fortunately, Ken's inner voice had told him about fifteen minutes earlier that he should leave the house. So when the officers started arresting the young men, my boy was long gone. However, with reports that he had been there and that one kid had been seen running away after the police arrived, Ken fell under immediate suspicion for two serious offenses—resisting arrest and fleeing the scene of a crime. The circumstantial evidence looked pretty bad.

But Ken told me, the school principal, and the investigating officer that he had walked in the house, stayed for a few minutes, and then left because he knew he shouldn't be there. He insisted that he was not there when the police arrived, so he could not have possibly been the one running away. I had my doubts, but my principle had been to build honesty and integrity into my son by showing that I would always default to a position of faith in him—unless or until he proved otherwise.

It was tough to adhere to that principle, given the circumstances. Outwardly I was supporting my son and his character with the police, but inwardly I was dying a thousand deaths from near despair that it was possible that he might now be compounding a horrible situation by lying about it to school and law enforcement officials. Fortunately for Ken, and me, more information soon came to light, and the guilty student was identified and later confessed. The lesson this taught me was that my principle of placing trust in my son in a visible manner was worth the risk. Ken learned to obey signs, but much more than that, he learned that I had not lied when I said that I would always stand by him, ready to protect his good name and his integrity.

I know from experience how failing to uphold your principles can cause regret: The trip was meant to be a bonding time for my daughter and me. Our favorite place in the world is a small bridgeless paradise along the Gulf coast of Florida known as Little Gasparilla Island. Kristin and I went there for a week one summer—just the two of us. We love the warm turquoise waters, the white sandy beaches, and the abundance of marine life. A key goal of the trip was to rent a Jet Ski for the day to explore the waters of the Intracoastal Waterway and the canals and passes that lead to the ocean and, in so doing, to have a great adventure by just being together.

As soon as we got hold of that Jet Ski, we started flying at what seemed to be light speed over the waves of the Gulf, bouncing and clinging for dear life. Kristin and I took turns at the wheel, which means I endured hours of fear that I just might go reeling off the back of that thing and crash into the churning waters with maximum impact while Kristin continued barreling away at breakneck speed. I learned very quickly that she is much more daring and confident than I am. She knows how to cut the Jet Ski sharply in any direction and take a wave head-on, propelling us into the air and slamming us back down as we lurch ever forward. It is a great ride whenever Kristin is driving, but I wonder why she isn't deaf, as I am prone to fits of uncontrollable high-pitched screams and squeals when she is in command!

Later in the day we beached the water bike on the end of the island and hopped off to look for shells and just sit awhile. It was glorious. When we got hungry, we decided to jet down the canal to a paradise called Palm Island. Tucked away in the middle of a snaking lagoon and behind clumps of mangroves, the dock that serves as the landing spot for the delightful restaurant awaited us. The problem is, when you dock a watercraft, you have to tie it up carefully so it doesn't float away. Or, worse yet, if you tie it up too loosely at low tide, you'll find that your boat or Jet Ski was pushed by the current under the dock with the rising tide and then crushed as the water continued to steadily lift it. It was during the process of tying down the twenty-thousand-dollar Jet Ski (that belonged to someone else) that I came close to wrecking the entire day.

Although I've been an island girl my entire life, I've never quite been able to get this docking and tying thing down. And even though my husband is an excellent sailor, Kristin is a novice at the knotting thing. As we were tying off the boat, I had determined there was a very specific piling Kristin's end should be anchored on. Not wanting to give her a direct command to tie it there, I said several times that it "might be a good idea to try it over there." This was really my way of telling her what I thought she should do without actually telling her what to do—if you know what I mean. But Kristin was still figuring out where she thought it would be safest to anchor it, her beautiful head calculating the many factors that would lead to success or disaster. While we worked to steady the craft and brace it from the motion of the ever-lapping waters that insisted on banging it into the side of the dock, the stress began to build.

We also had the added treat of working with ropes that were way too long—by about five feet. So there we were, one teenager with developing emotions and growing independence and one forty-something slightly stressed mom who was also a bit hot and hungry, trying to figure out how to keep this craft that didn't belong to us from getting crushed. (Which would have also, by the way, left us stranded on the island and at the mercy of the Jet Ski's owner, who would have had to close his shop several miles away in order to come rescue us by boat. But no pressure.)

Anyway, after some time I totally and completely blew it. I said, "Kristin, I've told you three times to tie the rope around that post and you just keep disobeying." Well, I might as well have told her that her best friend had just betrayed her.

What had been a problem-solving, team-building, bonding moment was obliterated. Kristin silently began tying up the Jet Ski where I said she should as her eyes filled with tears and sadness enveloped her lovely face.

Because I preferred to satisfy my immediate desire for food and comfort over practicing my principle to be patient with my kids, I cast a cloud over the otherwise sunny day and darkened my daughter's tender spirit.

Thankfully, we both believe in repentance, forgiveness, and redemption, so when I finally humbled myself and said I was so sorry, she heaped love and compassion on me. The day ended with us reunited, sitting on the beach absorbing the incredible beauty of another dazzling sunset. But I lost a few precious hours that day with my daughter that are now gone forever.

## Reflections from a Daughter

When my husband and I first got married, we wanted to do everything together. But it didn't take long for us to realize how exhausting that would be. It wasn't that we grew tired of each other's company; we just realized that with 100 percent togetherness we couldn't possibly create a single schedule that would provide the right balance of rest, exercise, and mental stimulation for both of us. We have different needs, desires, interests, and capabilities.

Marriage certainly involves sacrificing some preferences and even learning to enjoy the preferences of the other. But if Randy or I were to forget ourselves entirely (if that were even possible), we would essentially become the other person. I didn't marry Randy because he reminded me of myself. I married him because, though we share the same principles rooted in our Christian faith, he experiences that faith and expresses it in his life in very different ways than I do. By getting to know him, I got to understand more about the God we both worship.

It's tempting sometimes to want to conform Randy to my own image. But we better represent Christ in our marriage when we encourage one another, as much as possible, to express God's image in the unique ways he designed each of us to. In fact, when we do, we find more abundant life and deeper love for each other.

Ephesians 4:16 says, "He makes the whole body fit together perfectly. As each part does its own special work, it helps the other parts grow, so that the whole body is healthy and growing and full of love" (NLT).

# Act Now

Date _____

Today I began listing the principles I want to live out and instill in my children, and I pledge to do my best never to sacrifice them for the sake of convenience, desire, or doubt.

Signature _____

*Chapter 9*
# Write a Letter to Your Teens

## The Challenge

As children turn into teens, many parents find it difficult to express the deep love, warmth, and vision that they have for them. The fact is, a sullen teenager is hard to connect with! As moms and dads, we often forget that what our teens crave more than anything is genuine love, thoughtful words, and encouragement from us. Their peers aren't prone to provide the affirmation they need, and the culture seems to do everything possible to supply plenty of just the opposite. When we relinquish our power to encourage and advise them, we only contribute to their tendency of withdrawal and angst. The hopeful news is that research shows that teens desperately want parental affirmation, approval, and love. Although they may appear to be like bricks—cold and indifferent to your advice and counsel—they are actually more like seeds that are capable of tremendous growth when planted in a nurturing environment and constantly watered with words of love, encouragement, and counsel. Such words are never more powerful than when they are written down. But, my goodness, how many parents have ever written their children a single letter?

My guess is that most moms and dads have never penned more
than a few words on a birthday card. As valuable as those cards
may be, they are not enough.

Obviously, it's critical to begin building more time and discussion with your children into your day (see chapter 12, "Learn How
to Have Meaningful Discussions with Your Children"). But in the
meantime, there is something you can do to start bridging the communication gap and showing your teens just how much they mean
to you: write them a love letter.

It's one thing to talk to your kids, but writing down your
feelings and sharing the vision you have for their lives serves as a
tangible reminder of how much you care. In this day of text messages, handwritten letters are rare. If you take the time to write down
your thoughts, your children will take them seriously and will have
something to hold in their hands and read over and over again. You
will most likely create a treasure that they just might keep for the rest
of their lives.

## From My Home to Yours

If you don't think you are a gifted writer, please don't let that stop
you. Feel free to borrow ideas from others or to quote poetry or
verses from relevant songs. Don't let anything keep you from writing what might be the single most important letter of your life! Go
to a quiet place and start by writing down bullet points or the first
few things that come to your mind. Create draft after draft if you
need to, and if it makes you more comfortable, ask a trusted friend
to review your letter for you. Or you can ask a complete stranger:

I'm more than happy to give you feedback if you would like. You can email me at rebecca@30waystostrengthenyourfamily.com.

So what should your letter include? Here are a few thoughts to help you get started:

**A clear statement of your love.** This doesn't have to be poetic, but it can be. However you choose to state it, your kids need to walk away from the letter knowing that you love them. Even the simple words "I love you" written on a line all by themselves will suffice. But you must say it very clearly, one way or another. Teens today report that what they crave more than anything else in the world is to be loved. And to be blunt, if they doubt your love for them, then no matter what else you do, you have failed.

**Your vision statement for their future.** Remember that vision statement you wrote in chapter 2? Why not share it in your letter?

**A prayer for them.** While I won't share the entire contents of a letter I wrote to my children, I will include a small sample of how I used the words of another to help me express the prayer of my heart for my children. You might even want to include this in your letter to your own kids:

> This is my prayer for you: that your love will grow more and more; that you will have knowledge and understanding with your love; that you will see the difference between good and bad and will choose the good.

Written long ago by Paul to the Christian church in Philippi, this ancient prayer can be found in Philippians 1:9–10 (NCV). It is so applicable today that I can scarcely believe it was written ages ago.

My heart's desire is that Drew, Nick, Kristin, and our son-in-law, Randy, will love God and people more and more every day. I pray that they will gain knowledge, insight, and discernment on a daily basis, that they will continuously fine-tune their inner compasses by reading God's Word so they can always find their way, and that they will be so filled with understanding that they make good short- and long-term decisions. I want them to have the ability to always clearly see the difference between good and bad. The world likes to fuzz the boundaries between good and bad, between right and wrong. Mixed messages about sexual activity, respect, violence, and tolerance are so prevalent that today's kids and young adults are faced with a mesh of morality that makes it increasingly difficult to know where truth ends and injustice begins. I also pray that they will have the courage and strength to always choose the good. And when they find it difficult to summon courage and strength, I pray that they will place their faith in God and his promises so they will be able to do the right thing anyway. Isn't that what you pray for your children? If so, then tell them! Whatever it is you want them to know about you, your life, and your heart, write it down and tell them.

**A warm memory you have of their childhood.** Children and teens absolutely love stories—especially about them! It excites them to know that you have a special memory of their lives or personality stored away deep in your heart. If something doesn't come to mind right away, then just describe how you felt the first time you held them in your arms or the smell of their little fuzzy head or what you thought when they got on the school bus for the first time. Certainly you can think of something!

**Positive words about them as people.** Teens today are filled with doubt about their worth, abilities, and futures. As I mention later in this book, society confuses them even more by focusing on building their self-esteem (see chapter 19, "Teach Your Children Every Day That They Have God-Given Value"). What you need to do is tell them how much you think they are worth—how you value their personality, their talents, or their sense of humor. Something remarkable happens when you speak positively to teens: they start giving you more of the positive attribute you have praised. When they know you think they have value, then they start believing it.

You might also want to include the elements of the Jewish blessing that I describe in chapter 19 and let them know why you want to bless them every day in this manner.

**Any admissions of your mistakes or failings in your relationship with them.** Ouch. This one can hurt. But your admission to your kids of your own mistakes actually creates a strong emotional bond with them—after all, if you've made a huge mistake that has hurt them, they already know it! This would be a great time to bring it out in the open and to ask for their forgiveness. It also helps them open up and ask forgiveness for their own mistakes. It's important for us to admit that we aren't perfect and that we have a lot of work to do in order to become the parents God meant for us to be. We also need to let them know we will keep striving to be that mom or dad they can always count on.

**A strong commitment to be there for them, regardless of the circumstances that the future may bring.** After telling them straight out that you love them, the second most powerful element of your letter will be to let them know that as long as there is breath left in you, you will be there for them. Understanding what true commitment entails is something very foreign in today's world. With over half of all marriages ending in divorce, the epidemic of absentee parents, and relationships constantly portrayed only in sexual terms, your kids need to know they can count on you. Regardless of how many mistakes they make, regardless of what they have done in the past, regardless of what they may do in the future, they must have someone to rely on. That person is you—and you must tell them.

# In Your Shoes

My pastor, Steve King, tells a beautiful story about how a very short letter from his father served to guide his conscience and actions throughout his college years:

> My dad was a man of few words and did not typically write me letters. To get one from him was very unusual. When I graduated from high school and was preparing to go off to college, my father penned a letter that I will always cherish. It said something like this: "Dear Steve, through high school you

have been a fine Christian man and I am proud of
you. Now that you are going off to college you will
face temptations that you cannot even imagine. I
believe that you will remain a man of character and
will face them well." Then my father transitioned
and said, "But even if you do not, I want you to
know that I will always be on your side."

What I explain to people is that my dad's letter
kept me out of trouble in college because my greatest fear was that I would break my father's heart.

A dear friend shared with me a letter that her dad wrote before
she embarked on a new opportunity in her life. It reads, in part,

Dear Bek,

Thank you for your sincere love for your family.
Your mother and I are so proud of you!

Your best days are ahead. Let the Word of God
be on your breath. Your intoxication with his truth
will lead you into opportunities and people you
can never dream of. His truth will be your anchor
of faith and the wisdom you need to make wise
choices.

Be decisive and trust God with the results.
Fear God and serve people, but keep your security
wrapped up in your intimate relationship with him.
Your next few months will be exciting and scary,
but we are here for you.

Take time to think on quiet thoughts to balance your big dreams. Take time to do nothing, which will bring balance to your horrendous activity and sometimes torrid pace. Make sure to invest in people who can give you nothing in return to keep your motives pure and unselfish.

I love you, Rebekah! Look up to your heavenly Father for his direction, look out to others for their needs, look inward to yourself for a clear conscience, and look to your family for unconditional love and support. Yes, there are big days ahead, but you can make every day big.

Love, Dad

Mom and Dad, your children are hungry for your love, for your approval, and for your guidance. Please don't squander the influence and lasting impact you can have on their lives. Even if you aren't a great writer—or, like my pastor's dad, are a person of few words—take the time and give the effort to write your child a letter or brief note of your commitment to them. The few minutes you invest in this endeavor could reap a lifetime of wise choices and inspiration for generations to come.

## Reflections from a Daughter

I frequently received notes from my mom as I was growing up. It seems that at every major life event, and many of the small ones, I got one: birthdays, graduations, when I went off to study abroad, and sometimes just because. We both have an attraction to the written word, which may be part of the reason she loved writing the notes and I loved getting them. But what kid doesn't love getting words of praise and encouragement from his or her parents?

I have a box of memorabilia where I've kept many of the letters I've gotten from both of my parents over the years. From time to time I go through it, and the words written to me years ago never fail to bring me to tears. In fact, they mean much more to me now than they did when I first got them. Proverbs 16:24 says, "Gracious words are like a honeycomb, sweetness to the soul and health to the body" (ESV). I can attest to that truth. Words written in love are life giving. And they only get sweeter with time.

## Act Now

Date _____

Today I sat down and began a draft of a letter to each of my children. I vow to complete them within the next thirty days, and I pledge to continue communicating positive words of love to them in writing on a regular basis.

Signature _____

*Chapter 10*

# Battle the Culture, Not Your Children

## The Challenge

We all know how easy it is to get angry when we see our children make mistakes. While we cannot let our children entirely off the hook and must make consistent discipline a part of our homes, we also need to realize that our kids are the targets of pernicious media, fierce advertising, and an entire army of adults who think they know how to raise our children better than we do. From the media to educators, doctors, and child psychologists, it seems the very institution of parenthood is under attack. And when both the mass media and adults in positions of authority degrade the basic roles of mother and father, it undermines the validity of our authority and insight with our own children.

Ending the conflict in your home starts with taking on the enemy that fired the first shots: the culture, not your kids.

As I pointed out in chapter 1, "Commit to the Daily Battle," adults are the ones responsible for the difficult world our children must navigate.

But it's not just the adults who control the media that you need to battle. It's also the adults who control a growing number of professional associations, such as teachers' unions and medical organizations. There was a time in this country when institutions and the adults who ran them understood that their purpose was to help parents in parenting their children, not to subvert or replace them. The schools once worked hand in hand with parents and encouraged parental involvement, not just activity in the PTA to help raise money. Today, many (not all) educators believe they actually know what is best for your son or daughter. The fact is, they can't possibly understand the history, gifts, needs, habits, dreams, and unique personality of each kid shuffled through a system built for the masses. Our children come home to us at night. They grow in our presence, and we alone are equipped to look at the whole child and situation. You are the first and last defense for your child. Yet parents often believe they aren't smart enough to raise or educate their own kids. (Read more about this in the next chapter, "Direct Your Children's Education.") Tragically, it seems the medical community is adopting this position more and more too. As the health of our nation and our families has suffered because of an out-of-control media culture and a rejection of basic moral values, our children are paying the price. An epidemic number of teen pregnancies and sexually transmitted diseases and a record number of kids diagnosed with clinical depression, ADD, and ADHD only encourage the government and the medical community to step in and take yet more control and influence away from parents. It's a maddening cycle that causes more confusion and disarray while obscuring who is responsible for the inevitable increase of shattered families and damaged lives of young people. It will only become worse if parents become less relevant. I know the constant barrage of attacks upon our children can make us feel hopeless. The battle for our children's souls is never ending. But the good news is that we are the ones best equipped to make a difference in our children's lives. Realizing that the battle is not with our kids is critical for parents who truly want to take back their homes.

If you fight the culture war in a way that creates a hostile environment, perhaps with the idea that your teen is enemy number one, you will lose the battle and maybe even your child in the process. We must communicate to our kids that we, as their parents, are fighting for and not against them. We are fighting for their character, their futures, their innocence, and their childhood.

As Dr. James Dobson of Family Talk, who has perhaps done more to preserve families and help parents than any other single person in history (other than Christ, of course), explains in his wonderful book *Your Legacy: The Greatest Gift*, society is no longer supporting us in raising our children. Judeo-Christian values are fading, pop culture and politically correct ideology undermine parents, and harmful images and ideas slip into our kids' lives via the Internet. And social media has completely changed the game. Dr. Dobson explained:

> With every child having a cell phone with which to access each other beyond parental ears, and with the advent of the all-pervasive social media, there are just too many opportunities for kids to conspire and to get into trouble.... It still makes sense to prohibit harmful or immoral behavior, and to discipline and punish when appropriate. However, these time-honored approaches to child

management must be supplemented by an emotional connection that makes children *want* to do
what is right.... Your sons and daughters must
know that you love them unconditionally and that
everything you require is for their own good....
"Laying down the law" without this emotional
linkage is likely to fail.

We will win when we teach our children rather than fight with
them, when we protect them rather than wrestle with them, and
when we assert our authority over our children rather than relinquish
our roles to "the professionals."

# In Your Shoes

When my daughter, Kristin, was thirteen years old, I took her to a
pediatrician for a sports physical so she could join her middle school
track team. It was a standard, uneventful visit—until the doctor told
me that she needed to have a "private chat" with Kristin.

"Excuse me?" I asked. "What do you mean by private chat?"

"Oh, there are some things I need to talk to Kristin about and
you can't be in the room," she said matter-of-factly.

Incredulous, I shot back, "I need to be here for any conversation
you have with my daughter."

"But you can't," the doctor insisted. "We're going to be talking
about private things and you have to leave."

I bristled, "She's a minor. I'm her mother. And I will be in the
room for everything."

The doctor was stunned but continued anyway. "Okay, now I'm going to have that talk with you just like I would if your mom were not here."

She reminded Kristin that drinking is illegal until you turn twenty-one and that smoking is really, really bad. Then came the frustrating comments: "Sex is a little trickier. You're getting to the age where girls are having boyfriends, and some of them will be kissing and doing other things. You have to do what is right for you."

At this point, I had to interrupt. "Excuse me, but we've taught our children that sex isn't just about what feels right. We've taught them that it's important to save sex for marriage."

The doctor looked at me in disbelief. Then she turned to my thirteen-year-old daughter and said, "Well, that's what some people think, but you have to do what is comfortable for you."

Of course, that was the last time we went to that doctor! I still shudder when I think about it. The doctor obviously didn't expect to get my pushback any more than I expected her to challenge me on my own authority with my daughter. But you as a mom or dad must push back! On the way home in the car that day, I had the following conversation with Kristin:

"Kristin, do you know what just happened in there? That doctor tried to drive a wedge between us. She tried to isolate you from me and pass on her own values to you."

Kristin replied, "I know, Mom. And I know why you are upset."

"Good," I responded. "Because I want you to know that if something bad were to happen to you, it's not the doctor who will be there for you. It's me. It's me and your dad who will always be there for you. She might be a 'professional,' but she's not your mom. Your dad and I love you more than anyone else in the world possibly could. We know what's best for you. And I refuse to let anyone interfere with my commitment to you or with my ability to protect and teach you."

Kristin got it, and guess what? My bond with my daughter was actually strengthened that day. We won that battle over the adult who tried to impose her worldview on my precious child. It took courage and discomfort, but we did it.

Radio and television host and commentator Laura Ingraham included the story I just shared in her book *Power to the People*. She also wrote,

> It's not just forces in the popular culture that are trying to push parents out of the way. "Health care" professionals can also step way over the line. When doctors speak, most of us listen and trust them....
>
> Parents would be disturbed to know that it is common practice among pediatricians these days to tell the moms and dads to leave the room so the "professional" can have private chats with children—chats that involve controversial topics like abortion, premarital sex, masturbation, and birth control. Doctors think they can—and should— talk to children in a way that parents can't. It's a trend that extends from doctors' offices, to schools, to government. The "experts" know best. Parents are too ignorant, too "traditional," and too incompetent to be left "unsupervised" to direct the lives of their own children.

Good for Rebecca for saying "back away from my child!" It's difficult to stand up to experts, doctors, and supposed authority figures. And too many parents just take it. Think about what that approach communicates to your child.

# From My Home to Yours

In addition to making it clear that you are the authority figure in your children's lives, here are other ways you can fight the culture war without fighting your kids:

**Remind your children of who you are.** Regardless of what our children might tell us, they long to know that we are in control. The last thing they want is to be pulled back and forth between adults, manipulated by anyone, or led to believe that everything is relative. Teens are looking for boundaries, for a firm foundation they can count on, for solid advice, and for someone who can be responsible for them. They are looking for someone to believe in. Remind them through conversation and actions that you are that person. (See chapter 12, "Learn How to Have Meaningful Discussions with Your Children.")

**Assert your authority with other adults.** I just can't say this enough! As I was raising my children, it seemed that nearly every day I had to remind other adults that they had no right to instruct or advise my children without my permission! It's not the teacher, it's not the doctor, and it's not the social worker who will be held accountable if your children get in trouble. It is you.

**Interact with local media.** When you see something pernicious aimed at your children by a local radio or television outlet,
call the station manager and follow up with a letter demanding a
reply. Write an op-ed for your weekly newspaper or a letter to the
editor for your daily paper. You can find out how to do this by
reading the editorial page. Papers have rules for opinion pieces and
letters they may publish. You must follow them if you want to see
your piece in print. You may be surprised to find that you are voic-
ing what lots of other parents are feeling. (See chapter 14, "Secure
Allies in the Battle.")

**Organize a group of parents to visit the teacher.** If you have
issues with the way a teacher or school handles something, such as
sex education in the classroom, for example, chances are that other
parents feel the same way. Remember that the schools exist to help
you teach your children, not to dictate their brand of morality.
You have an absolute right to express your concerns, and if other
parents do it too, you will have a better chance of a positive out-
come. But above all else be kind and respectful and take only kind
and respectful parents with you. Make sure that if you point out a
problem you also offer a solution that would apply to your child
and the children of those who believe as you do. You are not there
to force your beliefs on other students any more than you would
want other parents to force their beliefs on your child. But you do
have an absolute right to make certain that your faith and moral
beliefs are not trampled by the public school that you, through
your tax dollars, are paying for.

**Organize boycotts with other parents.** Again, there is strength in numbers. You'd be amazed at how quickly a local business will respond to requests from customers and potential customers in their neighborhood. And you'll also probably be surprised by how many willing participants are out there. A survey of women by the Motherhood Project revealed that most moms wish parents would join forces in fighting the adults who seek to manipulate our kids. Even a short letter with twenty signatures of parents who share your concerns can get a local merchant to remove a product or stop an inappropriate marketing campaign aimed at your children. Just remember to be nice but firm. And if the owner does respond positively, reward him by shopping at his business in the future and encouraging others to do the same.

**Write to the CEOs and board members of companies negatively targeting your children.** Odds are you'll catch the attention of at least one empathetic parent who serves on the board or one executive who doesn't want angry parents denting quarterly earnings.

## Reflections from a Daughter

One thing my parents did incredibly well was communicate that they trusted me and were on my side. They gave my brothers and me a tremendous amount of freedom, even when we were very young. For example, we had to tell them where we were going on our bikes when we were younger or in our cars when we were older, but we didn't have to beg them for permission. They had their rules, to be

sure, many of which we didn't particularly enjoy, but the rules never
felt as though they were against us. When my parents said no to
movies, it was because of specific content. Their nos were predict-
able and consistent; they weren't the "because I said so" answers that
drove so many of my friends to want to lie to their parents about
what they were doing.

What I appreciate most is that when situations turned sour, they
gave us the benefit of the doubt. If we were ever wrongly accused or
believed we were unjustly punished by some authority, they took our
word for it and put themselves on the line to stand up for us. They
never took sides against us. Because they displayed that kind of trust,
it made me very reluctant to do anything that would disappoint them.

My mom's advice to "battle the culture, not your children" is,
I believe, one of the most important pieces of advice in this book.
I have friends with parents everywhere on the spectrum. On one
extreme, I have dear friends whose parents embrace, rather than
reject, the unwholesome parts of the culture. While some of those
friends grew to discern and filter through negative aspects of the culture on their own, they now feel they have taken on the parental role
in their relationships with their moms and dads, which understandably creates a lot of tension and heartache within their families. On
the other extreme, I have friends whose parents were so controlling,
overprotective, or mistrusting as they were growing up that they
never felt they could be honest or open with them. Those friends are
still reluctant to talk candidly with their parents and admit they are
struggling to find independence as adults. I've often been told that
the basis for any good relationship is trust, and that certainly doesn't
exclude parents and children.

# Act Now

Date _____

Today I pledged to protect my children by standing up to those who would attack them, our values, and their futures. In so doing, I reminded my kids that we are on the same team and that I will never, ever leave them to fend for themselves.

Signature _____

# More Help

**Dr. Bill Maier** is one of the leading experts on how you can battle the culture and, in so doing, actually cause your kids to love you more. One particular book he edited, *Help! My Teen Thinks I'm the Enemy*, explains, "Your teen really does want a good relationship with you, though at times it may feel like you're enduring the Cold War. [This] can help you build a strong and lasting relationship with your child, through the teen years and beyond." I suggest ordering this great resource and others by Dr. Maier. He knows what he is talking about and should be one of your first resources.

***So Sexy So Soon: The New Sexualized Childhood and What Parents Can Do to Protect Their Kids*** is a wonderful book filled with great ideas on how to battle the culture. Written by Diane Levin and Jean Kilbourne, it is filled with tips and stories of success to equip and encourage you.

**Bill O'Reilly,** in his book *Culture Warrior*, covers the battleground for our culture by outlining a number of issues and decrying the erosion of societal discipline.

*Power to the People* by Laura Ingraham is a powerful handbook that outlines your rights as both a parent and a citizen and explains how to stop the creep of influence that undermines your authority.

The website of the **American Family Association** (afa.net) has a great section called "Activism," where you can get tips on how to approach businesses when you feel they are degrading community standards and how to fight marketing campaigns and businesses that corrupt decency.

*Chapter 11*

# Direct Your Children's Education

## The Challenge

With free education offered everywhere in the United States, a plethora of teachers who seem to be more than willing to take a role of authority in place of parents, and the convenience of sending our children to someone else to educate them, many parents have relinquished their role as the primary directors of their children's education. Our kids spend more awake time in schoolrooms during their formative years than just about any place else other than home. But it seems most parents don't have a clue what their children are being taught.

Even the most expensive private school can be a moral wasteland. Although a high price tag might indicate academic excellence, it can also indicate that the school may contain a level of intellectual snobbery or an air of superiority that assumes that faith in God and traditional moral values are foolishness. Conversely, many nurturing religious schools lack an emphasis on academic achievement. The bottom line is, you have to do your homework before you can be certain the private schools in your area are all that you hope for. Don't get me wrong—with the growing failures of the public schools, there has been a rise in the number of private schools across the nation that can help our children excel both spiritually and academically. You just have to find out what is available to you.

Of course, everyone knows—though few want to face it—that the performance level of the public school system is dismal. Study after study shows that American public education is failing when compared to the rest of the civilized world.

Add to that the rampant behavioral problems and sexually explicit "family life education" materials that teach our kids they are expected to have sex as teens, and you've got a host of reasons not to send your children to public school.

This chapter is not meant to discourage you if your children are in a public school setting. My own children attended our local public high schools. The reality is, however, that you must be diligent about finding out what goes on in the classroom, what your kids are reading, and whether your values are under attack. If you have the slightest indication that your children are susceptible to manipulation or may be influenced by the lack of morality on display in the public schools, then I strongly urge you to look for other educational options. If you determine that your children should attend public school, then I hope to help you begin to navigate those treacherous waters and I encourage you to maximize your parental rights. Warning: this chapter merely scratches the surface of how you can affect what goes on in the classroom. It is not meant to be an all-encompassing, foolproof method for your situation. It is intended, however, to encourage you to take control of your children's education by becoming an active participant. Your commitment in taking on that responsibility is the first, and most important, of the many steps you will need to take over the years.

It's time to take an active role in your children's education. Read their textbooks, interact with their teachers, understand your rights as a parent, question materials, and never, ever assume that someone knows how to teach your children better than you do.

The Heritage Foundation reports that parental involvement is a

robust influence on educational outcomes. It is multidimensional. Ways to be involved include monitoring children's activities outside home and school; setting rules; having conversations about and helping children with schoolwork and school-related issues; holding high educational expectations; discussing future planning with children and helping them with important decision making; participating in school-related activities such as meeting with teachers and volunteering in the classroom; and reading to children or engaging in other enrichment or leisure activities together.

Education expert Christine Kim of the Heritage Foundation reports,

While academic research has consistently shown that increased spending does not correlate with educational gains, the research does show a strong relationship between parental influences and children's educational outcomes, from school readiness to college completion. Two compelling parental factors emerge:

1. family structure, i.e., the number of parents living in the student's home and their relationships to the child, and

2. parents' involvement in their children's schoolwork.

Consequently, the solution to improving educational outcomes begins at home, by strengthening marriage and promoting stable family formation and parental involvement.

# From My Home to Yours

**Evaluate each of your children's needs and your academic choices.** I'm the mom of three, and I know from experience that my children are not cookie-cutter images of each other. They displayed different academic strengths and weaknesses and different tolerance levels and had very different personalities. And they have not maintained the exact same levels of interests and needs over the years. Different children have different ways of learning, and it's up to you—not some educator who can't possibly know or love them as you do—to make the decisions about how and where they should learn. Every parent should have the choice and freedom to select the educational setting that is best for each of their children.

We educated our three children in virtually every possible setting over the years—homeschool, private school, and public schools. My husband and I determined long ago that our family would march to the beat of our own drummer. We refused to be victims of the snobbery of those parents who insisted that private schools are the best. We didn't allow ourselves to be shamed by well-meaning parents who insisted that if we didn't homeschool then we were less committed to our kids than they were to theirs. And we absolutely rejected both the conventional wisdom that public education is the answer and the notion that all public schools are failing schools. We never forced all our children into one educational mold out of a desire for convenience. It makes life a little more complicated to actually evaluate what situations are best for your kids, but it is absolutely worth it.

**Seriously consider every option, including homeschooling.** Research the schools in your area. What are the test scores? What are the behavior problems? How are students disciplined? How much parental involvement is allowed? What textbooks are used? Is abstinence education—or something else—the basis for sex ed? The bottom line is that if a school is keeping you in the dark about materials, classroom procedures, or personal involvement, they probably have an agenda they are hiding. It might be academic content that emerges as the problem, or it might be an attitude of superiority that seeks to keep you effectively locked out of your child's education. In either case, I have one piece of advice: grab your kids and run! If an adult in authority ever tries to force his or her brand of morality on your children, if any system that has your children in their care says that you as the parent don't belong, then just get up and go.

For a season, taking control of our children's education meant homeschooling them. Homeschooling certainly presented its own set of challenges, but it was the best option for our family at the time and our children thrived in the freedom it allowed us.

Homeschooling might not be right for your family. It might not be the best option for your child. But I encourage you to consider it as a possibility. There is a huge body of research that proves that homeschooled children as a whole soar over their peers academically, psychologically, and socially.

The Home School Legal Defense Association (hslda.org) has compiled studies from around the nation to show how the individual attention and atmosphere that homeschooled children enjoy is superior to a system of mass education. The *Homeschool Progress Report 2009: Academic Achievement and Demographics*, which can be accessed on their website, reported that homeschoolers, on average, scored thirty-seven percentile points above public school students on standardized achievement tests. Even children whose parents did not have college degrees scored in the eighty-third percentile, which is well above the national average for public school students. Homeschooled children whose parents both had college degrees scored in the ninetieth percentile.

The average public school spends nearly ten thousand dollars per child per year, whereas the progress report stated that the average home-school parent spends about five hundred dollars per child per year.

If you decide it is time to take full control of your kids' education, know that homeschooling isn't what the mass media would have you believe it is. And the word *homeschooling* is actually a misnomer; much of it is now done through co-ops, by hiring tutors skilled in a specific area, in group settings with others, and online through acclaimed institutions. Given all the support and technology available to parents today, you just might be surprised to find that homeschooling is right for you and your children.

**Vigilance is the key to success.** No matter which settings you choose for your children, constant vigilance is necessary if you are to succeed in developing your children's emotional, intellectual, and spiritual abilities to their fullest. Hands-on interaction is critical. If you find something offensive or incorrect in their textbooks, challenge it with the teacher. Volunteer during school hours so you can see what is really going on. Know your rights, such as opting your children out of sex education/family life classes.

As a matter of fact, exploring the content of the sex education materials in your children's school should be a priority for you. These classes often start in grade school and set the stage for an entire worldview that may be contrary to yours. Go to the school today and find out the content of the curriculum. My guess is you will want to opt your child out. If you don't like what you see or how you are treated, please email me at rebecca@30waystostrengthenyourfamily.com. I am so concerned about the content of these classes that I pledge to connect you with someone who can help you figure out what to do to keep your children from being indoctrinated. You should also alert others who share your concerns and beliefs and work together to find solutions that fit your particular situation.

## In Your Shoes

Because the vast majority of children in the United States are educated in public schools at some time in their lives, I believe it is important to share inspiring stories from parents who have refused to relinquish their parental control or beliefs in such settings. My public education hero is a man I have never met. Via email he shared with me his story about how he worked with the system in order to protect his family's intellectual and faith beliefs. Gary wrote:

> When our son was in grade school, we received a call from the teacher explaining that he had been disruptive in class. He had challenged the teacher during a science lesson and said she was wrong when stating that the earth is billions of years old. He would not back down, so she escorted him to the office. I also knew this teacher had a masters in geology, so I prayed really hard that night.
>
> When I met with her I was humble and had my son repeat what had occurred. He also stated, "But that's what *you* told me, Dad!" I agreed and she added, "I understand your religious beliefs say one thing, but science shows us otherwise."
>
> I politely disagreed, saying science really is not able to state such, and gave her a couple of video tapes including *Young Age* and *Mt. St. Helens* by the Institute for Creation Research and *The Secret of Dinosaurs* by Master Books, as well as some technical articles.... We had a very polite and agreeable half-hour meeting.
>
> I never attacked her or railed about evolution/indoctrination/secularism but treated her like I would like to be treated.

At the end of this she shocked me by saying,
"Perhaps for now instead of saying billions or mil-
lions of years instead I will just say 'really ancient.'"

I added, "Yes, some of these kids might think
their grandparents are ancient."

She laughed at that and thanked me for staying understanding and polite, as she had been
confronted before by other parents and was dread-
ing another angry confrontation. She was truly
impressed with the reasons I presented to help her
see the other side of this debate.

Gary also wrote that this same teacher later invited him to give
a presentation before her class. He said, "She still held to evolution,
but for the rest of the school year presented both sides whenever she
talked over anything about origins or evolution of life issues. In fact
she even showed some of the videos to her class and to other teachers
so they could become more aware of this 'controversy.'" Gary is a
wonderful example of how it is possible to influence the teacher if
you come equipped with information and the right attitude.

Most teachers teach because they love children and knowledge.
But others have an agenda and can even trample on your rights or
practice intimidation if you let them. It is absolutely essential that
you never allow the public schools to infringe upon the religious
beliefs you are trying to pass on to your children, or deny your
children the right to free speech. In the "More Help" section at the
end of this chapter I have listed legal organizations that provide free
services to families who have had their constitutional rights infringed

upon. They don't accept every case, but they will hear you out and offer thoughtful, sound advice on how to handle your situation.

# Reflections from a Daughter

For the first half of kindergarten I was homeschooled.

Then I started at the local public school, which I loved.

A couple of years later I decided I wanted to be homeschooled again, and my parents welcomed the idea. (Meanwhile, my two older brothers attended a private middle school.)

The next year we were all homeschooled, but we took classes at an academy with other homeschooled students a couple of days a week (my mom even sat in on a Spanish class with us).

Finally, we moved from Richmond to Arlington, where we stayed in the public school system until our high school graduations.

That may sound too complicated for you, but I'm so happy my family did it that way. Every stage seemed very fitting, especially now when I look back on the way each one shaped me. When we were homeschooled we were under our parents' direction, and they gave us the important lifelong gift of learning how to teach ourselves. The principle of learning how to self-govern was also practiced, even without my always knowing it. It caused me to become an independent learner and allowed me to spend a lot more quality time with my mom when I was a young girl. It also freed us to travel as a family for some hands-on education. In public school, I gained confidence, expanded my social circles, and got to choose from all the extracurricular activities.

What I appreciate most is that I experienced a great sense of freedom in my education. Our parents were in charge, which meant we had a lot more input than most kids get. What we did certainly wouldn't work for most families, and I wouldn't try to claim it is the best way to do things. But it was custom fit, which means it was absolutely the best for us.

# Act Now

Date _____

Today I pledged to direct my children's education. I began to evaluate each of my children and their needs in order to determine what is best for them and our family.

Signature _____

# More Help

If you believe your children's constitutional rights have been infringed upon by your local public school, these organizations provide free advice and, in some cases, legal action. The best bet is to contact them through their websites:

- Alliance Defending Freedom (adflegal.org)
- American Center for Law and Justice (aclj.org)
- The Rutherford Institute (rutherford.org)

If you homeschool and believe you are being denied your rights, the **Home School Legal Defense Association (hslda.org)** can help.

You should also visit and join their parent organization, the **Home School Foundation (homeschoolfoundation.org)**, because they offer practical advice on everything from curriculum to teaching tips to support groups in your area. Both organizations were founded by Mike Farris, the guru of the modern homeschooling movement, and membership in them is a must for any family who has taken complete control of their children's education. I just can't say enough good things about their resources, conferences, website, and camaraderie. They even have real help for single parents and the parents of disabled children who want to homeschool their kids.

*Chapter 12*

# Learn How to Have Meaningful Discussions with Your Children

## The Challenge

Do you ever feel that talking to your child is like talking to a wall? Does it seem as if things go in one ear and out the other? Or do you ever feel as though every time you say something to your child a fireworks display of emotion is likely to ensue?

You are not alone. Learning the art of meaningful discussion with your children can be the hardest part of being a parent. Engaging your child without talking down to him or talking at a level too complex for her to grasp is truly an art, and getting your children to feel comfortable talking to you about their joys or concerns is challenging. Finding the balance between providing love, security, and nurture and being a disciplinarian may sometimes seem nearly impossible.

The very nature of conversation requires it to be a two-way street. If one person is blah, blah, blahing and the other is sulking nearby on the couch, arms folded and rolling his eyes, it's not a discussion. It just doesn't count. Believe me, as a mother of three, I've had those chats before, and they usually don't end well.

Having meaningful conversations with your children is critical to developing strong relationships that will last into adulthood. Such chats can also lead to important discussions about safety, and can provide opportunities for you to teach them values and principles that will protect their futures.

An article published in *Adolescence* reported,

> Considerable research has been devoted to forms of communication between parents and children. Several studies have reported that youth from families with frequent, open (bidirectional), and positive communication are less likely to become involved with drugs. These youth are also more likely to have abstinence-based norms than are youth from families in which this kind of dialogue is absent.... Discussions that involve both children's and parents' perspectives have been found to promote the development of conventional standards of conduct.

There is an undeniable direct and positive correlation between learning how to reach your children in a discussion and how they will do in the future.

# In Your Shoes

The following story, sent to me by Ana, describes a few ways to get the conversation rolling. She wrote:

When I turned fifteen, communication with my mother began to break down. Talking about the tough issues that typically arise during the teenage years devolved into regular fights, ending usually with tears and yelling. When I wanted to see a movie my mother did not agree on or wear a swimsuit that she did not approve of, a war of words was bound to ensue.

We essentially stopped discussing things. Instead, we would fight, argue, talk over each other's heads, yell, slam doors, and cry.

It did not take long for both of us to realize that it had to stop.

We did two things to work toward solving the problem.

First, we formed a discussion group with my three closest girlfriends and their mothers. We selected readings that walked through many of the common struggles between parents and teenagers, such as clothing and dating. The books covered numerous topics with discussion questions and real-life stories, some modern, some biblical.

Our group began meeting every other week, each daughter taking turns selecting a fun coffee shop or restaurant. For the first forty-five minutes of our get-together, we would socialize, laugh, and have a good time. After we were all feeling comfortable and in good spirits, we would begin our discussions. It could not have been a more healthy experience. For the girls, it provided an open and fun forum for expressing our feelings on "hot topics." For our mothers, they got the chance to express their concerns. We got to hear about their own life experiences, their own regrets in dating, dressing, and other choices they wanted to share. The conversations remained under control because no one wanted to cry or yell in front of everyone else. And the best part—we got to laugh through it all. We formed bonds with each other and learned what meaningful and positive discussion about hard issues can look like. We read about women who have gone before us and been faced with making hard ethical choices.

The ice began to thaw with my mother as we both had an outlet for positive expression and dialogue.

The second thing that we did was write contracts together for issues that we were fighting about. We regularly fought about how clean I had to keep my room. My mother felt like it had to be spic and span; I couldn't understand why I could not have privacy and some leeway to make choices about how I lived. Clothes on my floor were not hurting anyone, after all!

After one tear-filled fight that ensued when I was grounded for leaving out some clothes, we decided to sit down and work through a plan. I wrote out what I thought was a fair standard for room cleanliness and privacy, and she wrote out her version. We then, with my dad acting as a moderator, worked out a final standard that was a compromise between our two ideals, got it in writing, and then signed it.

We never fought about the cleanliness of my room again. But, better yet, we learned something about a great way to have a meaningful discussion about a topic causing us strife and a potential way to resolve it.

Writing a contract is probably not the best way for everyone to work out a problem. But having both sides put their thoughts in writing is a great way to get a meaningful conversation off to a good start.

The way you talk to your children may end up being unique to your relationship. When I was a preteen, my mother developed a very unusual but effective way to talk to me about difficult issues. She would offer to wash my hair—no kidding. I would stand at the bathroom counter, lean over, and put my head in the sink. Mom would usually use a cup to drench my hair with warm water and then soap up my head, and then the discussion would begin. It sounds odd, but I was actually comforted by the process. For me, it was a matter of being removed from the glare of an interrogation light—because in reality, I was under a spigot. No one was watching my expression, there was no eye contact, and it didn't matter if I cried—my face was wet anyway. She would always gently massage my head and say positive words of encouragement. But if it was an issue or concern or big life fact she needed to tell me, you can sure bet I heard it, even through water in my ears.

## From My Home to Yours

As a mother, I've always tried to keep my eyes open in search of opportunities to communicate with my kids. Here are a few tips I learned along the way:

**Make yourself available.** When your kids are home, do whatever you can to be home too. I've spent many an evening just relaxing on the sofa when I knew they were going to be hanging out. The kitchen is also a good place to plant yourself on a weekend—hungry teens in search of food will enter sooner or later, and most likely a comfortable opportunity to converse will usually present itself.

**Always offer to drive the masses.** Okay, so this one sounds nuts. But as often as possible, I offered to be the driver when my children and their friends were headed out. It was so much fun to listen to childhood and teen banter—and almost miraculously, when lots of bodies are in the car, you become a natural part of the conversation and laughter.

**Drive your children to school for as long as you can.** My husband always made a point of driving our kids to school in the mornings whenever he could. He found that our daughter was willing to start the day out with Dad despite her often sleepy disposition because it meant she didn't have to ride the school bus! When she became old enough to drive herself, she truly treasured all those early mornings alone with her dad. In fact, she and my husband still treasure those days. The rides were short, but she got the message loud and clear that Dad was always there, ready and willing to chat. Even though she didn't always choose to take advantage of the conversation opportunity, she knew she could if she wanted to. And that made a huge difference.

**Turn off the television when eating meals.** I wish this were more obvious than it seems to be. According to surveys, almost two-thirds of teens say their parents keep the television on when having family dinners—which don't happen very often to begin with. Having the tube on means an opportunity for conversation is lost forever.

**Initiate, initiate, initiate.** Did I make my point? Kids often feel a bit awkward about broaching a difficult subject. You're the parent, and part of your job is to take the initiative and teach them how to communicate. Be sensitive to their moods and the conditions. Actively look for opportunities to engage them in meaningful conversations. If your normally hyperactive teen son is unusually pensive, sit by his side and find out what is going on in his head. If your child walks in the door joyous, for goodness' sake, put down what you are doing and find out the source of her joy so you can share in it! And always end every conversation with a positive and encouraging comment. Then seal it with a quick

hug or some other physical contact, such as a squeeze of the hand
or a pat on the back.

**Another key to developing a habit of significant discussions
with your children is learning their own special way of communicating.** Gary Chapman wrote in his renowned book *The 5 Love
Languages* that "each child develops unique emotional patterns." He
argues that most people communicate and feel love in one or two
predominant languages: quality time, words of affirmation, gifts,
acts of service, or physical touch. Chapman urges parents to spend
time observing their children. How do they communicate? Do they
ask to spend special time alone with you? Do they run up and give
you hugs? Do they quietly do a chore without being asked? Looking
for these cues can help you speak to your children on a very deep
and intimate level. Knowing their special way of communicating can
help you reach out to them and begin meaningful discussions in a
way that speaks to them deeply.

# Reflections from a Daughter

Some of my sweetest memories from my relationship with my parents
are of late nights up talking. Most of the time, those conversations
weren't about anything in particular. And though I don't necessarily
remember everything we talked about, I do remember that I never
wanted to go to bed.

Throughout the day most of us aren't big talkers, but we tend
to open up a little more at night when the distractions of the day
fall away. I think my parents noticed the trend, and I know they

have always enjoyed our conversations as much, if not more, than I have. They could have been strict about sending my brothers and me to bed so they could get some downtime when we were kids, but instead they chose to let us stay up together. Sometimes the timing of a conversation makes all the difference, and if the time is right, why lose the opportunity?

# Act Now

Date _____

Today I let my children know that I want to hear more of what they have to say and I want to be available to share more openly with them. I initiated meaningful conversation with _____ about _____ on _____ (date).

Signature _____

*Chapter 13*

# Vow to Be the Parent (Not Your Children's Best Friend)

## The Challenge

It's one of the first words children learn to say: no. Yet no matter how much their offspring misbehave, many parents can't seem to bear using it themselves.

Maybe these permissive mothers and fathers are too tired after a long day at work to stand their ground. Perhaps they're so accustomed to dealing with other adults that compromise has become second nature to them. Whatever the reason, I can tell you this: these doormats are doing their children—not to mention themselves and the rest of society—no favors. As night follows day, their selfish, unhappy tots are going to grow into selfish, unhappy teenagers.

That's one more unfortunate result of our politically correct culture. We've swung from the old Victorian extreme ("children are to be seen, not heard") to another ("children are to be catered to, lest you bruise their fragile egos"). Look at all the books and magazines on childrearing that focus only on the short-term goal of getting past one particular battle. They recommend various ways to distract your child or bargain with him. In short, anything to avoid saying no. Never mind that by not acting like the parent, you've lost crucial ground in the larger effort to raise a thoughtful, well-behaved, independent teen who will go on to become a responsible adult.

Of course, it could be that the publishers of these books and magazines know their audience—and its hunger for pat answers. "We want guarantees," says syndicated columnist Betsy Hart in her book *It Takes a Parent.* "But the only thing we really know is that we have a duty as parents to persevere. And in that perseverance lies the best hope for our children."

I can truly appreciate her point. Most parents have solid instincts about what's right and wrong, and they have a pretty good sense of how to raise their children to tell one from the other. As parents we make mistakes, but we can learn from them. The trick is in sticking with it, day after day, for years.

And stick with it we must. Why? Because we love our children, even when they're acting unlovable. And because, as Hart put it in a theme that recurs throughout her book, "we need to be on a rescue mission for our children's hearts." The reason is simple: what we do is a reflection of our character. If we persevere in planting good virtues in our children—and we do that by being their parents, not their friends—we won't have to worry so much about how they will behave under pressure. (Of course, we'll never stop worrying altogether—we are parents, after all.)

Consider two people Hart used as examples to show that "training can take over when it comes to the heart": Bruce Ismay and Todd Beamer. Ismay was chairman and managing director of the White Star Line, which owned the *Titanic*, and was on the ship when it began to sink. But unlike hundreds of his passengers, he survived. Why? Because, Hart said, he was able to board a lifeboat "ahead of other potential male passengers because of his status." Contrast that with Todd Beamer, who was on United Airlines Flight 93 on September 11, 2001. When it became apparent that terrorists were using the plane for a suicide mission, Beamer rallied his fellow passengers to stop their attackers. We know the result. Instead of slamming into the US Capitol or a similar target, the plane crashed into a Pennsylvania field.

Was Bruce Ismay a born coward and was Todd Beamer a born hero? No. But in a moment of supreme peril, both showed their true character. Vice and virtue had no doubt been reinforced time and again during their lifetimes. When the big moment came, each acted accordingly. A hero, let's remember, acts unselfishly—and that's the kind of character trait that develops when parents take the time and the trouble to be the parent. It's hard, of course. But as the saying goes, nothing worthwhile is ever easy. There will be a few tears here and there, even some hurt feelings from time to time, but, believe it or not, the sky won't fall.

In fact, on some level, your children will appreciate it. They may not admit it, but deep down they're longing for guidance and boundaries. Some interesting public service announcements that aired years ago made this point nicely. They depicted several older teenagers, each telling the viewer how upset he was when his parents said no to staying out too late, hanging with the wrong crowd, or doing drugs. The message is loud and clear. They were angry that their parents didn't give in. But at the end of the video, they looked into the camera, paused, and said, "Thanks."

In retrospect, kids appreciate when their parents lay down the law. They realize, years after the fact, that it was done out of love (although you can be sure they were convinced at the time that their parents hated them). And that's the point. You're the adult, and it's your job to look down that road and do what it takes to ensure their future happiness. And that means acting like a parent.

Having the guts to say no when appropriate is also a good way to save your children from the "anything goes" culture that surrounds us. Modern parents seem to enthrone their children and constantly reinforce the notion that the world revolves around them. In the process, they create monsters who are a terror not only to others but to themselves, if the rising rates of depression are any indication.

These spoiled children are filled with false self-esteem (see chapter 19, "Teach Your Children Every Day That They Have God-Given Value") and have no real sense that personal dignity comes with treating others as you would like to be treated (see chapter 27, "Let the Golden Rule Rule Your Home").

You have authority simply because you are a parent. Our children need us to guide and direct them with the experience that comes from the school of hard knocks and from a position of authority. Your children need you to be their mom or dad—not just another drifting peer trying to figure out your way in the world.

# From My Home to Yours

**Set clear boundaries.** Take something like nonhomework computer time. Teens need to know how much of it they're allowed to have. A vaguely worded caution, such as "Don't be on there too long," followed by irritation when they've passed some time marker that's only in your own head, doesn't help. Tell them clearly, "You can only be online for X minutes"—and stick to it. The same principle applies to other areas of life. Let them know as clearly as possible what you expect.

**Enforce the rules.** Rules without enforcement are meaningless. Yet we constantly hear parents saying, "Don't do that" again and again—as their children, of course, do it repeatedly with no consequences. It would actually be better for these parents to say nothing and let their kids simply do whatever they wanted. That way, at least the parents wouldn't be teaching their children contempt for authority.

Don't plead with your children to behave. Make it clear that you expect them to obey. Obedience is a dirty word in our pop culture. But if you don't require it with your kids, you will all be in trouble. You will set them up for failure in life now and in the future. Teens have to obey the rules at school or they could get suspended; teens and adults have to obey the rules of the workplace or they could get fired. As a parent, teaching your children or teens to obey means (brace yourself, modern parents) saying a well-considered no and remaining firm. Despite what many parenting "experts" say, your children won't be scarred for life. Indeed, they'll be much better off. If you really love them, you're more concerned with shaping their character and teaching them how to succeed in life than you are with winning a popularity contest. Let's face it: there's no other reason to bother being the parent, because setting rules and enforcing them is hard work. Nothing could be easier than just sitting back and letting our children become tyrants. We do the work of being parents because we love our children.

**Don't discipline in anger.** I know—easier said than done. We've all had moments when we've flown off the handle and reacted in anger. But it's important for your children to realize that their punishment is just and that it's not coming simply because you're upset. Take some time to cool off before you say or do something you might regret. There's nothing wrong with saying, "We'll talk about this later, young man." (Make sure you do, of course!)

**Find a mentor—for you.** Many of you reading this book have come from less-than-perfect homes. You may have horrible memories of your mother and father, or you may have no memories of them at all because they weren't there. Regardless of your circumstances and heartache, you can become the parent your children need. Mentors are important for people of all ages, especially for parents who are single, struggling, or have bad childhood memories of their own. Moms, find an older, respected mother in your church or community and let her know you would like to learn from her. Dads, seek out grandfathers and older men of strong moral character to help you succeed at being a loving father. The point is, you don't have to make it up as you go or do it alone. Get help, and, in turn, your interest can bless the one who is mentoring you. (See the next chapter, "Secure Allies in the Battle," for more tips.)

# In Your Shoes

When I encouraged readers of my column to submit their stories for
this book, I received insight, wisdom, and encouragement and have
shared much of it with you. This letter, from a woman who wanted
to be identified only as L.C., is a poignant reminder of just how desperately our children want us to truly parent them. I share it for two
reasons: (1) to remind you that you have the power to shape your
children forever, and (2) to comfort you if you grew up in a home with
a parent who was hurtful. God offers healing for those who suffer from
negligent parenting, and part of that healing can come from becoming
the parent to your kids that you always dreamed of having.

> Mrs. Hagelin,
>
> I've read your columns ever since I discovered
> Townhall.com, and I loved *Home Invasion*. I wrote
> today because everyone should know how impor-
> tant it is for parents to be parents.
>
> In high school, I would hear girls complain
> about how their parents were too strict; some would
> change into clothes that showed noticeably more
> skin once they got to school, complaining that their
> parents wouldn't let them out the door if they knew
> that's what they were wearing that day. Sometimes I
> couldn't stay silent anymore and I would say, "You
> really don't know how blessed you are." You see, I
> was one of the girls who didn't have that, and I suf-
> fered for it.

My mom was absent for most of my childhood, and the times when she was there were characterized by extreme dysfunction more than anything else. She would buy and encourage me to wear the short little skirts and then turn around and tell me that I looked like a hooker the next day when she changed her mind about them. The one thing I wanted growing up was a clear standard. One moment my mom wanted to be my friend instead of my mom, and the next she was a completely unreasonable authoritarian. I never knew where I stood with her. God heals a lot of scars, and today I'm twenty-two years old and in grad school, but I still yearn for that guidance that I know I'll never have from her.

Please keep up the good work; I hope many children will grow up not knowing how blessed they are to have good parents, because the only ones who know what a blessing it is are too often the ones who never had it.

God bless,

L.C.

## Reflections from a Daughter

I can't say my brothers or I heard the word no very often. I think that's part of the reason it always held so much weight. There was no use arguing once Mom or Dad said the word. They wouldn't say it if they didn't mean it. It wasn't the frequency with which the word was used that made me respect it; it was the finality of it. But even though I respected it, I can't say I appreciated it. At least not in the moment.

With regard to saying no, my mom wrote, "There will be a few tears here and there, even some hurt feelings from time to time, but, believe it or not, the sky won't fall."

Sometimes it did feel like the sky was falling. I remember the cringe-worthy embarrassment of telling my friends I couldn't see the movie with them because my mom wouldn't let me.

But even though it felt like the sky was falling, it never did. I moved on.

Mom went on to say, "In retrospect, kids appreciate when their parents lay down the law. They realize, years after the fact, that it was done out of love."

She was right. Not long ago my husband and I walked out of a movie because we didn't feel like sitting there, awkwardly pretending not to be bothered by what was repeatedly happening on the screen. If my mom had bought me a ticket to the same movie when I was twelve, I would have been just as uncomfortable sitting there with my friends, but I would have been too worried about what they would think to get up and leave.

Now that I'm old enough to buy my own tickets, I understand why my parents sometimes said no, and I'm thankful they did. I'm also thankful that I learned from them how to say no for myself.

# Act Now

Date _____

Today I began being the parent in my home. I pledged to give my children the boundaries and discipline they need and, in so doing, to show the depth of my love for them.

Signature _____

# More Help

***The Epidemic: Raising Secure, Loving, Happy, and Responsible Children in an Era of Absentee and Permissive Parenting*** by Dr. Robert Shaw is a book sorely needed in today's culture. As a child and family psychiatrist, Shaw has seen, up close and personal, the pain caused by parents who won't do their job. Written with Stephanie Wood, a former executive editor of *Child* magazine, *The Epidemic* is packed with insights and useful tips.

***Christian Fatherhood*** by Stephen Wood and James Burnham is a bestselling book that was endorsed by Mother Teresa, Cardinal Stafford, and Cardinal O'Connor, to name a few. Wood is a dynamic speaker who challenges dads to stop shirking their duties and truly fulfill their role as father.

*Chapter 14*

# Secure Allies in the Battle

## The Challenge

Fighting the culture and seemingly everything in it can be a lonely battle. Of course, the trick of a formidable enemy is to make you think you are the only one—it's a classic tactic to make you want to give up, give in, or run away!

At first you might actually seem like the only one—you've probably heard it from your kids a thousand times if you've ventured even slightly into the culture war. "You're the only mom who won't let her kid go to that movie." "You're the only dad who won't let his son play that video game." "You're the only parents who want to talk to the teacher."

If you've heard these words, your children just might have an unintended but important point: Why are you the only parent your children know who has your values? Isn't it up to you to find other adults who do? Taking time to secure allies who share your worldview will make life easier not only for you but also for your children. No teen wants to feel isolated, left out, or weird. There are probably many parents who share your concerns, but they may not have dared to venture out and ask for help.

A Gallup poll revealed that 82 percent of Republicans and 78 percent of Democrats believe that American values today are fair to downright poor because of the pop culture. In another study, two thousand mothers were interviewed by researchers at the University of Minnesota on behalf of the Motherhood Project. The women were from all walks of life and included moms who work outside the home and those who work inside the home. They were from many different socioeconomic classes and various races. Yet they all shared the common worry about the harmful effects the modern culture is having on America's kids. The good news is that although the world would have you feel ostracized for your concerns, you are in good company. There is a silent army, probably many in your sphere of influence, looking for leadership and reinforcement in fighting the cultural battle.

We weren't meant to do this alone—to face the world by ourselves with our families standing vulnerable to the onslaught of a toxic culture. There has always been strength in numbers and comfort in camaraderie.

You must find allies in this battle for the hearts and souls of your children. Be bold. Take the first step. Start the conversation with other parents, and you just might be surprised at how many of them are actually longing for help and a return to the time when neighbors helped neighbors reinforce strong moral values for their kids. Here are just a few places to look for allies.

**In a faith community:** The first place you should look for allies is in your faith community. A large and growing body of social science research shows what a huge difference religious faith makes in our everyday lives. It's no overstatement, in fact, to say that religion makes civil society possible. Without it, just about every indicator of human misery would be off the charts.

My husband and I raised our three children in a loving Christian household and in a church with people who share our values. The friendships and support we have found there have done more to help us raise children of character than anything else, and the very act of attending church together also brings us closer as a family.

Pat Fagan, one of the nation's premier social science scholars and researchers, has sifted through countless studies that show the remarkable effect that religious practice (including attending church) has on marriage, divorce, child rearing, drug and alcohol abuse, out-of-wedlock births, and even mental and physical health.

I was pleased to see that there are many benefits of being involved in a faith community and that they are nearly universal. Fagan reported, for instance, on how practicing faith brings parents and children closer:

> Compared with mothers who did not consider religion important, those who deemed religion to be very important rated their relationship with their child significantly higher.... When mothers and their children share the same level of religious practice, they experience better relationships with one another. For instance, when eighteen-year-olds attended religious services with approximately the same frequency as their mothers, the mothers reported significantly better relationships with them, even many years later.... Moreover, mothers

who became more religious throughout the first eighteen years of their child's life reported a better relationship with that child, regardless of the level of their religious practice before the child was born.

The same holds true for fathers:

Compared with fathers who had no religious affiliation, those who attended religious services frequently were more likely to monitor their children, praise and hug their children, and spend time with their children. In fact, fathers' frequency of religious attendance was a stronger predictor of paternal involvement in one-on-one activities with children than were employment and income—the factors most frequently cited in the academic literature on fatherhood.

How about adolescent sexual behavior? Fagan noted that traditional values and religious beliefs are among the most common factors teens cite to explain why they are abstaining from sex. In addition, the use of cigarettes and the abuse of alcohol and drugs drop significantly among those who are religiously active.

He also wrote, "In the vast majority of the studies reviewed, an increase in religious practice was associated with having greater hope and a greater sense of purpose in life."

Here are a few of the other positive results Dr. Fagan pointed out as related to being in a community of faith:

> Churchgoers are more likely to be married, less likely to be divorced or single, and more likely to manifest high levels of satisfaction in marriage....
>
> Regular religious practice generally inoculates individuals against a host of social problems, including suicide, drug abuse, out-of-wedlock births, crime, and divorce....
>
> In repairing damage caused by alcoholism, drug addiction, and marital breakdown, religious belief and practice are a major source of strength and recovery.

Obviously, churches aren't perfect—they are, after all, composed of imperfect people—but the results of attending church are undeniable. Solid churches are composed of people whose faith in God guides them through troubles, whose values help steer them away from cultural garbage, and who are trying to protect their children's hearts, minds, and souls. If you're looking for the best possible environment for your family in this crazy culture, head to a good church.

**In your neighborhood:** Wow, how America's concept of neighborhood has changed over the years! We live such busy lives that many of us don't even know our neighbors, much less what is important to them. If you don't know everyone on your street and on the street behind your house, take the next six months to make your way around and have a chat with every family. Identifying possible allies right next door can help you—and them—in countless ways. You'll also be able to figure out which houses you and your children should avoid. In addition, you can identify the needs of those right outside your door and then create a plan with your teens for how to help. Are there elderly people down the street who need assistance with yard work? Is there a frazzled young mother who needs your counsel? Is there a single parent who could use a hand and a friend? Being involved in your neighborhood can expand the borders of your home and do you, your children, and your neighbors a world of good.

**Among the parents of your kids' friends:** As my children grew into teens I began to realize that I had no real information about many of the families of their new friends. When teens go to high school, they suddenly have a mile-long list of new friends and acquaintances. They start driving and end up visiting homes we, as parents, have not been to. My goodness, I found it so much easier to keep track when I had to drive them everywhere!

With the convenience of having a teen who could drive himself around (and run errands for me!) came an added level of parental responsibility. I had to work harder to gather information on the families and homes he was visiting. It took me awhile to figure out how to create a system. By the time our youngest, Kristin, was driving, she knew she needed to call me from the landline phone of any new friend's house that she visited.

This little trick did three things.

> 1. I knew exactly where she was calling from and
>    could add the number to my contact list.

2. I could introduce myself to the parent(s) and
have a quick discussion about adult supervision,
the activities that were going on in the home, etc.
3. It put the parent(s) on notice that I care.

(Now that most teenagers have their own phones and landlines are
less common, it's important to note that you aren't accomplishing the
same thing if you simply have them call you from their own phone.
The point is that you get to talk to the adults who are supervising, that
you have an emergency contact, or that you at least get to pinpoint a
physical location. Have them hand their phone over to an adult so you
can chat, or have them call you from the adult's cell phone. You may
also want to look into enabling GPS tracking on their cell phone so
you can always tell where they are. It's a great safety feature!)

And, of course, I had a discussion with Kristin about the three
uncompromising reasons she must immediately leave a home:

1. The presence of alcohol or drugs
2. A lack of adult supervision
3. Entertainment or behavior that is in conflict
with what we allowed in our home

I learned through the years that I could trust Kristin to make
wise choices about where she spent her free time, but knowing the
parents provided an extra level of intelligence for me and protection for her.

I also took extra effort to get to know the teens who came into
my home. Ours has always been a very open home filled with mobs

of children through the years: toddlers, then young children, then pre-
teens, then teenagers, then young adults, and now adult children on
their own! When our children's friends started driving themselves over
or catching rides with friends (rather than with their parents), I tried
to make it a point to ask newcomers to call their parents and hand me
the phone so I could say hello. You'd be amazed at how many parents
are pleasantly surprised to receive such a call. Once again, I found that
some of them had quiet concerns about whom their children spent
time with but for a variety of reasons had never bothered to find out.
Placing a quick call helped me identify which parents shared my values
and assured them that I would be vigilant about taking care of their
sons and daughters while they were guests in my home.

**Through sports and other group activities:** Whether your kids
run track, play in the orchestra, or participate in other group activities, it's always a great idea to spend time with the parents when you
attend the games, concerts, and other events. Make the effort to chat
with other moms and dads, give kids rides to practices, and help out
with the fund-raisers. Your children will love you for it (although they
may not tell you), and you will be able to find parents who share your
values. I'm amazed at how many parents are no longer involved in their
kid's group activities once they reach high school. This is exactly the
time you should be introducing yourself and looking for friendships
and allies. You will also be able to identify (through the lack of their
parents' involvement) children whose lives you can add meaning to.
Your goal here should be to have a solid presence that allows you to
be involved but does not cramp your teen's growing need for independence. It can be a delicate balance, but if you don't make the effort

to attend and connect with the kids and their families, you will miss a valuable opportunity to help create a community of parents who support and protect their children and uphold solid values.

# From My Home to Yours

If you're searching for fellow warriors to help you combat the culture and raise your children, the following tips can help you secure new friends and allies:

**Be joyful:** Do you remember the song "Don't Worry, Be Happy"? It's a great reminder of how hungry people are for happiness. But it can be extremely difficult to experience joy when you are in the midst of a cultural battle. People are drawn to those who are calm and filled with joy. No one wants to be around a complaining, bitter mom who is viewed as hating everything about the society around her! People seek to be with people who are positive. See it as your job to help parents, teachers, and youth group leaders be "happy warriors." Encourage other parents, build up their joy of parenting, and remind them that being a mom is the most wonderful blessing of all. The Bible teaches us that if we ask God for his help and thank him for his blessings, we will have a deep and abiding peace even in the midst of the battle. It also teaches us that the joy of God can be our strength.

**Be brave:** Work together with those who share your values, and refuse to be afraid of those who are against you. Fear is enemy number one. Fear of disapproval, snide remarks, and the evil thrown at you by the media can quickly kill your spirits and efforts. Think of yourself as a conqueror. You are a voice for the innocent, a champion for what is highest and best, and a warrior for truth. Don't let anyone steal your vision of the best possible childhood and future for your children.

**Be kind:** While you are standing strong, everyone around you, especially your spouse and children, should see that you are gentle and kind. But that's hard to do. When I'm frustrated or feel attacked or aggravated, it's very, very difficult to be gentle and kind. Our culture teaches us that it's enough to be tolerant. But the great command is to do far more than just tolerate others. We are charged to treat others with love and kindness. That doesn't mean we give in or pretend we approve of behavior we know is wrong. It means we love other people enough, even when they display beliefs we may disagree with, to show them a kindness that just might open their hearts to what we have to say.

# Reflections from a Daughter

As a kid, I certainly took my parents' values for granted. I had no concept of the struggles they must have faced in their daily battle to provide the kind of childhood they desired for us. I also didn't know how many others were fighting alongside my parents or how many countless friends and family members were cheering them on from a distance. But as my wedding approached, so many of my parents' friends, people I barely knew or had never even met, offered incredibly moving and heartfelt words and gifts of congratulations. For the first time, I saw a glimpse of the invisible army of believers who helped raise me by investing in my parents.

secure allies in the battle

Scripture teaches that we become sharper, more mature, and
more stable when we live our lives in community with other believers. The world has a dulling effect on our senses, our thinking, and
our consciences. But "as iron sharpens iron, so one person sharpens
another" (Prov. 27:17).

Ephesians 4 says that Christians are given a variety of strengths,
so we are meant to work together to build one another up. It says,
"This will continue until we all come to such unity in our faith and
knowledge of God's Son that we will be mature in the Lord, measuring up to the full and complete standard of Christ. Then we will no
longer be immature like children. We won't be tossed and blown
about by every wind of new teaching. We will not be influenced
when people try to trick us with lies so clever they sound like the
truth" (verses 13–14 NLT).

On our own, we are vulnerable to the world's corruption. But
when we come together, we look more and more like Jesus, who
overcame the world.

# Act Now

Date _____

Today I determined that I would not be silenced by fear and that
I would find allies to help me succeed in raising my kids to tower
above the culture.

Signature _____

I can find potential allies in

my church: _____

my neighbors: _____

parents of my children's friends: _____

parents at my children's activities: _____

A new thing I'm going to try in order to find allies in the battle:

_____

# More Help

**Concerned Families (Fathers, Mothers, and Youth)** is a unique three-tier organization that has developed a simple system based on the principle that the traditional family is a transforming power and thus a "community family" can also be transforming. Concerned Fathers against Crime, Concerned Mothers Alliance for Children, and Concerned Youth allow local churches to work together to bless their neighbors in targeted ways, from working with law enforcement to working with local businesses. The end goal is public safety, including protecting children from the negative influences of the culture. You can join forces with them or start a chapter in your area by visiting ConcernedFamilies.org.

*Chapter 15*

# Develop and Follow Your "Mother's Intuition" and "Father Knows Best" Instincts

## The Challenge

As I talk to parents (especially mothers) in my own community and around the country, I have come to realize that many of us are frustrated by an ongoing conflict: we experience an intangible discernment about people and situations but don't always know how to act on it.

If we are honest with each other, one problem is that we fear the possibility of our instincts being incorrect and the actions we take looked upon by other parents as overreacting, overbearing, or overreaching. This fear ultimately causes many of us to remain silent, ignoring our instincts and disregarding our intuition as a reliable source for decision making and parenting.

Society certainly does not help to convince us that our instincts are reliable. We're constantly told that we aren't smart enough or don't have the right skills to understand and raise our children. We are also accused of being overprotective and closed minded or judgmental. Name calling has always been an effective method for silencing people.

Another reason we often hesitate to take action is that it can lead to conflict with our children, especially our teens. If your mother's intuition gives you concern about one of your kid's friends, for instance, and you begin to delve deeper into the situation, your son or daughter may feel offended. If we already lack faith in our intuition in the first place, we tend to back away from acting on it in any way that would potentially lead to parent-child conflict.

But ask yourself this question: How many times has your stomach suddenly filled with knots or a flash of doubt gone through your mind about an issue, parent, or situation and later you wished you had acted on that feeling? Likely at least a few examples come to mind. Hindsight, of course, is always 20/20.

Listen to that voice inside you that says, "Something isn't right here," and then act on it. As a parent, you are the first and last line of defense for your children. And as the saying goes, "Better safe than sorry."

Regardless of what you may call it, it's undeniable that women, in particular, possess a unique and mysterious kind of discernment we often refer to as "women's intuition." It may be nearly impossible to define, but I think each of us can remember a specific time when we experienced a feeling of warning or discomfort that, upon reflection, could only be described as our intuition. And, ladies, when we become mothers, the ability to discern situations grows even sharper. I believe the Lord gives parents that instinct to protect our children. It can be trusted, and it should not be ignored. It is something God gave you in abundance as a mother, and, as mysterious as it is, it is very real. Our mother's intuition is something we need to come to trust as an essential tool we must use to protect our children. As mothers, we also have a need and ability to understand and connect with our kids as nobody else can. We should feel confident in acting on the warnings we experience from this connection.

And, fathers, there is a reason why a show like *Father Knows Best* was so popular. It's because loving dads do watch out for their families, and they do sacrifice and go the extra mile to connect to their sons and daughters. Loving dads have always weighed all the options to figure out what is best for their children. Of course, that show aired at a time when men were actually respected and expected to take care of their families. Many of today's television commercials and sitcoms portray dads as wimpy, ignorant, and stupid. We are led to believe that fathers are useless and disposable. I cringe every time I see fathers portrayed on television. It would be interesting to see the effect it would have on real dads if the media started showing more programs with intact family units in which television dads actually model what a good father looks like. It makes me wonder if television is imitating life or if life is imitating television. It was horribly wrong when shows of long ago portrayed women as weak; it was downright sexist. So why is it acceptable to turn around now and do the same to men? With a barrage of media aimed at destroying masculinity, it's no wonder it isn't politically correct to declare that "father knows best." Perhaps that's partly why many fathers fail to exert their opinions anymore.

I remember the first time I held each of my children in my arms. I was overcome by the urge to take care of my baby and would have done anything it took to protect the precious little bundle. Most of us would take a bullet for our kids. So we must ask ourselves, why aren't we also willing to do something a little less heroic, and a lot less

costly, like install an Internet filter to protect them from child predators who might stalk them online? When polled about Internet usage
in their homes, the majority of parents said they have concerns about
the content their children might be viewing. Yet these same parents
also said they had never taken any action to ensure their kids' online
safety. The intuition is right, but the inaction is puzzling. What has
caused them to ignore their instinct?

Proverbs 27:12 says, "The prudent see danger and take refuge,
but the simple keep going and pay the penalty." The warning here is
clear: When we understand there is danger and take action to protect
ourselves, we are wise. But when we sense harm and ignore it, we are
fools and will pay the price. The bigger problem is that when you are a
parent who exercises bad judgment, your children will often suffer too.

# In Your Shoes

We must also help our children develop their own intuition.

My friend Rebecca told me how her own father took great care to
develop her inner voice. Rebecca and her dad have always been very
close. She was an extremely verbal and socially mature child—sort of
like a mini-adult—by the age of five. She was often found conversing
with adults around her (much to their entertainment), and her father
consciously treated his carefree little princess like a person of intelligence and importance. He always asked her what she thought about
the people they encountered, and he invited her to do the same of
him. He didn't ask what she thought about someone's haircut, choice
of shoes, or other characteristics visible to the eye; instead, he helped
her cultivate a habit of looking deeper at people upon their first

meeting, and he constantly evaluated her initial intuitive reaction to them. In this way her father uniquely helped Rebecca develop an unprecedented relational maturity, bringing to her attention her women's intuition, if you will, from a very early age.

Through the years this continued, and Rebecca soon became acutely aware of a certain intangible yet distinct discomfort that filled her around certain people. Most often this first impression never fully went away, even after continued interaction or exposure to the person. It's important to note that this was something she experienced with only a handful of people and in a handful of situations. Every time she would express this uncomfortable feeling to her father, he would look her steadily in the eyes and say the same thing: "Trust that feeling, Rebecca. The Lord gives some people, and especially women, a discernment of people that should not be ignored. Whenever you sense this kind of discomfort, danger, or unease, trust it. It is very real."

And in her case it certainly turned out to be. She experienced this feeling with three "Christian" men with whom she became acquainted through church; later she discovered each had had affairs with other men's wives. She also trusted that deep warning and avoided going to dinner with someone who later put a friend in a threatening position. Over and over again she has seen how trusting her intuition has saved her from dangers that otherwise could not have been foreseen.

I am convinced that because Rebecca's father took great care to develop her intuition, she has a dependable inner compass that might have otherwise gone off kilter. Society, after all, does not encourage us to listen to our conscience, that still, small voice inside of us. Instead, it often lures us to danger with empty promises of

"Everyone's doing it; you'll be fine" or "That star (or politician) can't be that bad; he is so popular with masses of people." We are often led to believe that we are odd and alone in our misgivings about others. But Rebecca's story shows us that we can help our children develop discernment about people and situations.

## From My Home to Yours

Remember the prayer I quoted in chapter 9, "Write a Letter to Your Teens"? One of the basic skills the author of that prayer, the apostle Paul, wanted people to develop was their discernment. This is also referred to as judgment or understanding. How do we do that? Rebecca's father has shown us the truth of the biblical admonishment in Hebrews that teaching discernment comes from "constant practice to distinguish good from evil" (5:14 ESV).

Discernment can be defined as "acuteness of judgment and understanding." Intuition is described by Webster's as "a keen and quick insight." Thankfully for all of us, discernment isn't something we have to be born with; it's something we can all develop with lots of practice. We also become more able to have those "keen and quick" insights into people and situations when we listen to and act on our inner feeling. But beware: the more you set your intuition aside, don't exercise your own good judgment, or ignore the difference between good and evil, the weaker your power of discernment becomes. Plainly put, you lose the ability to know the difference between good and bad. And if you or your kids have lost the sensitivity to know right from wrong, it becomes less likely that you will choose what is good, fair, and just.

When I was a child, my mother used to tell me, "If you feel the hair rising on the back of your neck, then something isn't right." It was her way of warning me to learn to be discerning and to trust myself when I felt uncomfortable with a situation. She was right. There have been many times when I've walked away from an opportunity for no other reason than it didn't feel right. I try to teach my children to do the same. And you know what happens when you listen to your intuition? It gets better and better. When you use the insight you have, your ability to discern becomes stronger.

I heard a story on the radio that perfectly illustrates how easy it is to lose our way when we ignore our intuition and focus only on the pleasant. I didn't catch the name of the person sharing it, but I am eternally grateful that he did:

> A pastor was relating how he went to Hawaii and had the opportunity to go snorkeling. There, in crystal clear waters, he could put his head just under the surface and see amazingly beautiful, colorful fish all around him. He waded out about waist deep and was mesmerized by the beauty. The guide told him he would be able to get a far better view if he got on a raft and floated while he watched. The pastor complied, even though he knew the water was getting deep, and lay down on the raft in such a way that he could stick his face just below the surface and slightly lift it every now and then for a breath. He saw so many lovely creatures and got so caught up in the glory of it all that he no longer

paid attention to where he was. After some time, he heard a noise and looked up to see a rescue boat pulling toward him. Startled, he turned around and looked toward the shore, which was so far away that he could no longer see the people on the beach! He had ignored his initial warning system and focused instead on the fun he was having. He had become so mesmerized by the dazzling colors that he had drifted into grave danger before he knew it.

This is exactly what can happen to us and our children if we ignore our intuition—if we lose sight of the truth and become blinded by the dazzle.

# Reflections from a Daughter

When it comes time to make difficult decisions, it's easy to ask and hope for a sign from God. But when we don't receive one, we feel abandoned and fear we will lose our way.

James 1:5 says, "If any of you lacks wisdom, you should ask God, who gives generously to all without finding fault, and it will be given to you." Wisdom is defined as having good judgment. While God certainly does sometimes direct our minds on a conscious level, it seems he more often desires us to use the thinking, reasoning minds he gave to us to make creative decisions of our own, provided those decisions do not contradict the Scriptures. God sees our hearts. So when we operate under the goal of pleasing him, he is pleased.

Bob Benson wrote in his book *See You at the House*:

> If I do not seem to hear him speak from outside, and if there does not seem to be any message from the sky, then I must listen to the voice that is within me. For that voice, too, is the purposeful, calling voice of God to us.... Not many of us have enough confidence in ourselves to listen to that whispering voice that comes from within. Most of the time, we do not even hear it. But it doesn't matter because we wouldn't trust it. We cannot believe that this inner voice is capable of leading us due north.

## Act Now

Date _____

Today I vowed never to doubt my own conscience and intuition. I started to trust my ability to discern and pledged to practice following it.

Signature _____

*Chapter 16*

# Install Parental Controls on Your Televisions—and Be the Ultimate Control

## The Challenge

According to the Kaiser Family Foundation, the average eight- to eighteen-year-old views television for approximately four and a half hours a day. This astounding fact should be enough to give every parent cause for alarm.

Aside from the fact that every hour spent watching television is usually an hour wasted, it is also an hour that takes the place of doing something good or healthy, such as reading, exercising, interacting with family and peers, or enjoying the outdoors. To make matters worse, many of those wasted hours are saturated with violence, sexual activity, drug use, crafty advertisements, and other pernicious media material that your child—and probably you, in many cases—should simply not be watching.

The standards for what is permissible in prime time are at an all-time low on both broadcast and cable stations. Steamy sex-laden shows geared toward young people are now airing at the peak viewing hours, making them accessible to children of any age. To make matters worse, most television contracts come with scores of channels airing pornography and countless variations of MTV, VH1, and the like. Without limitations, television is simply not safe for anyone, especially those with developing minds.

And, of course, as every parent knows by now, it's not just the programming you have to worry about. It's often the commercials too. How many of us have frantically tried to grab the remote control in the middle of an ad on erectile dysfunction? How many preteen and teen girls have been embarrassed when an ad on feminine hygiene came on while boys were in the room? And how many of us are sick and tired of adult males being portrayed in commercials as lazy, ignorant, and stupid?

The fact is, in today's television world, you can never be certain that your family is safe from values that run counter to yours or that your kids will be protected from information far above their level of maturity.

The psychological damage done to children and teens by exposure to harmful television has been proved and documented by countless scientific and social studies. Research also shows how television programming can affect behavior.

A study by the RAND Corporation reveals what many parents have known in our guts for a long time: kids who watch sex on television are more likely to engage in sexual activity. The study followed the viewing habits of teenagers over a four-year period and found, specifically, that teens who watch high levels of sexual activity are twice as likely to be involved in a pregnancy as kids who have limited exposure. The report also revealed that such viewers are more likely to engage in sex at younger ages than their peers.

A list compiled by Kyla Boyse, RN, for the University of Michigan Health System included the following dangers to your children from overexposure to television:

- Television viewing is probably replacing activities in your children's life that you would rather they do.
- Kids who spend more time watching television (both with and without parents and siblings present) spend less time interacting with family members.
- Excessive television viewing can contribute to poor grades, sleep problems, behavior problems, obesity, and risky behavior.
- Most children's programming does not teach what parents say they want their children to learn.

The same University of Michigan website also lists a host of dangers from exposure to violence on television, pulled from various child health studies:

- An average American child will see two hundred thousand violent acts and sixteen thousand murders on television by age eighteen.
- Two-thirds of all programming contains violence.
- Programs designed for children more often contain violence than those designed for adult television.

The studies also point out that most violence on television goes unpunished, and a lot of it is portrayed as funny, with no concern for human suffering and loss. The violence on television is often glamorous. It's shown as "a fun and effective way to get what you want, without consequences." Even the heroes of G-rated animated movies use violence to solve their problems. The violence is nearly universal, and it's increasing.

That might not matter so much, except that, as the University of Michigan website reported, "Children imitate the violence they see on TV. It reduces inhibitions and leads to more aggressive behavior." And the effect is long term—lasting into adulthood.

The only real solution to these many problems is to take control of the television-viewing habits in your home. Some parents may choose to eliminate all television, but I don't recommend this. Television is not the problem; the problem is lack of parental oversight. There are so many wonderful, educational, and inspirational programs on television that it would be sad to block it all. There's also the risk of unintentionally glamorizing television and creating a taboo that your children may try to break in other places. Regardless of your tactic, you must take control. Fortunately, with the parental controls available today, it's easier than ever to screen out much of the harmful or objectionable material. It may take an hour or so to set up the controls and understand how they work, but, my goodness, one hour of your time can keep your children from watching thousands of hours of raunchy programming over many years. Just do it. And remember, you can't rely solely on the ratings system or the judgment of others. You have to set limits on hours and be available to help your kids sort through garbage on your own terms.

The first step is to install a blocking technology or use a tool such as TiVo to record worthwhile programming so you can skip commercials. The second step is to vow to be the ultimate control. You can't fully depend on any device to make personal judgments for you based on your children and your values, and you can't depend on the technology to always work. You've got to remember that your kids are much more technologically savvy than you will ever be. As one young man informed me while I was writing this book, "Kids can be pretty ingenious about breaking codes, and you will never know it—especially high schoolers." Of course, that statement got me to delve much deeper into what he was getting at. With some reluctance, but also with a level of maturity in understanding that parents need to know how easy codes are to break, he proceeded to tell me that it took him and his brother about an hour and a half to figure out a way to discover the code on the parental controls. "We put little marks of highlighter on each of the numbers on the controller. We told Dad we wanted to watch something from the movies-on-demand section, and we gave him the remote control to punch in the code. After he ordered the movie and left the room, we turned on a black light to see what numbers were smudged, and then we wrote out each possible combination. We punched them all in until we figured it out—the code was 3906."

So what are the lessons learned here? A few things:

- Change your code often.
- Your kids want to prove they are more technologically advanced than you are, and they will do it just to show that they are.

- No matter how good your kids are, the media are always there tempting them.
- Life is full of surprises! There's a lot going on that you don't know about!

# In Your Shoes

When Gwen was six, her mother left her in front of the television watching *Sesame Street* while she made dinner. While Mom was in the kitchen cooking, Gwen picked up the remote. She was at an observant age and had recently watched her father casually flipping channels and found it interesting. She flipped through some sports games, news, and family dramas. She couldn't quite figure out how to get back to *Sesame Street,* so she kept pressing the button.

Some channels later, she landed on a scene with a nude woman showering and eerie music playing in the background. A man with a large knife was slinking toward her in the dark.

Gwen had stumbled onto the infamous shower scene in the horror movie *Psycho*, in which a showering woman is brutally stabbed to death. Transfixed in horror, she watched the entire scene.

Her mother returned to find her blanched and unable to speak. By that time the commercials had come on, so her mother did not know what she had watched, but she knew Gwen had seen something she should not have.

That night Gwen sobbed for hours and was unable to sleep. For months she had trouble sleeping and ridding herself of the horrible images she had seen. Her mother frequently awoke to hear her crying and often had to lie in bed with her for hours to soothe her.

It wasn't until twenty years later that Gwen shared the scene that had haunted her throughout her childhood! Her story is a sad reminder that children cannot easily erase the images that are put into their minds. Television marks us like permanent ink. Whether it's gory violence, graphic sexual content, or some other garbage, once we have viewed it, it's there to stay. We may not remember it as often as Gwen, but it undoubtedly affects us in some negative way.

A man named Poppy shared with me via email the positive results that discussing, monitoring, and explaining viewing rules have had on his children:

> We have four boys and they are very active and interested in movies, cartoons, and video games like most kids. However, I have trained them that there are certain shows and games they won't be seeing, and I always explain why. So it thrills me now when something questionable will come on TV (they DO NOT, and NEVER WILL, have a TV in their rooms) and they will turn around and look at me, because they already know when something is not right. I have also overheard them telling their friends, "We're not allowed to watch that." I feel that when you explain the reasoning behind the rule, children begin to make informed and wise choices at an early age. Our boys regularly go to the movies and watch age-appropriate programming, so there is no sense of deprivation. They do

participate in the culture—but with wisdom and
guidance based on our worldview.

# From My Home to Yours

In addition to using parental controls, the American Academy of
Pediatrics (AAP) suggests practical ways that you can take control
of your family television set. First, set reasonable limits. Setting time
limits is a good idea for all electronic entertainment. No television in
a child's bedroom or while doing homework are also two good rules.
Second, plan what to watch. Surfing the channels idly isn't the way to
find good programming. Instead, use a program guide, confer with
your children, and make deliberate choices about which shows your
family will watch. Third, turn the television on to watch the program
and then turn it off when it is over. It's important to watch television
together with your kids so you can make what you see a springboard
for family discussion. Your children can benefit from your wisdom on
any questionable material they may see, from stereotypes to violence
to sexual images. As the AAP points out, you can also help them learn
to resist the ads by pointing out that "the purpose of commercials is to
make people want things they may not need."

The AAP also points out that you can help your kids break the
TV habit by suggesting substitute activities, from hobbies and books
to sports and music. This group also urges, "Set a good example. As
a role model, limiting your own TV viewing and choosing programs
carefully will help your children do the same." Finally, they point
out the importance of taking a public stand: "Stations, networks,
and sponsors pay attention to letters from the public. If you think a

commercial is misleading or inappropriately targeting children, write down the product name, channel, and time you saw the commercial and describe your concerns."

# Reflections from a Daughter

One day fairly early on in high school, I came home and turned on the television, as I often did. I watched the first ten or so minutes of a show, then commercials came on, and about halfway through the commercials, something weird happened. I suddenly couldn't remember what show I was watching. I sat there, blinking, dumbfounded, trying in vain to remember what it was even about, and then I got up and turned the thing off. There was nothing dramatic about it, but from then on, I simply didn't have any interest in watching TV.

Before that, we had parental controls on all the televisions in our house. To be honest, it was pretty embarrassing when friends came over and show after show, movie after movie they wanted to watch was blocked. But I got over the embarrassment, and we watched other shows (most of which I can't remember now), or we retreated to going outside instead.

My husband grew up without cable, and though he receives incredulous looks from time to time for not knowing our generation's popular childhood cartoons, he turned out okay. He's also much smarter than I am, and I suspect that might be why.

While television isn't all bad, and parental controls can help clean it up, I'm actually of the opinion that it's best to ditch the TV altogether.

# Act Now

Date _____

Today I learned how to use the V-chip (see "More Help" at the end of this chapter) or the parental controls on my remote control. I also vowed to be the one to determine what my children watch on television and when and how often they watch it.

Signature _____

# More Help

Unless you bought your television in the dark ages, it contains something called a V-chip, which allows you to filter television programs by rating. If you are unsure of how to use this great tool, visit **TheTVBoss.com** for a tutorial on how to program it. You can block individual channels and shows and lock them with a password. There are also several tamper-proof television time-management devices on the market that allow parents to set limits on how much time is spent watching television. You can even buy a special remote for children (a Weemote) with large, simple buttons that can be programmed to access only approved television channels.

The website **ControlWithCable.org** has great information about how you can gain control over your television and how you can improve your media literacy. Warning: please remember that although they can be incredibly helpful, the ratings the television industry gives itself probably do not reflect your personal ratings. These tools do *not* replace your responsibilities to "be the filter."

*Chapter 17*
# Be Your Family's Movie Critic

## The Challenge

There's nothing like a cold, rainy day to make you think about taking the family to the local multiplex to see a movie. Grab some popcorn, forget your worries for a couple of hours, and enter that larger-than-life world of imagination and spectacle, of heroes and villains. Warning: your choices are going to be somewhat limited if your aim is wholesome family entertainment. What's showing at the movies this week? Hmm, the story of how the world's most infamous cannibal acquired his taste for his fellow man? An apocalyptic future world in which the human race is threatened with extinction? How about spending the evening with a deranged killer who stalks young people? Why on earth do parents actually pay for their children to explore the depths of human depravity? Simply put, most parents just aren't paying attention. And what about the movies your kids watch on their own? Count how many titles you see that glorify violence, casual sex, or disloyalty. Way too many movies are filled with messages that undermine the strong character traits most parents want their children to develop. It's crazy to hope our children will grow up understanding the importance of fidelity, purity, and honesty when they are digesting a steady diet of garbage—usually paid for by Mom and Dad.

As the Dove Foundation, which offers an excellent family-friendly media rating system, notes on its website, Dove.org, "For years we have watched the morals and attitudes of the entertainment industry slowly creep into society."

They are right. And since Hollywood's standards are so low, we as parents must be diligent. It is up to us to determine what we will allow into our homes and how we will equip our children to make the right moral choices at the theater.

In his article "Marquee Madness," former Heritage Foundation president Dr. Edwin Feulner wrote about a Federal Trade Commission report documenting the damaging effects of American pop culture on children. Many were concerned that the report's findings might lead to calls for greater censorship. Dr. Feulner wrote, "If parents want to protect their kids and avoid censorship, they must be the ones pressuring Hollywood to change. It's the only way to guarantee a happy ending to what has so far been a sad, sad story."

If we want to live in an ownership society that emphasizes personal responsibility, we as parents cannot waste time wagging fingers at Hollywood. Parents must take responsibility for their own children. Hollywood will follow our cues. They want to make profitable films! PG-13- and R-rated films don't make the most money—not by a long shot. Ironically, it's G- and PG-rated films that prove to be the most lucrative. If parents continue to ramp up the demand for wholesome movies, Hollywood will produce them. There is hope.

But, left to their own devices, Hollywood moguls will continue to turn even the stories of childhood heroes into disturbingly dark films. The Batman movie *The Dark Knight* provides a perfect case in point. The film broke every box office record in history when it was released. It also heavily targeted youth. It was, after all, a film about a comic book hero! Yet there was wide-ranging agreement among critics that the film, rated PG-13, should have been rated R and was definitely not kid friendly. Christopher Orr wrote for *The Atlantic*, "This is *not* a film for children, and the MPAA should be ashamed of its PG-13 acquiescence."

What does the movie actually contain? Many shooting scenes, graphic injuries, violent and disturbing deaths, sexual innuendo, countless curse words, and scenes of brutal and bloody combat, just to list a few. It got off the hook, though, because there were no instances of the F-word.

One twenty-four-year-old man wrote to me that it was by far "the most hauntingly disturbing PG-13" movie he had ever seen and would "recommend exercising great discretion before seeing the film, even as an adult." Yet the movie industry would like you to think it's perfectly appropriate for your thirteen-year-old son or daughter, and the movie makers intended for kids of all ages to come and see it.

Something is wrong with this picture.

The fact is, you can't rely on the Hollywood rating system to make wise viewing choices for your family. To begin with, there has been a steady decline in the ratings system, with industry standards becoming more lax as the years go by. A movie that would have received a PG rating ten years ago, for instance, could easily be a G-rated movie today.

On the flip side, some movies that receive an R rating might actually contain stories of violence and war that are a critical part of a larger story with a positive message. Two examples of R-rated movies that might be appropriate and actually beneficial in teaching values to teens come to mind: *The Passion of the Christ*, the story of the crucifixion of Jesus, and *The Patriot*, a historical fiction movie that underscores the valiant vision and sacrifices in the struggle for America's freedom.

The point is that you as the parent need to be the movie critic for your children. What might be inappropriate for your eleven-year-old might be incredibly valuable in helping to underscore lessons of morality for your sixteen-year-old. Don't let other adults make the final decisions for you! The easiest way to make selections is to start with a trusted source for movie reviews and then go from there in making your decisions. Several great resources are listed in the "More Help" section at the end of this chapter.

# In Your Shoes

I wonder how many conversations about movies between parents and children have ended in tears. Children, especially teenagers, see movies as an opportunity to exercise freedom and choice along with the right to engage with today's culture and their friends. In a time when the social community in America is in serious decline, the movie theater has become one of the most popular places for children to hang out.

But gore and promiscuity seem to have become the keystone and bedrock of most flicks being produced these days. The key is to find an age-appropriate system that lets your children have a say while allowing you to take responsible steps to protect your sons and daughters from the whims of crazy moviemakers who despise your worldview.

Alice, a young adult, recently shared with me how movies were the greatest strain on her relationship with her mother as a teen, and what her family did to tackle the problem and teach her to use discretion.

Alice was independent and responsible and took pride in making good choices; she also loved films. Her mother was also strong willed, and she took pride in making sure that Hollywood trash stayed far away from her daughter.

When Friday nights rolled around, Alice loved heading to the theater with friends or to the store to pick out something lively and engaging to watch at home. But she dreaded the impending conversation with Mom, and Mom dreaded the argument, and tears, that almost always ensued. Most of the arguments centered on whether Alice should be allowed to watch R-rated movies.

One night the argument over a weekend flick went too far. Both mom and daughter wound up in tears, and Alice's father had had enough.

They all sat down for a brainstorming session and after several hours decided on a "movie contract." Alice, who was then sixteen, was given full discretion over PG-13 movies. There was one caveat: for every PG-13 movie she chose, she was required to write a brief summary about why she chose it, why it was rated PG-13, and whether it was a worthwhile movie.

When it came to R-rated movies, Alice could select three a year, all of which had to have some grounding in historical accuracy. The same reporting requirement stood.

If her parents felt she was making thoughtful and responsible choices, Alice's movie-selection rights would be reevaluated and
expanded after the course of one year. If she failed to produce a report
or continually made unwise choices, her movie-choosing rights would
be constricted.

They never had another argument over movies again. Now, that
is a happy ending!

Alice's parents basically gave her ownership rights over part of her
decisions about films. They shifted a significant portion of the responsibility of making ethical choices to her, with some guidance. They
familiarized her with their movie guide and its objective standards,
which allowed her to better judge how to make a good decision about
a PG-13 or R movie. They made it clear that her choices would be
measured in large part against their criteria for a wholesome film. They
established a clear and consistent policy that took into account their
daughter's level of maturity, their parental responsibility to impart their
values to her, and their parental right to make the final decisions. Best of
all, they were able to come up with a solution they were all happy with.

# Reflections from a Daughter

If it had been up to me as a kid, I would have seen every movie my
friends were seeing, just so I wouldn't miss out. I didn't believe the
movies I watched could have any effect on me. Now I don't feel like
I missed out in the slightest. I also recognize that I am not immune
to the influence of the things I watch.

A lot of parents avoid saying no to the movies their kids want
to see, even if they would say no for themselves. They avoid it

because they (quite understandably) want to prevent their kids from becoming "sheltered." But there's a great difference between filtering through Hollywood's portrayal of the world and sheltering kids from the real world. (Chapter 13, "Vow to Be the Parent [Not Your Children's Best Friend]," contains a few more thoughts on the topic of saying no.)

# Act Now

Date _____

Today I deliberately began to establish a movie-rating system for my children based on our values and their ages and maturity.

Signature _____

# More Help

Take heart, parents: There are great films made by great artists featuring great stories that your family will enjoy. Lots of them. But you owe it to your children and their developing character to do your homework in finding them.

One of my favorite sites for information about movies is **PluggedInOnline.org.** I used it many times when my daughter or sons called from a friend's house to ask for permission to watch a movie. When it is necessary to give an answer very quickly, all you have to do is go to the site and type in the name of the movie in question, and a thorough review pops up on the screen. The site also enables you to make alternative suggestions if your gut tells you the particular requested movie isn't right for your family.

**Dove.org,** run by the Dove Foundation, promotes family-friendly entertainment in a refreshingly positive way. It also encourages the creation of good movies by reviewing films for parents and by putting its "Family-Approved" seal on those that actually provide clean entertainment. And the message gets through. According to Ralph Winter, producer of the X-Men films, among other titles, "The Dove Foundation provides a valuable service for those of us working in Hollywood. They dig for the facts and show us trends for reaching the values-based audiences that are underserved." If you count yourself among that audience, you owe it to yourself and your children to speak up in support of good films and to vote with your wallet. That's the best way to ensure a happy ending.

**MovieGuide.org and the Movieguide magazine** are dedicated to "redeeming the values of the mass media according to biblical principles by influencing media executives to adopt higher standards imbued with Christian and traditional family values, and by informing and equipping moral people in America and around the world, especially parents, families and Christians, to make wise media choices based on the biblical worldview." Many reviews are available for no charge on the website, and a subscription to the site or the magazine will provide you with more in-depth information.

**ClearPlay.com** is also an excellent source for vetting your family's entertainment. A membership allows you to stream movies online and have them filtered based on your personal preferences. If you purchase a ClearPlay Player, it will even allow you to play your own collection of DVDs and have them filtered based on your preferences.

*Chapter 18*

# Tell Your Children What Makes a True Hero, and Pledge to Be a Hero Too

## The Challenge

Have you seen any true heroes lately?

By definition, a hero is someone who has done something noble and good, something worthy of our admiration and respect. Right?

Nowadays, the answer to that question is not so clear. Today's generation is redefining heroism, and not for the better. But who can blame them? The pickings are slim when choosing a hero from modern culture, be it pop or political, athletic or artistic.

It seems like every day we hear about a once-upstanding politician mired in a sex scandal or a Hall of Fame athlete caught doping. Even comic book superheroes are turned into haunting and violent characters for the big screen in films such as *The Dark Knight* or *Iron Man*.

Janet, a young woman teaching in the New York public school system, learned just how low the hero bar has fallen for today's children when she did an exercise on role models with her fourth grade social studies class.

She assigned as homework a small project where her students had to think about someone they considered to be their role model, someone they aspired to be like when they grew up. They then had to draw a picture and give a presentation to the class.

Janet was curious to see whom the children looked up to. The next day, the class came in with their drawings. As the presentations began, Janet was horrified.

Students chose figures such as Madonna, 50 Cent, and James Bond. One student wrote that he wanted to be a hit man when he grew up.

More than half of the boys' drawings included violent imagery such as guns or blood. And most of the girls drew a woman who was in some way a pop icon, dressed in something skimpy a majority of the time.

If these are the figures our children seek to emulate, then we are in serious trouble.

As the primary adults in our kids' lives, we can begin to teach our children about the true meaning of heroism by modeling virtue in the home. We must aspire to be role models to our children and teach them where to look for true heroism.

And if you are a single parent or a grandparent raising a child or teen, don't ever let society tell you that you can't be a hero too.

## In Your Shoes

We cannot afford to let our children grow up worshipping Playboy Bunnies and explicit rap artists. As US Supreme Court justice Clarence Thomas remarked in a speech about his wonderful book

*My Grandfather's Son*, "A free society will not survive without people of character who foster virtue through example. Doing good deeds and hard work is habit forming and ultimately builds character." Indeed. Justice Thomas's entire book is a testament and tribute to the power of his personal hero, his grandfather. Abandoned by his own father at a very young age, the justice describes how even a poor, black, fatherless child in the segregated South was able to rise above his circumstances because there was a powerful force for good that guided him. Justice Thomas speaks eloquently and respectfully of the man who rescued him from the life of waste that so often claimed the souls of young black males in the 1950s. His grandfather was the steely, emotionally distant "Daddy"—a man who wouldn't take no for an answer (from his grandson or society) and who taught the young Thomas how hard work, character, and loyalty could overcome even the worst of circumstances. Thomas recalls one of his grandfather's favorite sayings: "Old Man Can't is dead—I helped bury him."

Teaching children about the role models within our own families is a great way to talk about heroism. It can help your child connect to noble behavior in a personal way and see that everyday, imperfect people can do things worthy of great esteem. My life has been filled with heroes. My own father was a giant of a man who understood that fathers and mothers are the most important forces in their children's lives. And when I married my knight in shining armor over twenty years ago, God blessed me with another hero: my father-in-law.

Papa John quickly became an important part of my life. As I grew to know and love him and my mother-in-law over the years, it became quite evident why my husband is a man of strong character and selfless love.

What follows is an excerpt from a column I wrote about my father-in-law. I share it again as a reminder that we often forget that real heroes can be found within our own families.

> Quite a few years ago, my husband and I took his parents and our kids to the Fantasy of Flight Museum, a private collection in Polk City, Florida, boasting what may be the world's largest assemblage of airworthy vintage aircraft. Andy and I felt the trip would bring a better understanding of what Papa John, a World War II vet, and the rest of the Greatest Generation went through to protect America's freedom years ago.
>
> Papa John wore his best poker face as he climbed carefully through the bomb-bay doors and into the fuselage, his grandsons scrambling in close behind. But it had to have been an emotional moment for him. During World War II, he served with the 450th Bomb Group as a nose gunner in a B-24 Liberator, making runs from Italy into southern Europe. Unlike many, he returned to wed, raise a family, and see his kids raise families of their own.
>
> Even with its bomb racks empty, the bomb bay was surprisingly cramped. Between the racks, the only way forward to the flight deck and to

Papa John's former battle station was a narrow girder, not even wide enough to be called a cat-walk. Negotiating that, then hunching down, and finally crawling forward, Papa John advanced as far toward the nose turret as his now-creaky knees would let him, just far enough to brush aside a patch of spider webs and peer inside through its double hatch.

He had certainly had a good view from that position, as far forward as one could possibly be in an airplane, with only a bubble of Plexiglas between him and the frigid, onrushing air. How had he folded himself, his parachute, and other gear into that tiny space? How could he stay in that position for up to eight hours? How did it feel to be shot at the first time? What did it feel like to climb back in for a second mission? A third? And what did you do to come to terms with the thought that the next mission might be your last?

True to form, Papa John was a fount of knowl-edge about all things technical. He pointed out the dials and knobs and handles, explaining their pur-poses and how they worked. Those things seemed to come back to him pretty easily. But how it all felt was more difficult to put into words, maybe even to remember.

As for most of those who made it back, there has rarely been an appropriate moment to share details of those days. Even if the moment presented itself, the story is not an easy one to tell. How does one present the full context of the experience? Wanting above all to be accurate, how do you weave a complete and coherent story out of a collection of memories, some vivid and some vague, particularly when you never knew the whole story anyway—how do you tell your story knowing that it is only a very small part of a very large undertaking? So, more often than not, these stories go untold.

The silence is part of what makes Papa John—and so many like him in the Greatest Generation—so great. It is our duty, not theirs, to collect and preserve their story. That is why it's good to build museums, write books, produce documentary films, and teach our children. It's right to recognize these heroes' sacrifice. That is the reason we establish memorial days and create memorial monuments in Washington and in hometowns across America. And it's right to thank them by stepping forward to take up the banner of service they carried so faithfully, and by working to restore an America of virtue and strong moral values.

They are the heroes about whom we must begin to teach our children.

# From My Home to Yours

Mom and Dad, you can be the most effective hero for your kids. Despite what the educators, the social scientists, or the culture may tell you, the truth is that you are the primary force in your children's lives. You can inspire them, teach them, care for them on a daily basis, and protect them from heartache and danger countless times. Sometimes you will see the result of your heroism and hard work in small bits and pieces. But mostly you can take comfort in the fact that although your son might not recognize you as his role model right now, and though your daughter may not tell you how much she appreciates your endless sacrifices, you are having a tremendous influence. It's true that the hand that rocks the cradle rules the world. And that's also true of the hand that takes the car keys away from a son who has been disrespectful, the finger that hits the button on the remote control when degrading material appears on the television screen, and the arms that wrap around the teenage daughter when she has experienced hurt or disappointment.

My gut has always told me that my children need my husband and me to be an active part of their daily lives. Thank the Lord we listened to our quiet instincts over the myriad other boisterous voices whose constant hectoring tells parents that we are irrelevant, replaceable, and even harmful. I realized all too quickly that the opportunity I had to mold and shape the hearts and lives entrusted to my care was the greatest privilege and challenge of my life. It's a challenge worthy of a hero. Yours is too.

# Reflections from a Daughter

Frederick Buechner created a beautiful picture of the effect a real hero can have on someone's life. In his book *A Room Called Remember* he wrote:

> You sit at the feet of the wise and learn what they have to teach, and our debts to them are so great that, if your experience is like mine, even twenty-five years later you will draw on the depth and breadth of their insights, and their voices will speak in you still, and again and again you will find yourself speaking in their voices. You learn as much as you can from the wise until finally, if you do it right and things break your way, you are wise enough to be yourself, and brave enough to speak with your own voice, and foolish enough, for Christ's sake, to live and serve out of the uniqueness of your own vision of Him and out of your own passion.

Real-life heroes, the kind of heroes who actually exist and truly influence the way others live, are simply ordinary people who live wisely and sincerely. We hang on to their words and ways, and when we soak in their wisdom, it becomes as much a part of who we are as it was a part of them. The beauty of real-life heroes is that their heroism is infectious. If we spend enough time in their company, we may one day become like them. So if we want to live as good examples, or if we want our children to, a good place to start is by finding some heroes of our own.

## Act Now

Date _____

Today I told my children about one of my life heroes. I discussed with them what makes true heroism and vowed I would always strive to be a hero for them.

Signature _____

## More Help

One excellent way to teach your children about heroes is by simply picking up a good biography. Try reading a biography of a great historical or contemporary figure together as a family. A good one to start with is John Keegan's short but excellent biography *Winston Churchill: A Life* or David McCullough's book on John Adams. Hillsdale College has the most expansive collection on Churchill ever written—his official biography—in numerous volumes. It's a fabulous collection to start adding to your personal library. Hillsdale also offers one of the largest collections of speeches by modern leaders from many different fields who are heroes in their own right. The speeches are published in a monthly newsletter, *Imprimis*, to which you can subscribe, free of charge, at hillsdale.edu. If your child is a sports enthusiast, find books about players and coaches who are known for their skill and character. Stories about great people present a wonderful opportunity to teach your children about the material and makeup of heroes.

Perhaps one of the best books written in recent years about a real-life hero is Eric Metaxas's terrific work *Bonhoeffer: Pastor, Martyr, Prophet, Spy*. For a potentially life-changing and enriching experience for you and your teens, read it with them.

## Chapter 19

# Teach Your Children Every Day That They Have God-Given Value

## The Challenge

In today's highly competitive and busy world, kids can easily believe their value comes from what they do versus who they are. Well-meaning moms and dads hustle and bustle their kids around to countless sports, clubs, social activities, and shopping, then back home for homework, quick dinners, and weary evenings. We wake up the next morning and start the day with stress and mayhem, only to do the whole thing all over again. In the busyness and good things we do in life, we often overlook that what our children crave is a sense of personal meaning—some signal that they are loved and valued just as they are.

The world often confuses self-esteem with worth. We know today's teens struggle with doubts and feelings of inadequacy, so we create special programs and school events that gloss over the problem with "feel good" language. Our local high school had a day-long program they called ROCS—an acronym for Respect Others, Community, and Self. While such a program may sound wonderful and be filled with good intentions, it teaches exactly the wrong message: that our value comes from how we view ourselves. It is a man-made message that is contrary to reality. Of course we should view ourselves as having value, but the essence of our true value can't be found in our own high opinion of ourselves, which is a subjective standard that's vulnerable to shifting feelings. It is impossible to teach the true worth of human beings without teaching them about God, who does not change.

Of course, the public schools are now forbidden to teach about the One who can truly provide our children with a sense of their ultimate value. This wasn't always the case. Many public schools in this country were originally started in order to teach children how to read the Bible. Prayer was a daily activity, and God was acknowledged as the source of wisdom, love, and the ability to live harmoniously with others.

Our schools today and the modern pop culture's message are void of any recognition of the intrinsic value of the individual. Our kids are taught that they are here only as a result of evolution—that they have the same worth as ancient apes; that they are simply a by-product of an accidental big bang; or that they are just some advanced form of a primordial ooze that appeared billions of years ago. But they should feel really, really good about themselves anyway!

They are also taught that a human life is of value only when it is wanted and is disposable when it is inconvenient. The mantra of abortion on demand at any time, for any reason, has led to the devaluation of children and humanity in general. If a baby can be killed at will by her own mother just because she has yet to take a first breath of air, how on earth can she be of any real value after she is born? We live in a world where the elderly, the sick, and the disabled are often shoved off to nursing homes, away from people who can actually "contribute" to society. Many of them are left to die in loneliness or, worse yet, to feel as if they have been asked to die by virtue of the fact that they have been abandoned. We even, in a growing number of cases, actively euthanize them.

Add to this stark reality the onslaught of media messages that teach our kids that they are nothing more than animals in heat, that relationships are as disposable as tattered clothes, and that "love" is based on temporary cravings and emotions, and it's no wonder we have a generation of kids who don't know they are precious individuals with a sacred calling.

Such empty messages and vain imaginings have wreaked horrible consequences on the lives of our sons and daughters. Consider these sad facts:

- According to the Centers for Disease Control and Prevention, a full 50 percent of the new cases of sexually transmitted diseases reported every year are in teenagers and young adults ages fifteen to twenty-four.
- *The Chronicle of Higher Education*, which monitors trends on college campuses, reports that today's college students have a higher suicide rate than any generation before them.
- *The Chronicle* also reports that higher and higher numbers of incoming freshmen have been diagnosed with clinical depression.

- Cutting—the act of slicing your arms or legs with
  a razor or some other sharp object—has become
  a tragic trend among teenage girls. When one
  middle-class teen girl was asked why she cuts herself, she said, "I do it when I'm sad or lonely. It
  makes me feel alive." Columnist Michelle Malkin
  reported that one school counselor said, "Seventy
  percent of the kids here cut or know someone
  who does. It's cool, a trend, and acceptable."

Marian, a public school teacher in Maryland, observed, "Parents
and politicians would do well to spend a noon hour in the cafeteria
of a public school. Kids in supertight or droopy jeans and T-shirts
reading 'Yes—but not with you' or 'You forgot to ask if I care' shuffle
through food lines. But bad fashion and rude comments are not their
only common denominators. Their more defining trait is the forlorn
look they share."

The fact is, every person is made in the image of God. Every
child is fashioned by a loving Creator who knows and calls him by
name. What a powerful message to share with our children! If God
made you and knows you, then you had value before you were even
born—that's before you brought home one good grade or scored a
goal for the team or did your first good deed.

The value of human life is most beautifully stated in Psalm
139:13–15: "For you created my inmost being; you knit me together
in my mother's womb. I praise you because I am fearfully and won-
derfully made; your works are wonderful, I know that full well. My
frame was not hidden from you when I was made in the secret place."

I believe, as pastor Steve King of Cherrydale Baptist Church in Arlington, Virginia, said, "Every human life has infinite value and limitless potential." Our children need to know this is true, regardless of their IQ, physical abilities, successes, failures, popularity, or emotional state at any given time.

Teaching your children they have value in God's eyes is the single greatest thing you can do for your kids. Let them know there is a God who loves them, who knows and calls them by name. He knows how many hairs are on their head, how many concerns they have in their heart, and what issues they struggle over.

If a child knows he has intrinsic value just because he exists, he begins to understand that his life has meaning and purpose. Our children must know they are important just as they are. Kids who know they are of value are less likely to do drugs, are less likely to sleep around, and are able to gather a sense of purpose and mission for their futures.

And you know what else happens? They begin to love, value, and help others just for who they are. A deep sense and understanding of the love of God is something you just can't help spreading to others. Your view of your community changes. You understand that other people are of value, not because you happen to respect them, but because God has decided it is so. Such an understanding by our children could change their generation overnight.

There is a very simple five-step process you can begin today that will without doubt teach your children their value and worth. Practicing what is known as a blessing, dating way back to Abraham's day, will instill in your children a sense of well-being, purpose, and abiding love and will also strengthen your relationship with them in the process.

The church I attend has what our pastor calls a dedication ceremony for parents of new babies. But it is also applicable and highly powerful for children of all ages. Every time I sit through the brief charge, I am reminded that my young adult children need me, as their mom, to bless them on a daily basis. Here are five very basic—but very powerful—actions you can perform every day that will change your child's life:

- Bless your child with loving, meaningful physical touch.
- Bless your child with positive words spoken to and about them.
- Bless your child by expressing that she is a person of high value.
- Bless your child by painting a vision of a bright future for him.
- Bless your child by making an active, permanent commitment to her as a person.

## In Your Shoes

I asked the readers of my column to share how they teach their children that they have intrinsic value in God's eyes. Among the very thoughtful and simple tips that came in are these:

Jim said,

> We go to church. I also talk about the heart—a lot.
> I am always saying, 'I always love you,' 'You are

always important,' 'You are always special.' That, taken with the church community, makes the jump to God a very small step.

Mary offered this advice:

> To help my children know that they (and others) have value in God's eyes, I listen to them, reflective listening in which I try to articulate what they're telling me. I also take my children to parish visitations so they understand that people are rich and poor, young and old, wise and foolish—and sometimes the wise ones are the ones you least expect to be. Most of all, I turn down any activities for myself that I don't see as vital, especially if they're at night. I have seen that if I can talk to my children before I put them to bed, they see themselves as important to me.

Several readers suggested the importance of teaching our children to pray. A reader named Gary shared this beautiful story about how the hearts of even the smallest children respond to the news that God values them and desires to communicate with them. In the process of sharing the story, Gary also offered a creative idea for how to further connect our children to God through prayer:

> Our youth group gave us all a gift, a Prayer Jar, as a thanks for helping them with a project. Not knowing exactly what a Prayer Jar was for, I got the

inspiration to instruct our grandchildren that the Prayer Jar was for whispering our prayers to God.

The next day we passed the Prayer Jar around the breakfast table and everyone thanked God for his many blessings. My grandchildren were really excited about saying prayers into the jar and continued to add prayers to it the entire day.

That night we offered up our prayers to Jesus. By whispering them into the Prayer Jar [that morning], we not only prayed then, but now we released them to him all over again. So, we prayed twice!

The story could end happily there, but there was more. The next day our grandson reported that his little brother had pulled a chair over to the kitchen counter and moved the Prayer Jar to the floor.

We rushed into the room fearing we'd find a broken jar. What we saw made our hearts melt. Sitting in the middle of the floor, being as gentle as he could, our tiny grandson was leaning over the open Prayer Jar, babbling his heart out to God, who was definitely present with him right there in the jar!

Finally, Mary wrote a letter to her children on Mother's Day as a reminder of God's love. It very much reflects the prayer of my own heart. It reads, in part:

I must confess that so many times I have knelt in the dark of yet another day's end, begging God's forgiveness for my failures with you: my abruptness, harsh words, the ears that hear but tune out your silent pleas for understanding, the eyes that don't see the hurts of your little hearts, the omissions of simple pleasures and commissions of parental sins. I beg your forgiveness! I want to give you something this Mother's Day: a will of hope and a testament of God's love and mine.

My dear ones, I won't always be with you on the earth. You will go through crucibles of sorrows and trials. Don't allow them to defeat you! God has promised his strength to those who wait on him. Man may fail, you may fail at times, but your loving Father will never fail you. I haven't always given you what you wanted—perhaps not even what you needed. I pray God will be the Sufficiency for my lacks, the Gentleness for my impatience, the Compassion for my misunderstandings, the Calm for my restlessness.

Dear ones, I want for you what God wants for you. He wants you to be his heroes, armed with faith, purity, and humility in a disbelieving, pleasure-seeking, vain world. God wants you to reflect his care and love to those who will cross your path of life. I thank you, dear precious gifts, for giving my life an eternal dimension—for giving me something to live, work, and strive for. You have inspired me and I love you deeply.

# Reflections from a Daughter

I am tremendously thankful that I never felt pressure from my parents as I was growing up to become anything in particular. As long as my brothers and I were working hard at whatever it was we were doing, Mom and Dad were happy. I never felt I had to force myself into something or achieve anything spectacular to win their approval. Unless I was breaking some established rule or courtesy, I never felt even a hint of disappointment from them. I knew my parents loved me and were proud of me simply because I was their child, and that security increased my desire—and I believe even my ability—to work hard.

In his book *Let Your Life Speak*, Parker Palmer wrote that "identity does not depend on the role we play or the power it gives us over others. It depends only on the simple fact that we are children of God, valued in and for ourselves. When a leader is grounded in that knowledge, what happens in the family, the office, the classroom, the hospital can be life-giving for all concerned."

Looking back, I can see that my parents have always been confident in their own identities, and I believe that confidence comes from their faith in a God who is leading them step by step into his perfect plan for their lives. Because of their own confidence and contentment, they never projected any image of who they thought I should be onto me. Instead, they encouraged me to follow God wherever he would lead me. They passed on their confidence by passing on their faith.

# Act Now

Date _____

Today I committed to "bless" my children on a daily basis, thus instilling the reality that God's love for them and the value he has given them can never be taken away.

Signature _____

# More Help

Gary Smalley, noted family counselor, and Dr. John Trent co-wrote *The Blessing: Giving the Gift of Unconditional Love and Acceptance*, which no parent should be without. It describes the life-changing impact blessing can have on your family and fleshes out the blessing described earlier. They summarized how anyone can bless others, especially their children and family members:

> Today, as in centuries past, orthodox Jewish homes bestow a special family blessing on their children. This blessing is much like the patriarchal blessing we were introduced to in the story of Esau. This blessing has been an important part of providing a sense of acceptance for generations of children. But recently, it has also provided an important source of protection to those children.

However, the blessing is not just an important tool for parents to use. The blessing is also of critical importance for anyone who desires to cleave, or draw close, to another person in an intimate relationship.

**Brad Bright,** a true leader in shaping the culture and teaching people of all ages about the high value God places on all of us, developed a program just for children to help them know God. "The most important thing you can teach your children is who God really is and why it matters. Every decision they make in life will be influenced by their view of God. Discover God 4Kids uses a unique, interactive approach to wrap the message of who God really is into your everyday family life." Brad's many fabulous resources for parents and kids can be found at DG4Kids.com.

**Mercy Multiplied** provides a residential counseling program free of charge to young women who have life-controlling issues such as eating disorders, self-harm, unplanned pregnancy, sexual abuse, addictions, and depression. The program is voluntary and lasts approximately six months. Young women receive biblically based counseling, nutrition and fitness education, and life-skills classes in areas such as budgeting, setting boundaries, and preparation for parenting if they are pregnant. The Mercy Multiplied program takes a nonconventional approach to treatment by getting to the root issues of the problems and then helping the young women move past their debilitating circumstances, recognize and accept their self-worth, and prepare themselves to reach their full potential. Mercy

Multiplied has helped thousands of young women find freedom from very difficult issues, and graduates of their program are found in universities, on the mission field, working, raising children, and giving back to their communities. Visit MercyMultiplied.com for more information about how to apply.

*Chapter 20*

# Establish a Family Tradition of a Daily Quiet Time

## The Challenge

It's hard to stay sane in a world where we are bombarded nonstop by stimuli of all variations. When your kids come home from school, odds are they can choose from a smartphone, video games, a computer, a television, Netflix, YouTube, Facebook, and many other modes of entertainment and distraction.

Jeffrey Brantley, an MD at Duke's department of psychiatry and the author of *Calming Your Anxious Mind*, wrote,

> Uncertainty seems to grow daily in life all around us. Newspaper headlines scream of terrorist threats, international conflict, environmental disasters, dishonesty and corruption in government and business. Catholic priests are accused of sexual abuse. Schoolchildren are searched for weapons because some of their fellows have chosen to become mass murderers.
>
> Life grows busier for people everywhere. Information streams at us from all directions and

knows no boundary. Phones that connect to the Internet, tablets and laptop computers contribute to the never ending workday as people can be reached anytime, anywhere, for any reason. Personal life can feel more and more out of control and out of balance.

Our children are growing up in a world with an unprecedented level of distractions and potential threats coming from nearly every direction. They see it in the world of their parents as well.

It seems almost impossible to make it through a family dinner without technology calling someone, physically or mentally, away from the table. Our phones are always buzzing, and our kids want to finish eating as soon as possible to race off and watch television or get to the next level on their favorite video game.

Kids and adults need to take moments to just ... breathe. Children especially need to learn the value of taking pause for reflection, as they have not yet learned how to fully grapple with the demands of everyday life.

Do you remember those carefree days of summer in your youth? Some of my fondest memories are of lying in the warm grass and just watching the clouds go by. Like many children, when I was young I had countless opportunities to let my imagination soar. I turned those clouds into castles and animals, and I wondered about the depth of the skies and universe. I delighted in the gentle breeze and smell of the freshly cut fields. It was pure magic—peaceful and inspiring.

My favorite place in the world is the beach, and growing up in Florida I had many blessed opportunities to walk long stretches of an island shore in solitude. It was in these moments that I thought about the many blessings in life, let my mind absorb the beauty around me, and began to form words and thoughts into the poems and stories of my heart. When I was in fourth grade I started taking a notebook with me and often sat near the sandy dunes and wrote. I still have some of the poetry I composed in those early years, and today writing is one of my most therapeutic activities. I am convinced that many of the skills I developed came as a result of my parents encouraging me to be still.

One of the most powerful Bible verses is Psalm 46:10, "Be still, and know that I am God."

It is in the quiet moments of our lives that God reveals himself most intimately to us. If we meditate on and consider his words in our place of solitude, our faith begins to soar and we can sense his presence. How many teens do you know who say they have felt a closeness with God? If they spend all their time in frantic activity or watching television, then although they may be good kids, chances are they may never have experienced a divine personal connection.

Making daily quiet times a part of your home can bring benefits to the physical and mental well-being of everyone. Quiet times also offer the opportunity to bond more deeply with your family as you master the art of simply spending time together. And quiet times don't have to be silent. They are often most powerful when they are filled with our sincere prayers to the living God.

# In Your Shoes

Alice, a reader from New York City, wrote to me about her own experience with enforced quiet times as a child and their impact on her adult life:

Quiet times were something my parents emphasized from an early age. They used to frustrate
me, because I was always very fidgety as a child.
I wanted to spend my free time running around,
playing games, singing, playing with other children, and in other wild, boisterous activities. But
every day, my parents would make me spend an
hour of quiet time. I had to spend the first thirty
minutes lying down. If I did not fall asleep, then
I could spend the remaining thirty minutes doing
something still and quiet in my room. Ninety-five
percent of the time, I spent the remaining thirty
minutes reading.

A few things happened as a result, but I did not
notice them until I was an adult. First, I developed
a deep-seated passion for reading. Spending that
thirty minutes a day reading got me hooked. Often
I would enjoy my book so much that I would read
it longer than the required thirty minutes. That
love for reading has extended into my adult life.
Now that I live a busy and fast-paced life in New
York City, this time spent alone reading is a little
gem buried in the rough of day-to-day life. When
I am feeling anxious or overwhelmed, I know that
just picking up something to read will relax me.
I think that association between calmness and
reading goes all the way back to my regular habit
of quiet time and reading in my youth. I have

noticed that most of my peers do not have the same love for reading, and they were not required to spend time being quiet as children. I think the link is definitely there.

In addition to developing a love for reading, I learned the simple art of clearing my head in the middle of the day. Even when I do not feel stressed, I am often amazed at how spending some time with the TV off, in silence, will give me a great sense of refreshment. It's like letting your mind take a nap. Sometimes our minds are so jumbled that they don't even know how to tell us to give it a rest for a few minutes. The habit of calming my mind daily began in childhood, so I learned from an early age the necessity of taking just a little bit of time, and the difference it can make during the day. Even in college, I made a big point of taking at least thirty minutes to myself. Sometimes I would walk down to the nearby coffee shop and people-watch or read. Other times I would go to the quiet room of the library with a magazine. People thought I was crazy to do this during busy times like finals, but the only thing that got me through those stressful periods was taking a little "time out."

One reader, Leslie, a mother of five, recently wrote to me about how her family established a time for reflection after dinner and how it changed her family for the better:

My family grew up eating dinner together six nights a week. I knew that this was a highly uncommon practice in the American social landscape, but I cherished it. After all the craziness of each school day, sports practices, theater and choir practice, scrimmages, and the like, my kids would come tumbling into the house and we would sit down, pray, and eat together.

That worked until my oldest kids got into their late teenage years. They began staying late at school, heading out with their friends, and needing to skip dinner to study. Our family dinners began to fall apart. My youngest boys also began to play video games and spend more time on the computer. As soon as they finished shoveling food down their throats they would jump up and ask to be excused and race downstairs. After a while, I grew exasperated and gave up trying to keep everyone in their seats.

One night, after I had spent an hour preparing dinner, one child showed up at the dinner table. My husband was in his office working, two children were at school, one was out with a friend, and another was still playing sports with the neighbor kids despite being told what time we would sit down.

I decided that enough was enough.

The following night I told each member of my family that if they wanted to eat anything at all the next night, they would be at dinner for an important announcement, otherwise the kitchen would close shortly afterward, and they would be unable to eat.

The next night I told my family that we had to start working toward spending some time together. I told them I understood that it could not be every night. I understood that everyone has important commitments. But commitment to family should be the number one priority.

I proposed that every person commit to dinner with the family four nights a week. That commitment included staying at the table for thirty full minutes, followed by fifteen minutes of reading, silence, or quiet discussion in the living room. We could tell each other about our days, read the newspaper together, or read a Scripture passage and discuss it for ten minutes. Anything.

It was hard but it worked. Now my three oldest are off at college, but I feel like for the rest of their time in my house, they spent more time just unwinding at the end of each day and getting to spend some quality time with their family. I treasured those quiet moments with them after dinner and am so glad I had the chance to know them a little better and teach them the value of reflection and family before they left to go out into the world.

# From My Home to Yours

One of my greatest regrets as a mom is not making family devotionals a daily habit throughout our children's lives. Don't make the same mistake. You have the chance to build their faith on a daily basis when they live in your home, and when those days are gone, they are gone forever. Quiet times are important too. Sometimes our teens and kids feel so much pressure to be busy that they just might find it refreshing to know you believe they need time to relax. Since every family is unique, you should evaluate yours and sit down to discuss how you can carve out time for reflection. Here are just a few tips for creating successful quiet times in your home:

- Create a monthly chart to record the amount of time spent in silence each day and what quiet activity was done.
- Have a list on hand of ways to spend quality time in silence, such as "Everyone reads a book" or "Go for a walk."
- Make prayer a part of your quiet time.
- Have each member in your family keep a journal for their thoughts during quiet time.
- Make sure you have a space that is comfortable for sitting and relaxing and conducive to reflection. A room with no tempting electronic devices is ideal.
- When you plan family vacations and outings, choose places that offer both activities to do and lovely natural surroundings in which to quiet yourselves.

- Purchase a family devotional or access one online. *Our Daily Bread*, available at OurDailyBread.org, is a daily devotion that includes a small passage and thought to meditate on for each day of the month. Reading it at the start of a family quiet time will enable you to plant seeds of truth in the minds of your kids that they can then nurture through reflection and prayer after the reading is over.

# Reflections from a Daughter

We hardly hear God in our loud, busy world because his voice is a gentle whisper (see 1 Kings 19:12). But he is speaking, reaching out to us all the time, ready to meet with us if we simply slow down and start listening. Spending quiet time in the Lord's presence and getting into Scripture doesn't come naturally for anyone, so it makes sense that it would be even more of a challenge for families with crazy schedules. My parents made reading the Bible a priority for themselves, and when they first started introducing family devotionals into our time after dinner, I started wondering why it hadn't been one of my personal priorities.

M. Craig Barnes wrote in his book *Sacred Thirst*, "We were created with a need to satisfy our physical thirst, and every morning of our lives we are reminded of this thirst. But this physical thirst is a symbol, maybe even a sacrament, that points to the deeper spiritual thirst of the soul. So also is our longing for better families and more satisfying jobs a symbol of our deeper yearning to be a part of the family and mission of God."

Though eating and drinking come naturally, healthy diets require discipline. In the same way, we naturally try to satisfy our souls with convenient and pleasurable things, but going to God's Word requires a form of spiritual discipline that has to be learned. You can do the teaching.

# Act Now

Date _____

Today my family and I began having quiet time. I also pledged to set the example by being still and reflective and encouraging my family to do the same.

Signature _____

# More Help

***Certain Peace in Uncertain Times*** is a moving book by Shirley Dobson that will teach you the power and peace of prayer. Mrs. Dobson reminds us that the God of the universe desires to hear from us and that his peace awaits those who call on him. As Mrs. Dobson pointed out, "Yet God does not abandon us. He keeps His promise: 'Never will I leave you; never will I forsake you' (Heb. 13:5). Even during the storms, He stands just to the side, ever watchful, waiting to embrace us the moment we again seek His presence. His words to Jeremiah apply to us all: 'Call to me and I will answer you' (Jer. 33:3)."

*Chapter 21*

# Set the Example

## The Challenge

We all know stories of bad parents.

We hear about mothers who criticize teachers for daring to give their little darlings a failing grade and about fathers who scream obscenities at umpires from the sidelines of Little League baseball games. Perhaps we've witnessed such incidents ourselves. All around us are parents behaving in a rude and crass manner that would have been deemed unthinkable a generation or two ago. We shake our heads and wonder what the world is coming to.

But before we point the finger of blame, let's ask ourselves, Are we good models for our children—and other people's children, for that matter?

It's not enough to simply refrain from flagrantly bad behavior. That, quite frankly, sets the standard far too low. I'm starting from the assumption that you're not acting like some substance-abusing celebrity mother who has just had her parenting techniques dissected in the supermarket tabloids. No, you're a mother or father who works hard, at home and on the job, and you truly want what's best for your children.

And what do they need, besides food, clothes, shelter, and all the material things we strive after so mightily, day in and day out? They need you to provide a good example. And you do that primarily with your actions.

We've all heard the old adage "Do as I say, not as I do." Of course, the reason that's a joke is precisely because you can't expect children to do that at all. If anything, it's the opposite. If your actions don't match your words, they'll ignore the latter, no matter how carefully you couch your "pearls of wisdom." As Ralph Waldo Emerson once said, "Don't say things. What you are stands over you the while, and thunders so that I cannot hear what you say to the contrary."

Show me a child who doesn't interrupt, for example. I guarantee you his parents haven't simply said, "Don't interrupt—it isn't nice." That child has seen his parents listen patiently when other people are talking, and he has learned to imitate their good behavior. Show me a teenager who is generous, and I know to expect the same trait from her mother and father, who—and this is a crucial point—may not even realize they're being watched and copied.

What we have to keep in mind is that our children are watching and learning, for good or for ill. They watch our interactions and reactions with others. For instance, when they hear us refuse to listen to a dirty joke, that makes an impression. When we watch our language, they do likewise. When we lose a game graciously, they learn how to react when the same thing happens to them.

Obviously—perhaps unfortunately, given our fallen human nature—the same principle applies when we model bad behavior. Take driving, for instance. State Farm insurance company released a study in September 2008 showing that most teenagers report seeing their parents drive in an unsafe manner. More than two-thirds said their parents were speeding, talking on their cell phones, or driving while tired. If you're one of those teenagers, what are you going to think when your parents turn around and give you a big lecture about safe driving?

I'm not suggesting you have to be perfect. We all make mistakes from time to time. But remember, children learn from what they see and hear you doing. They pick up on patterns. So we've got to try our best to make those patterns worth emulating.

That can be quite a challenge in a culture that celebrates childish and boorish behavior. In movies, books, and television shows, today's stars prefer impulse to self-control. "Everywhere I turn today I see men who refuse to grow up," wrote Gary Cross, a history professor at Pennsylvania State University, in his book *Men to Boys: The Making of Modern Immaturity*. Boys today are looking up to actors like Adam Sandler and Will Ferrell, and the popular female actresses are almost all sex symbols. There is a serious shortage of honorable role models in the media.

You must set a good example. Your children are looking to you for guidance, whether you or they even realize it. If you're not already taking that responsibility seriously, now is the time to start.

The good news is that common sense will take you a good part of the way. Most parents instinctively modify their behavior when children come along. But others don't realize that even the smallest of children will start copying their behavior. One of my friends is a teacher, and she has said she can tell by her students' language whose parents use foul words at home and whose don't. She also knows which parents model good manners and which ones don't. Of this you can be certain: your children will tell on you. Maybe not literally, but their attitudes and actions will reflect what they see and hear. And no matter how good or wholesome you are, if they consume rotten media messages, their lives will model that too. You have to work extra hard to model good behavior for your kids because you are up against a culture of garbage that is trying to influence them to behave like garbage too.

# From My Home to Yours

Nearly all of us can use a little help beyond these basics. After all, we're aiming for something higher: to turn the next generation into men and women of pride and accomplishment and to help them become the people God intends for them to be. To that end, I have a few suggestions:

**Always model honesty and truth.** There is no difference between a little white lie and a big fat lie, and our kids know it. If you are dishonest in your speech or actions, even a tad bit, you are modeling complete dishonesty for your children. You are teaching them to practice situational ethics versus absolute honesty. Speaking truth and being a person of integrity in all that you do is the right way to live, and it will also have a tremendous impact on your children and how they treat others. Doing otherwise is not only wrong, but it can cause mass confusion in a child's developing sense of morality. It's very frustrating to children when you punish them for telling you a lie if they have seen or heard you be less than honest with your friends or them. Always be true and faithful in word and deed, and your children will respect you, trust you, and grow up to emulate you.

**Speak up when you see or hear something wrong.** When you encounter something that offends your values, don't simply look the other way. Let your children know how you feel and why. I'm not saying you should always be ready to launch into a lecture—just a sentence or two will usually do. If you're passing one of those soft-porn Victoria's Secret displays at the mall, for instance, shake your head and say something like, "I can't believe they'd want to show pictures of women half-naked in public. That's just wrong." The same principle applies when you run across bad movies or television shows. Don't just assume they'll understand something is wrong. They're looking for guidance. Provide it.

**Let your kids see you reading good material.** Children and teens notice what their parents read. Every time you pick up a trashy magazine at the grocery store checkout stand or in the waiting room at the dentist's office, they notice. If you read those popular romance novels, chances are your daughter has picked one up when you weren't looking and read parts of it too. Look for quality books of history, faith, and fiction and make it a point to let your kids see you reading them.

**Show good sportsmanship.** Whatever activities your family enjoys, from softball games to football, from Monopoly to Scrabble, teach your kids how to win and how to lose. A good winner doesn't gloat (although a little good-natured ribbing is okay), and a good loser doesn't pitch a fit but is gracious and congratulates the winner.

**Be a good listener.** If you're always lecturing instead of listening, chances are your kids will avoid having these one-way conversations with you. Your kids should know they can always talk to you about what's on their minds. Ask questions that get them started, avoid immediate negative reactions, and try to make it natural. (In other words, don't just sit at the table and say you want to talk; ask them to help you with dinner and engage them in conversation while they're filling the glasses with ice.) When you listen to them, they will learn to listen to you!

**When you make a mistake, apologize.** There's nothing wrong with saying, "Honey, I'm sorry I lost my temper like that." That itself sets a good example, reminding them they shouldn't let pride interfere with doing what's right.

**Don't whine!** Okay, so I said it. Parents (especially moms) can get so frustrated with the pains and annoyances of everyday life that before we know it, we have turned into Wendy Whiner. Be bold and vocal about what is wrong and then work to change it if you can. But never, ever endlessly whine and complain around your kids. If you do, you will get massive amounts of whining in return.

**Learn to forgive and forget.** Nothing will destroy a human being faster than bitterness. Harboring resentment and anger also robs us of the opportunity to enjoy life and its many beautiful moments. Your children will be harmed by many people in their lives, and how they learn to deal with it depends largely on you. When you are betrayed or tricked or hurt in any way, it's critical for you to seek justice, practice forgiveness, and then move on. Dwelling on the mistakes of others not only drains you of energy but also can cause your children to wonder if you will ever really forgive them when they do something wrong. Teaching your children to forgive and forget will free them from the future bondage of bitterness and vengefulness.

**Mind your manners.** Need I say more? Probably. Always practice kindness and thoughtfulness. Open the door for others, go out of your way to be helpful.

**Be generous.** Regardless of financial circumstances, everyone can be generous with something. Ours is a materialistic, selfish society where each person is taught to fend for himself. Show your kids that you don't wait for the government to tax you to help others—you give freely of your blessings. Whether it is money, time, kindness, or displaying a cheerful spirit, show your kids by your daily life how important it is to give.

## Reflections from a Daughter

I'm not sure where this saying came from originally, but my husband and I love to quote it: "The opposite of integrity is hypocrisy. Hypocrisy is the gap that exists between the public and the private life."

And what is integrity? Well, my parents' lives define it beautifully. Their beliefs, actions, and words have always been consistent, as were their expectations and rules while we were growing up. I believe they set good examples for my brothers and me primarily because they were *clear* examples. We were free to make our own decisions, and we were responsible for our own actions, but they didn't leave us with any confusion about what is right and what is wrong.

# Act Now

Date _____

Today I began consciously setting the example in my home.

Signature _____

# More Help

**Family Talk (drjamesdobson.org):** This wonderful organization, run by the terrific Dr. James Dobson, has many helpful resources for parents. The "Parenting" section on its website carries a wealth of good information for time-strapped mothers and fathers. The site also offers many good articles, videos, books, and publications.

***Stop Whining, Start Living:*** This terrific book by Dr. Laura Schlessinger reminds us that whining and complaining will not bring about change in our lives or families. It's only when we take action that change comes. I believe one of the greatest skills a parent can master is the art of not whining or complaining endlessly about their kids and their behavior. Dr. Laura's book is a great place to start in learning how to master your own life and then modeling for your kids every day the type of character and attitude it takes to live life to its fullest. If you take Dr. Laura's advice to heart, you will have a more fulfilled life and will naturally become a powerful example for your kids.

***Strong Fathers, Strong Daughters: 10 Secrets Every Father Should Know:*** This book by Dr. Meg Meeker, a teen health expert, is one that every father with daughters ought to read. Chapters include "She Needs a Hero," "Be the Man You Want Her to Marry," and "Protect Her, Defend Her (and use a shotgun if necessary)." It's loaded with good advice for fathers who want to counteract the insidious and disgraceful way that modern radical feminism has tried to exclude the most important man in every girl's life.

*Chapter 22*

# Follow Ten Simple Steps with Your Teens to Provide Support for Their Purity

## The Challenge

We live in a culture that is saturated in sex.

Stores in the malls sell T-shirts advertising promiscuity with writing such as "Everyone Loves a Slutty Girl" sprawled across the chest. An Internet search for "slutty T-shirts" returns close to a million hits for online stores selling degrading tops.

Television shows bombard young women with the idea that for today's modern woman, men and sex go together like city sidewalks and a pair of expensive heels.

Sexuality today has been reduced to little more than an amusing hobby, and the concept of sexual purity has come to be thought of as backward and outdated. In fact, today's culture teaches that self-respect and sexual liberation (a nicer word for promiscuity) go hand in hand.

Wendy Shalit, author of *A Return to Modesty: Discovering the Lost Virtue*, noted that radical feminist Naomi Wolf wrote in one of her novels that "there are no good girls; we are all bad girls" and we all should just admit it and "explore the shadow slut who walks alongside us."

As Shalit pointed out, "We certainly feel the pressure and get the message that we are supposed to be bad—we, after all, started our sex education in elementary school—but when everyone is saying the same thing, it makes us wonder: isn't there anything more to life, to love?"

Our sons and daughters are growing up asking this very question. And the answer society gives them could not be more wrong or more dangerous.

Shalit explained that "the woes besetting the modern young woman—sexual harassment, stalking, rape, even 'whirlpooling' (when a group of guys surround a girl who is swimming, and then sexually assault her)—are all expressions of a society which has lost its respect for female modesty."

What are you teaching your daughter about the origin of her self-worth and the value of her purity? What are you teaching your son about his?

The bottom line is that you are your son's and daughter's first and last line of defense against the sexual pressures that are closing in around them. You can't rely on the schools to do it. As a matter of fact, much of the "abstinence-based" curriculum in schools today is exactly the opposite. The vast majority of comprehensive sex education teaches our children to think sexual activity is fine as long as they can handle it. You owe it to your son and daughter to actually take the time to read their sex education materials. You might just be shocked at what you find.

As a culture, we have lost appreciation for the virtue of modesty and chastity. Many scientific and sociological studies are emerging that demonstrate the physical and psychological problems resulting from young women abandoning the virtue of chastity.

The American Psychological Association released a seventy-two-page report on the damaging effects of the sexualization of our children. According to the study, sexualization occurs when:

- a person's value comes only from his or her sexual appeal or behavior, to the exclusion of other characteristics;
- a person is held to a standard that equates physical attractiveness (narrowly defined) with being sexy;
- a person is sexually objectified—that is, made into a thing for others' sexual use, rather than seen as a person with the capacity for independent action and decision making; and/or
- sexuality is inappropriately imposed upon a person.

All four conditions need not be present; any one is an indication of sexualization.

Our children are undeniably saturated in all four kinds of sexualization in nearly every aspect of culture, ranging from schools to shopping malls.

Need I say more?

But here is the clincher: a study done by the National Campaign to Prevent Teen and Unplanned Pregnancy found that a majority of both girls and boys who are sexually active wish they had waited.

In fact, "more than one-half of teen boys (55 percent) and the over-whelming majority of teen girls (72 percent) said they wish they had waited longer to have sex."

Mom and Dad, your kids need your active involvement to help keep them from having such regrets. Your influence must not be underestimated. Just read the following personal stories and see how much impact you can have on your teens.

# In Your Shoes

This comes from a wonderful woman and former colleague from my years at the Heritage Foundation, Rebekah Coons. She is an amazing woman whose wisdom, faith, and strong moral convictions I deeply admire. When I read this story about her father, I suddenly knew why she is such a remarkable person:

> My dad was very influential in my life from as far back as I can remember. From sharing his personal faith to reading my three sisters and me Bible stories as we fell to sleep at night, he was slowly but consistently making little character investments in us that would pay off the rest of our lives. The biggest deposit my dad made in my life was when I turned thirteen years old.
>
> Dad asked me out on a "special daddy-daughter date night" and asked me to dress up because we were going to a fancy restaurant. Needless to say, I felt like a princess … the evening couldn't have

been more magical. During dinner we talked about my birthday and how excited I was about becoming a teenager. He mostly let me do all the talking and quietly guided the conversation to the topic of boys and love toward the end of our meal. As we were discussing the subject, the waiter quietly interrupted us and presented me with a silver tray, which had a small wrapped box sitting in the middle of it. It was a gift from my dad. I unwrapped it and opened the box to find a poem and a gold heart locket and key necklace. The poem stated how much he and my heavenly Father loved me and how important it was to remain pure for my future husband, a man who would vow to love, cherish, and protect my heart for the rest of my life. Until I met that man, dad would guard the key to my heart and protect me.

Fast-forward ten years. I graduated college with the key and locket still around my neck. I will never forget my dad's words: "save yourself for your husband, a man who will vow to love, cherish, and protect you for the rest of your life."

Not long after graduation, it came time to give my key away. It was my wedding day, and as an ordained minister my dad conducted the ceremony. After leading us in our vows, it came time for Dad to make his second presentation of the heart and key necklace, except this time, he left just the heart with me.

He said, "We are so proud of you. The Bible says it like this: 'I have no greater joy than to hear that my children are walking in the truth' (3 John 1:4). The two of you from the outset of your relationship have wanted to honor the Lord and honor each other. Keep this as your number one goal and it will serve you well throughout your marriage."

With a tear in his eye my dad presented my new husband with the key to my heart.

At that moment it hit me: my dad had been preparing me for this moment since my thirteenth birthday. Honoring the Lord by remaining pure until marriage was merely laying the solid foundation for a marriage that is being built to last a lifetime.

Recently I was talking with a beautiful teenage girl I know. We were discussing what motivates her to remain sexually pure. She said it was, simply, "my sense of morality, which is based on my faith and the values my mother and father have taught me." This young woman is very active in her church, and her parents have always been very frank in their discussions with her about sex, abstinence, and wanting the very best for her life. It was exciting and encouraging to hear that her parents and faith have more influence on this young woman than even massive amounts of media that glorify sexual promiscuity! When I asked her what the second reason is for her decision to remain chaste, she said, "Respect. I know that I will have more respect from my peers if I uphold high standards."

So there you have it in a nutshell. Morality, faith, and the values that we as parents pass on to our kids, along with the need to be respected, can provide all the protection our children need in this hypersexed world. This is the recipe for teaching our children how to remain sexually pure until marriage. If you think this young woman is an anomaly, think again.

In study after study, when asked what influences them the most, teenagers said their parents. Even though our kids are consuming some seven and a half hours of media a day, they still say their parents have the greatest impact on them. So the point here isn't whether you have an influence, Mom and Dad. The question is, How are you going to use it? Your silence on issues of sexual activity will be taken as an endorsement of the status quo. But your active involvement and discussions with your teens on the subject can be the greatest force for good.

Ashley Samelson McGuire, an outstanding young woman I know, graduated from Tufts University, which, like most colleges today, is a hotbed of liberalism. During her senior year, she stumbled across a "sex fair" on Valentine's Day. Disgusted, she wrote a piece for her school newspaper. She pointed out that on Valentine's Day she had expected to see people on campus

> selling flowers that one could buy for a friend or
> sweetheart, chocolates, kiss-o-grams, candy hearts....
> What I discovered instead was a disgrace....
>
> Buckets of condoms, sex toys, sex games,
> genitalia cookies and masturbation tables sent the
> message that sex is virtually meaningless, something
> to joke about, and that sexual awareness comes

through learning to be free and detached mentally
and emotionally by ridding oneself of any moral
and emotional barriers that may accompany sex.

But, as Ashley pointed out in her article, "Encouraging women to be free and casual with their sex (so long as it's 'safe') sends the message to men that women are available as sexual objects, merely instruments for obtaining meaningless pleasure. If women are careless and emotion-free about sex, why should they be treated with any care at all?" She made an impassioned plea for a completely different approach: "Reteaching love, respect, and reverence is the first step towards … restoring chivalry in men and true awareness and self-esteem in women."

Ashley's inbox was flooded with positive responses. She said that for days young women showed up at the door of her dorm room, shyly agreeing that they, too, wished there were greater respect for chastity on campus, some tearfully telling stories of some promiscuous encounter that had left them feeling lonely and empty.

You can help keep your daughter or son from becoming a sexual statistic by following these practical tips:

- Have frequent discussions and give gentle reminders to your children about how sex was created by God for marriage.
- Nurture a culture of openness in your home where your children can feel comfortable coming to you with questions about their developing sexuality.
- Filter out any publications or media that treat women like sex objects or that glorify promiscuity.

- Go through an age-appropriate program on abstinence education with your preteen and/or teenager (see "Even More Help" at the end of the book for suggestions).
- Encourage group activities versus couple dating.
- Make your home the place where kids hang out.
- Keep your teenagers active in sports, volunteer activities, church, work, or, better yet, with you.
- Monitor where your teens go and with whom they hang out. As long as your teens live under your roof, you have the responsibility and right to know where they are.
- Opt your kids and teens out of the graphic sex education taught in many public schools. (Call your local school to learn how, and don't let them discourage you.)
- Find a strong faith-based or church-based youth group and encourage your teens to become involved. Young Life is one fantastic organization for high school students. You can access their website (younglife.org) to find a group near you.

# Reflections from a Daughter

When I turned fifteen, my dad took me out to dinner and gave me a ring. He has a talent for picking out jewelry, and I immediately loved it for its unique beauty, but the meaning he gave the gift is what makes me cherish it.

I had heard of dads giving their daughters purity rings, and, to be honest, the idea had never really appealed to me. Though I believed in the value of purity, a purity ring came across as a bit superficial, even awkward.

So when my dad pulled out a ring, I braced myself for "the talk." But instead, he simply told me that it was a promise ring representing his promise to always be there for me, no matter what.

The ring (that I don't plan on taking off any time soon) represents the pure, unconditional love of a good father. And when a girl grows up under a love like that, she knows better than to settle for anything less than an equally pure love.

## Act Now

Date _____

Today I pledged that I will be bold in passing on the value of sexual purity to my children and will foster an atmosphere that helps them overcome the cultural pressures.

Signature _____

## More Help

Thankfully, there is now a world of excellent abstinence materials for you and your sons and daughters. These are two of the best sites for all kinds of resources related to abstinence:

- Abstinence Clearinghouse (abstinence.net)
- Family Talk (drjamesdobson.org)

And here are just a few of the great books for guys and girls:

- *Why Wait?* by Josh McDowell
- *For Young Women Only* by Shaunti Feldhahn and Lisa Rice (Note: this book is absolutely perfect for teenage girls.)
- *Passion and Purity* by Elisabeth Elliott
- *Secret Keeper* by Dannah Gresh
- Dr. Meg Meeker has written several helpful books on this subject. I strongly encourage you to go to Amazon.com and search under her name for the many titles to choose from. You will find everything you need to prepare you for discussing sexuality with your children.

## Chapter 23

# Set Clothing Standards for Your Daughter That Reflect She Is to Be Respected and Admired for Who She Truly Is

## The Challenge

Too many young girls today are dressing like streetwalkers. It used to be a father's greatest privilege to protect his daughter's virtue. Yet dads across America are allowing their innocent young daughters—many as young as seven or eight—to dress in a manner that degrades them, oversexualizes their image, and portrays them as nothing more than an object to be used. Mothers are driving their little girls to the mall and plunking down big bucks for thongs, tight pants, and tiny tops that reveal tons of skin. Have we gone mad? Face the facts: Most twelve- to sixteen-year-olds don't have access to a lot of cash, unless their parents give it to them. And, last I heard, in most states, if you're below the age of sixteen, you can't simply hop in a car and drive yourself to the local mall. Nope, it's not the kids' money that is being spent; it's their parents'. And it's usually the mom who happily drives the little darlings to the mall for a fun day of shopping.

Let's face it: little girls dress according to what their mommies allow. I thought mothers were supposed to model virtue for their daughters, to teach them to value themselves and their bodies. What chance does a little girl stand of keeping her childhood or innocence intact when it's Mommy who's driving her to the store and paying for the thongs, the itty-bitty skirts, the yoga pants, and the plunging necklines?

A 2007 study by the American Psychological Association entitled *Report of the APA Task Force on the Sexualization of Girls* reveals the harm of treating our young daughters as sex objects. The report says, in part,

> Sexualization [is linked] to a variety of harmful consequences. These consequences include harm to the sexualized individuals themselves, to their interpersonal relationships, and to society. For example, there is evidence that sexualization contributes to impaired cognitive performance in college-aged women, and related research suggests that viewing material that is sexually objectifying can contribute to body dissatisfaction, eating disorders, low self-esteem, depressive affect, and even physical health problems in high-school-aged girls and in young women. The sexualization of girls may not only reflect sexist attitudes, a societal tolerance of sexual violence, and the exploitation of girls and women but may also contribute to these phenomena.

That should be enough for parents to regain their common sense. It's just plain dumb to dress our little girls in ways that degrade them. Refuse to allow the mass marketers to define your daughter's value. Let your daughter know, in loving but uncompromising terms, what clothing will and will not be acceptable.

# In Your Shoes

Our daughters need to understand that they are all beautiful and valuable creations. They need to know that they are to be respected and should be judged by their character. They need to understand that they can be tasteful and still look fabulous. The conversation I had several times with my daughter about clothing when she was a teenager went something like this: "Kristin, God made you lovely and special. You are someone to be respected. And I, as your mom—the one who loves you more than anyone else in the world could possible love you and who deeply understands the need and desire to feel attractive—commit to you that I'm going to help make sure that you dress in a way that shows your inner character and reveals your true beauty and individuality and the fact that you are not just a toy. So we'll have only one rule before we buy something: we both have to like it. That's it. That means that you won't try to convince me to buy an item that I think is inappropriate. And it also means that I will not try to force you to wear something that you think is dorky."

Guess what? This method works. Yes, I had to repeat it several times as the new shopping seasons and styles arrived. And, yes, my daughter and I shed a few tears of stress during unfruitful shopping trips. And, of course, we were often tempted after a long day of trudging from store to store to give in. But we didn't because my daughter and I know that our values don't change with the trends or when we're tired or when some designer in New York lowers the bar (yet again). And each time we upheld our standards instead of the shifting standards of the world, my daughter was reminded of her true value and of my undying love for her.

It's not easy for anyone, even my daughter and me. Despite her keen sense of morality, Kristin, like any teenager, was still subject to the pressures of our modern toxic culture.

One day we were shopping for swimwear and shorts for our summer vacation, and the last two hours of the trip almost made me want to bag the whole vacation. If you don't have young girls, you probably can't understand the dilemma. It's quite simple, really. The problem is that there are virtually no swimsuits, tops, or shorts designed for tweens and teens that don't resemble something a streetwalker would wear. As a capitalist, I find it very strange that an entire segment of the American population is so underserved—very strange indeed. Most of the moms and dads I know are thoroughly frustrated with the poor selection of clothing. But in the end they shrug their shoulders, cast aside their best judgment, and purchase the teeny-weeny bikinis for their innocent young daughters anyway.

We tried on item after item, hoping against hope that maybe the next pair of shorts would actually cover her bottom or that the next bathing suit wouldn't really be as tiny and revealing as it looked on the hanger. But time after time I had to shake my head and say no, which is why tears started to well up in Kristin's beautiful green eyes.

For a moment I thought of ignoring the reddening eyes as we continued our mission to find something decent. But I thought better of it, sighed, and softly said, "Sweetheart," as I stepped forward and hugged her close. This act of understanding was enough to send the pooled waters spilling down her cheeks. We remained in our silent embrace for several minutes, and then I stepped back and wiped away her tears. She sweetly smiled as I said, "We'll keep on looking—no matter how long it takes—until we find something you like that also reflects the honor and respect for your body that you deserve." Later, with only two items having passed muster—as I was putting the dozens of items that didn't work back on the hangers—Kristin came to me. She put her arms around my neck and said, "I'm sorry I was being so difficult." Again, she shed a few tears, and I marveled at the incredible gift, privilege, and responsibility of being a mother.

"Kristin," I said, "you weren't difficult at all. I'm sorry you live in a world where so many adults have failed in their responsibility to treat children like the treasures you are. Thanks for allowing me to be the mom, Kristin. The mom who loves you more than anyone in the world could possibly love you. The mom who wants what is best for you." She stepped back, looked directly in my eyes, and said, "I love you, Mom." We left the store a bit more determined to fight for our values, a bit more disgusted that there has to be a battle at all, and a lot closer to each other. All in all, it was a day I will long remember and even cherish as a reminder that fighting the culture is sometimes frustrating and exhausting but always, always worth the effort.

Your daughters are looking to you for direction and protection. Your little girls want you to set loving standards, to let them know they are of value. And there isn't anyone else who's going to do it. Our culture has sold our daughters short—will you be guilty of it too?

You can fight back. A few years ago, a story written by Nick Perry of the *Seattle Times* caught my attention. It shows just how much impact one little girl can have in the culture war. The article was about an eleven-year-old named Ella Gunderson who was "frustrated trying to find something fashionable—yet modest—in a world where she seems to be surrounded by low-riding jeans and tight, revealing tops." So she wrote a letter to the department store:

> "Dear Nordstrom, ... I am an eleven-year-old girl who has tried shopping at your store for clothes (in particular jeans), but all of them ride way under my hips, and the next size up is too big and falls down. I see all of these girls who walk around with pants that show their belly button and underwear," she wrote. "Your clearks sugjest [*sic*] that there is only one look. If that is true, then girls are suppost [*sic*] to walk around half naked. I think that you should change that."

As Perry reported, this letter made it to the desk of Pete Nordstrom, an executive vice president, and elicited a promise that Nordstrom would do a better job with options in fashions for girls. "'Wow,' wrote back Kris Allan, manager of Nordstrom's Bellevue Square store, where Ella shopped. 'Your letter really got my attention.... I think you are absolutely right. There should not be just one look for everyone. This look is not particularly a modest one and there should be choices for everyone.'"

Just think what you and a few friends and your daughters could do to change your local store's clothing choices!

## Reflections from a Daughter

Years ago, my mom published an article encouraging parents to stick to modest standards when buying clothing for their daughters. In the article, she shared the same story she shared above, telling about a shopping trip we went on to find me a new summer swimsuit. She detailed how we both became frustrated (and I may have shed a few tears) because there didn't seem to be a single option that fit her standards for my modesty and my pre-teen standards for what was stylish.

Well anyway, a year or so after my mom's article was published, I Googled my name and came across an angry post someone had written in response to my mom's. The post began with, "I can picture it now: Kristin, sobbing beneath her burqa in the corner, as mom chased away yet another friend, resolved to leave home as soon as possible and become a porn star in L.A."

I burst out laughing when I read it because of how ridiculous the sentiment behind it was. Some people believe that imposing even moderately conservative standards on your children is a surefire way to ruin their lives and destroy your relationship with them. And they may try to guilt you into believing that too. But as a child of a champion of conservative principles, I can tell you that my respect and thankfulness for my parents has grown exponentially throughout the years because I have seen them consistently abide by (and lovingly explain the reasons behind) the values they profess.

# Act Now

Date _____

Today I pledged to help ensure that my daughter knows she is of value and is to be respected. She understands that rule number one when we go shopping is that we both have to like it.

Signature _____

# More Help

You aren't alone! Thousands of families are going through the same thing. So don't give up. And don't despair—there are modest alternatives. Some readers of my column recommend Lands' End and L.L. Bean, both of which offer one-piece suits and tankinis.

**PureFashion.com** is also a tremendous resource. Pure Fashion even sponsors fashion shows in many cities across the country that uplift, rather than degrade, the value of young women. There are many other resources too. As one reader of my column said, "If you Google 'modest swimsuits,' you'll find literally thousands of options."

**4EveryGirl** is an organization that works for "media images that value, respect, empower and promote the true value of every girl." Their website, 4EveryGirl.com, includes current statistics on how media influence our daughters, and there's even a section on the website where you and your daughter can become involved right away in the effort to influence media programming. It's called "Change the World Around You." One thing I love about this approach is that it helps you show your daughter how she can take her personal beliefs and her own struggles against the pressures that come with negative female media images and use her stories to help create change. In other words, while building within your daughter the strength and courage to be different from the negative female role models and images the media force on her, you are showing her a way to actually change those images into positive ones. Yes, it is an uphill battle. Yes, it may seem impossible. But we must teach our daughters that their voices matter and that they don't just have to play defense. They can be offensive in the battle for their own dignity and respect too.

Another great resource for your daughter is the book *Dressing with Dignity* by former model Colleen Hammond. Colleen offers positive reinforcement about how men and boys treat girls who dress themselves with respect differently from how they treat those who dress as if all they have to offer the world is their sexual organs: "I believe it is because, subconsciously, men can read women's body language. If they see a woman who dresses with dignity and carries herself with grace and femininity, they pick up on that. They take it as a sign to approach her with the respect, reverence and honor a woman ought to have."

Finally, you must read the story of former supermodel Kim Alexis. She is a delightful person and freely shares her spiritual journey in her fantastic book *A Model for a Better Future*. Kim has graced the covers of hundreds of magazines over the years and continues to be one of the most beautiful women in the world. But she is lovely on the inside too. I once had the pleasure of sharing a room with her on a women's retreat and found that her true beauty lies in her heart for our nation's young women.

One very candid admission Kim made in her book about her modeling career is this:

> The worst part of this business is that you are constantly asked to compromise your moral standards. There are pictures I look back on today and think, *Oh, why did I let them talk me into that?* I made some choices I'm not proud of.

She went on to say,

> Many women are playing with fire in the way they dress. Dressing like a floozy tells the world, "Look at me, want me, lust after me. I'm easy and you can have me." Displaying intimate parts of the body is a form of advertising for sex—so if you dress to attract sexual attention, you can hardly blame anyone else if that kind of attention comes your way. Dressing modestly tells the world, "I respect myself and I insist on being treated with respect."

## Chapter 24
# Dress Your Son in Respect

## The Challenge

Let's face it: chivalry in young men is hard to come by these days. Radical feminism has taught us that holding doors and other such examples of genteel behavior are part of rigid gender roles that should just be thrown out the door. And to further erode civility, just look at how young boys are taught to behave by the mass media. What you get is a generation of young males who are confused or have no idea how they are supposed to treat young women or their elders. Battling a culture that devalues civility and purposefully attacks tradition makes it nearly impossible to teach our sons to be gentlemen. One of the most eye-opening videos I've ever seen, *The Merchants of Cool*, carefully documents why and how the modern media rob young males of their dignity. The marketing industry deliberately cultivates a grotesque male image known as a Mook—their definition of modern teen boys. As I described in chapter 4, "Understand How Marketers Target Your Children," programmers have discovered that the best way to increase viewership among teen boys is by showing rude, crude behavior by other boys. It also reinforces the behavior as normal, acceptable—even desirable—for our nation's young men.

The bottom line is the bottom dollar: those who market to our teens seek to manipulate their raw emotions and prey on their raging sexual curiosity and the natural confusion of identity and insecurity that comes in the teen years—all in order to boost ratings and make money. In her book *The War Against Boys*, Christina Hoff Sommers documented the moral fallout that has occurred in the wake of the decline of respectful young men. She told countless stories, including the story of Tawnya Brady, a high school student in Petaluma, California. When Tawnya would walk down the hallways of her school, her male peers would actually moo at her, a crude reference to the size of her breasts. Of course, such crude and hurtful behavior has always been displayed by some preteen and teen boys. The difference is that kids used to be punished for such rudeness and even ostracized by their peers as the "bad kids." It seems that in many cases, girls have just learned to put up with the behavior, teachers have given up, and parents don't have a clue. As for the boys themselves? Well, they don't seem to have any place to look for direction, boundaries, and what their role should be. Society doesn't teach them to be gentlemen anymore. No one tells them to open the door for girls, to offer a chair, or even to watch their language and banter around their female friends. Such acts of respect and thoughtfulness are all but gone, thrown out when radical feminism started demanding equal treatment in every aspect of the word. Equal pay for equal work? Of course. Equal opportunity for the sexes? Absolutely. But treating our daughters like "one of the boys"? I think we've robbed both our young males and females of their dignity and pride by allowing manners to be discarded in the name of equality.

Barney Brawer, director of the Boys' Project at Tufts University, told *Education Week*, "We've deconstructed the old version of manhood, but we've not constructed a new version." Mr. Brawer could not be more right. Radical feminism and the media have created a cultural vacuum on the topic of manhood. Respectful behavior is treated as sexist and backward. And the sex education taught in most public schools only adds to the problem. Young men are expected to have sex with our daughters but are taught that the most respectful way to treat our little girls is to wear a condom.

The problem is a failure to teach our sons what it truly means to be a strong, masculine, respectful male. And, of course, if disrespectful behavior continues to increase in the teen years, it will only manifest itself more powerfully and negatively after marriage. The sons of today are the husbands and fathers of tomorrow. If we want to reclaim the family as the healthy nucleus of American society, we must reclaim our sons.

Refuse to allow modern culture to be the etiquette class for your son. Teach him that a respectful attitude and being a gentleman are necessary to succeed in all facets of life. Your son must learn that respect entails protecting the women in his life, honoring a woman's chastity and name, and acting like a gentleman toward other men and his elders.

# In Your Shoes

My friend Amy went to a restaurant with her family, which included her eleven-year-old brother, Lyde. Next to her family, the waiters were setting up a large table for what was clearly going to be a big group event. After about ten minutes, a group of high school–aged young women and men came bounding up the stairs, laughing and chatting. After some loud shuffling and scuffling, they all found their seats and began ordering. Lyde, who had just finished a cotillion (dance) class, had been watching and closely observing how this young social group interacted. He took Amy's family by surprise when he indignantly chimed in with, "Those boys are not very respectful!" The family slowly put down their forks, caught a bit off guard by the remark. Lyde's mother asked, "Why do you say that?" He replied, "Well, all of the boys came in and grabbed the best seats for themselves and then made the girls climb around them for their chairs. The boys should have waited until all the girls picked a seat, pulled out their chairs for them, and then took the leftover seats. What they did was really disrespectful to the girls." The parents sat in stunned silence. The good news about this example is that boys can be taught! It doesn't take much to open even the youngest of eyes to the reality that there is honor in honoring others.

Julie, a recent college graduate, shared how young men frequently bolt in the door ahead of her, and even reported that one slammed the door in her face, causing her to fall down. Unfortunately, those are only her mild encounters with young men who have been taught nothing of manners. She also shared about overhearing college men referring to women, saying things like "last night I smacked that a**" or making fun of women's appearance or physical flaws.

When did young men start getting away with acting so disrespect- fully? You can pretty much trace it to the simultaneous breakdown of the family, the rise of radical feminism, and the onslaught of crude media. These dynamics have created the perfect storm, and our young men are being flung around like garbage. Of course if people are treated like garbage, they have a tendency to treat others that way. While we as parents can't magically turn back the clock to a more civilized society in general, we can control what we teach about how to treat others. We have a responsibility to teach that degrading or even thoughtless behavior toward others will not happen on our watch and should never happen even when no one is watching. We must be proactive in teaching that thoughtfulness is next to godliness and that considering others and their feelings is a mark of the highest character. Not all young men are rude and crass. There are plenty of kind and gracious young men with strong character out there, but they are becoming an increasingly rare find. Sadly, parents who do not teach their sons to be considerate rob them of a virtue, the loss of which will harm them the rest of their lives. They will find it harder to please their teachers and bosses and will be less able to find the type of woman who will stand by them, admire them, and give them the respect that men so deeply crave.

## From My Home to Yours

One tool, which seems to be losing popularity these days but could use a good comeback, is the concept of cotillion or etiquette classes for your preteen sons. There's just something delightful about watching them put on coats and ties and be forced to interact with girls in a room run by adults with old-fashioned manners. If you stay and watch, you just might be reminded of a few good rules of civility yourself.

Look for media examples (although they are few and far between) that show the power and masculinity of men who are loyal and true.

Take Mel Gibson's *The Patriot* or his epic movie *Braveheart*. (Note: I think these are appropriate for teenagers but not younger boys.) In both movies Gibson's character was loyal and true to his family, his faith, and his belief in freedom. Although far from perfect, the characters Gibson portrayed believed in fidelity and marriage. Speak to your son frequently about the power and strong character that come from being a person of undying commitment and absolute loyalty to someone else. You must also teach him the value of being loyal and true to an ideal that is bigger than himself—to ideas such as freedom, equality, and standing up for the defenseless.

The most natural way to teach manners is at home at your own dinner table. See every meal as an opportunity to practice dining etiquette for your sons and daughters. And, as my son Drew reminds me, the most effective thing you can tell your sons about having thoughtful behavior and good manners is "The girls really do like it."

One of the finest youth organizations for boys and young men used to be the Boy Scouts. It provided parents with amazing opportunities to work with their kids and each other to raise young men of character and responsibility. Recently, however, the Boy Scouts changed the entire way they operate, abandoning their time-honored principles of teaching fidelity and helping support boys to be "morally straight." It was one of the saddest days of my parental life when the Scouts decided to become politically correct and abandon their principles and the boys and families who believe in them. Thankfully, a new, wonderful, solid organization has sprung up to fill the void, and it now has chapters across the county. The group is called Trail Life USA—you can find the closest chapter near you at TrailLifeUSA.com. In Trail Life, parents (primarily dads or other male mentors) help their sons, and the boys help each other. This was true of Scouting, and I could tell story after story about how wonderful it was to be part of a network of parents who worked hard to help their sons and the other boys in the troop succeed. Because of my husband's hard work and leadership with Scouts, and with the dedication and support of other parents, our two sons and ten other boys in their age range went through the teen years as Scouts and every one of them became Eagles. Trail Life is set up with the same support network, but even better. Trail Life is built on several core values. Although you can find a complete listing at their website, here are a few:

- Outdoor focused: "We believe there is something special about being in the outdoors. This enables our program to instill 'Adventure, Character, and Leadership' traits in boys and young men. Camping, hiking, and other outdoor activities help build deep relationships and provide a special context for leadership, problem solving, conflict resolution, and character building."
- Servant leadership: "Leadership with a servant's attitude by both adults and youth is a core value."
- Courage: "We will continually commit ourselves to the truths found in the scriptures, that we are to fear God and not man, and that the fear of the Lord is the beginning of wisdom and understanding."

You can count on Trail Life to help build the following values into the lives of your son: purity, service, stewardship, and integrity. Scouting created countless wonderful memories of fun times with our boys that we will forever cherish. Identifying and becoming involved with this new organization for young men will be time well spent for you and your son—and it is even more important for the single parent.

Of course, the best way to teach your son to be a gentleman is to model it yourself. If you've been negligent in either directly teaching your son about basic manners and respect or practicing it for him, vow to change your ways this very day.

When talking to your son about respect, begin by teaching him that the principle of respect is rooted in an understanding of the inherent dignity of other people. The Golden Rule (see chapter 27, "Let the Golden Rule Rule Your Home") teaches us to treat others as we would like to be treated—a concept based on the idea that each of us is endowed with dignity by our Creator and is worthy of being treated with honor.

## Reflections from a Daughter

I can't think of any better grounds for the principle of respect than 2 Timothy 1:7, which says, "God gave us a spirit not of fear but of power and love and self-control" (ESV).

Mankind has been gifted with a spirit that is capable of incredible power, unending love, and the ability to tame and cultivate itself through self-discipline. Those immense capabilities practically require men and women to respect themselves and one another. But respect doesn't always come naturally, so it must be taught. And it must be taught especially to boys, who seem to have a greater desire for it.

The most respectful and respectable guys I knew while growing up were the ones whose parents taught them to take life seriously. Many of them also began taking God seriously, considering the ways they decided to treat others in light of their eternal consequences. People respected them, their actions, and their faith because they actively respected those around them and because they lived their lives according to a spirit of power, love, and self-control.

## Act Now

Date _____

Today I sat down with my son and talked about the lifelong value of treating others with respect. We began working through a book on manners or I enrolled him/us in an etiquette class.

Signature _____

## More Help

Dr. James Dobson of Family Talk has two wonderful resources on parenting boys, *Bringing Up Boys* and *Dare to Discipline*. Family Talk also has a section on their website (drjamesdobson.org) called "Parenting," which is devoted to parenting and discipline tips broken down by age groups and specific topics.

There are also a few great books on manners that you can use with your son. The very best method for using such books is to read them with your son. When doing so, make sure your son realizes that learning manners and respect should not be seen as a burden but rather as something that will set him apart from his peers and help him succeed in school, dating, and his career. Respect given is respect earned. My favorite books on manners for men and boys are John Bridges's *How to Be a Gentleman: A Timely Guide to Timeless Manners* and *50 Things Every Young Gentleman Should Know*. Emily Post's *Emily Post's Etiquette*, her revised book on manners, is also a classic with simple and digestible sections. The website for the Emily Post Institute, EmilyPost.com, is full of excellent resources for parents and children of all ages on a wide range of topics, such as etiquette in the workplace for teens.

*Chapter 25*
# Install a Reliable Internet Filter

## The Challenge

According to a study by the London School of Economics, nine out of ten children who go online (many of them just doing their homework, by the way) will view pornography. A study by the Kaiser Family Foundation shows that seven out of ten view porn unintentionally—at least the first time. In other words, even when kids are acting responsibly and innocently, the pornographers are so fixated on creating new porn addicts that they have made it virtually impossible for children to escape their grasp. Think about it: 90 percent of all kids on the Internet will be subjected to the sexual images and values of the perverted pornographers that are rampant in the online world. And, tragically, according to a 2006 report by the National Center for Missing and Exploited Children, one out of three children who views pornography is doing it intentionally.

Our culture has become so obsessed with sexualizing everything that our children's innocence is extremely vulnerable. I believe there should be a protected space in childhood where kids don't have sex forced upon them—physically or mentally. And, for crying out loud, if we as moms and dads aren't building that space in our own homes, how on earth can we expect them to have it anyplace else? Let me be clear: if your kids consume hard-core pornography in your home, you are the one to blame. The fantastic news is that this is one problem you have some control over.

Mere exposure to pornography inflicts a great deal of damage on developing attitudes, psyches, and morality. Dr. Jill Manning, family therapist and author of *What's the Big Deal about Pornography? A Guide for the Internet Generation*, outlined the personal cost of pornography to children in a study she presented to a special US Senate subcommittee. Her analysis of the peer-reviewed research reveals that pornography consumption by children is associated with the following trends (just to name a few). In Dr. Manning's words:

- Developing tolerance toward sexually explicit material, thereby requiring more novel or bizarre material to achieve the same level of arousal or interest
- Overestimating the prevalence of less common, harmful sexual practices (such as group sex, bestiality, and sadomasochistic activity)
- Abandoning the goal of sexual activity with exclusivity to one partner
- Perceiving promiscuity as a normal state of interaction
- Developing cynical attitudes about love
- Believing that raising children and having a family is an unattractive prospect

- Developing a negative body image, especially for girls

According to Dr. Manning, a multipronged solution is needed, including the following:

- Install reliable filters on each of your kids' electronic devices.
- Set limits on the amount of time your children spend with their electronics. Quality matters, but so does quantity. This is their precious youth they're spending on these activities!
- Keep up with the technology, because it keeps changing.

## From My Home to Yours

Thankfully, there are now many great parental control mechanisms that you can install on the computers, laptops, email services, social networks, gaming systems, and cell phones used by your family members. It will take quite a bit of your time and brainpower to understand what is available, but you owe it to your children and to what you say you believe to review the options and install what is right for your family. David Burt, an Internet and tech guru, has compiled a Parental Controls Guide that can be found on his website, DavidBurt.us. In this report, Mr. Burt has analyzed filters and controls for virtually every electronic gizmo you can think of. It takes only a few minutes and a few keystrokes to download and install many of the systems. Some even send reports via email letting you know what sites users have attempted to visit—a very useful tool when you have guests in your home. I used such a filter on the Internet when my kids lived at home, so they knew about the tracking system. However, the week that two friends were visiting us from out of town, my report revealed that someone had attempted to visit six hard-core porn sites. Thank the good Lord, their attempts were blocked. Had I not taken the time to secure the Internet for those in my care, these two young boys would have consumed hard-core pornography in my own home and possibly exposed my children while the rest of us slept peacefully just down the hallway. Think about it: we go to great lengths as parents to secure our doors and windows at night, yet for far too many parents the open portal of the Internet allows every kind of perversion to enter their home and attack the innocence and sensibilities of their kids.

Some parents who want to protect their kids online may have concerns that a filter would block health and reproductive information that might actually help their sons and daughters understand more about their ever-changing bodies. But there is good news on this front: there is no need for concern. FamilyFacts.org summarized a study on blocking software that was detailed in the article "Does Pornography-Blocking Software Block Access to Health Information on the Internet?" Published in the *Journal of the American Medical Association*, the summary details that pornography-blocking software has minimal impact on one's access to information about sexual and reproductive health. For example, filtering software set at moderate settings blocks only 5 percent of health information while blocking 90 percent of pornographic content online. Effective filters also contain password-protected override systems in case you, as a parent, believe a safe site has been mistakenly blocked. With a simple password and verification from you, the site becomes accessible. So what are you waiting for?

If your child has a smartphone, you also have the option to use apps that allow you to track his or her location through the phone. You can find the newest apps by searching through the Apple App Store or through a Google search online. Some mobile service providers also have their own tracking functions, so make sure you ask your cell phone provider for the options. By the way, tracking functions have the added benefit of helping you locate a lost cell phone.

# In Your Shoes

After a lecture about my book *Home Invasion* at the Heritage Foundation, a mother of five with whom I have been friends for many years approached me with distress etched across her face. She asked, "Can I meet with you privately for a few minutes? I feel so convicted about something." My friend has been heavily involved in the battle for decency in our culture for as many years as I have. Yet, as is the case with most parents, she is technologically challenged. She spoke with tears in her eyes as she shared an all too familiar horror story:

> I've known that I need a filter on our Internet. But my husband and I always seem to be having computer problems and we just feel overwhelmed by all the technology. I thought I could keep my kids safe by

monitoring their usage myself. But several weeks ago
our eight-year-old daughter awoke us in the middle
of the night crying her heart out. We thought she
was sick. Our precious little girl then said between
sobs, "I've done something very bad. I was on the
computer and saw some very bad pictures."

The mother then tried to assure her daughter that it wasn't her
fault she had stumbled across the photos—that she shouldn't feel
guilty or think she is a bad girl. The daughter responded between
breaths, "But, Mommy, I stayed and looked for a very long time."
What a tragedy. An innocent eight-year-old girl from a responsible,
conscientious family had vivid sex acts etched in her brain even
before she knew what sex was. The child had been suffering for days
with her own torment and guilt, replaying over and over in her mind
the horrible scenes that she didn't understand but instinctively knew
were wrong. And it all could have been avoided with the simple ten-
minute act of downloading a filter.

# From My Home to Yours

Here are some other online safety tips that I think you will find
helpful.

- Never allow your children to have Internet connections in their bedrooms. You can put the
  Internet connection in one common room so
  that everyone in the family is accountable for how

they are spending their time online. One reader
of my column, Julia, suggested a great tip: "We
have an older, slower computer in our sixteen-
year-old son's room, but no Internet connection.
He can write papers and make spreadsheets, and
that's about all! He has to bring his disk down
to the 'big computer' to print out his work."
In our era where nearly everyone seems to have
smartphones and instant access to the Internet
from the palm of their hand, it is admittedly
incredibly difficult to control what your sons and
daughters see and with whom they communicate
online. This makes your efforts and conversations
about technology with your children ever more
important.

- Make the resources of InternetSafety101.org your
  go-to source to help you protect your children
  and to strengthen their character in the process.
- If you have Wi-Fi at home, use a password that
  only you know (and be sure to "uncheck" the box
  when you enter the password on a child's computer and it asks if you want to save it), or change
  the password regularly.
- Don't give kids their own laptops, smartphones,
  or tablets until they are mature enough to be
  responsible on the Internet.
- When you do decide to give them access to the
  Internet, always use filters.

- Set limits on Internet usage. The problem is not just with content but with the hours and hours many kids spend online when they should be in face-to-face interactions with family and friends. You can turn off your family's Wi-Fi at bedtime to limit their access at night.
- Talk to your children about safety on the World Wide Web. Teach them how to navigate the web safely and to recognize areas of danger (more on this in the next chapter, "Keep Your Children Safe in Online Social Media"). The very best tools and resources I know come from InternetSafety101.org.
- Make it a rule that children never give out family or personal contact information on the web.
- Make it a rule that children never share passwords to social media sites, even with their friends, and insist that your children provide you with their passwords for Facebook or any other sites they use. Your mantra should be, "I'm paying for the computer, the cell phone, the room, the electricity, the Internet connection, and everything else you see. No password—no access." Let them know you will be checking their sites often in order to keep them safe. There is no room for compromise here, and you should never, ever let the world or your own friends tell you otherwise.

- Have rules for which games and apps your children can download or buy. Understand that many are violent, sexual, or just plain time wasters. For the ones you do allow them to have, make time to use them with your kids on occasion.
- Remind your children that not everything they read online is accurate. Encourage them to double-check facts across multiple sites and against trusted sources.
- Explain the concepts of intellectual property and plagiarism. Let your kids know it is stealing to use someone else's music, art, or words without purchasing them or crediting them.
- Remember that many fast food restaurants and other places teens visit often have free Wi-Fi access. Make it a point to ask the managers if they have a filter on their Internet services and, if they don't, request that they install one. If they resist, why not start a friendly petition drive with your friends to ask the manager to do so? Enough Is Enough (enough.org) has led the charge in successfully convincing many coffeehouses and restaurants to take such safety measures. You can get an up-to-date listing of places that have adopted this commonsense approach and learn how you can add your voice to convince the CEOs of national chains to create safer atmospheres for their customers.

Remember, no filtering system is foolproof. Kristin's admission in the next section (which I read right before we turned in this manuscript) made me laugh—now that the danger has passed! And it reminded me to remind you of this simple advice: Do the best you can. And do it every day.

# Reflections from a Daughter

Your kids will likely always be at least one step ahead of you when it comes to technology. Actually, the first time my mom reads this will be the first time I tell her that I figured out the password for our Internet filter early on. (Honestly, I did it just to prove to myself that I could. Sorry, Mom.) But don't let that discourage you. As long as you are doing something to filter and manage what comes into your house, two things will take place. First, your kids will learn that you care about what they come across online (knowing you care about it affects them more than you may realize), and second, they'll gain some idea as to what the boundaries are. They may break the rules you set or even outsmart the filters, but as long as there are rules and filters, there is a clear sense of right and wrong. (If you have to break through a filter to view something online, there can't be any excuses.)

And, yes, some objectionable material may slip through the cracks and show up on the screen unsolicited from time to time. Filters aren't ever going to entirely shelter kids on the Internet, but they absolutely help protect the innocent browser, and they absolutely help reinforce standards.

# Act Now

Date _____

Today I pledged to research available filters.

I researched filters and parental controls on _____ (date).

I installed the following safeguards on the electronics my kids use:

_____ (safeguard) _____ (device)

_____ (child) _____ (date)

_____ (safeguard) _____ (device)

_____ (child) _____ (date)

_____ (safeguard) _____ (device)

_____ (child) _____ (date)

_____ (safeguard) _____ (device)

_____ (child) _____ (date)

Signature _____

# More Help

I serve as a volunteer on the Internet Safety Council for Enough Is Enough (EIE), an organization I was very proud to help found way back in 1992 (when I was pregnant with Kristin!). Even before the Internet era, it was obvious to me that pornography was making victims and addicts of many people. My dear friends Dee Jepsen, Becky Norton Dunlop, Sarah Blanken, and others worked very hard with the National Coalition Against Pornography (now the National Coalition for the Protection of Children and Families) to inform women of the dangers of pornography on our lives, safety, self-esteem, and culture. Today, Enough Is Enough is run by Donna Rice Hughes and has refocused its efforts on keeping kids safe from online dangers. No one has done a better job of compiling resources for parents to use in keeping their kids safe online than Donna. No one. Enough Is Enough's many invaluable tools include *Internet Safety 101*, a video and workbook for empowering parents. The DVD and book contain list after list of gadgets you can use to protect your kids online, on their cell phones, and on their smartphones. They also provide facts, testimonials, age-based guidelines, simple-to-understand explanations of all the latest technologies, and even a look at what is to come. EIE actually maintains two great sites: Enough.org and InternetSafety101.org, which serve as clearinghouses for Internet safety and victim assistance resources. Their purpose is to educate the public about the dangers of Internet pornography and sexual predators as it relates to children and families. In addition, the websites are designed to promote and provide prevention awareness and empower parents and other adult childcare givers to implement safety measures needed to protect children from online dangers.

*Chapter 26*
# Keep Your Children Safe in Online Social Media

## The Challenge

There's no question that the Internet is a huge blessing. A world of information can be found at our fingertips; more moms and dads get to work in their homes instead of spending so much time in the office; we can access the world and many of its wonders and explore new cultures without leaving our living rooms. Social networking sites such as Facebook, Instagram, Twitter, and many others allow people of all ages to easily stay in touch with family and friends—and to make new acquaintances.

For the most part, such contact is harmless. But, parents, beware: like any public playground or theme park, social networks are also places where pedophiles and other perverts like to prowl.

It seems that nearly every week there's a news story about some sick individual who has preyed on children and teens via the Internet. While we often think the youngest of children are at the greatest risk, the fact is that the average age for child abduction is twelve years old. Why? This is the age when our kids are more independent and are first learning to protect themselves. The sad truth is that our teens are also increasingly vulnerable to victimization because they are spending more and more time online talking with strangers, and parents seem to be unaware of the fact that evil adults often anonymously search the Internet and quietly spy on conversations in search of prey. Social networks are playgrounds for sexual predators who can lure kids into situations of abuse and even death. The problem is so extensive that there have even been a plethora of television shows, such as *America's Most Wanted*, that feature sting operations and horror stories of adults meeting kids to have sex with them. According to the National Center for Missing and Exploited Children, two out of every five missing children ages fifteen to seventeen are abducted in connection with Internet activity.

The online dangers aren't confined to chat rooms and social media networks. Unfortunately, parents who have found porn in their email inboxes, been tormented by raunchy pop-up images, or unwittingly—and way too easily—stumbled across a porn site must realize that any kid who spends time on the Internet will not only be victimized by such images but will, because of natural childhood curiosity, be drawn into them.

The Internet is a place for perverts to "shop" for children without detection. These perverts have cunningly studied how to present themselves as friends to your kids. They often pretend to be teenagers and know just how to pry and push into the emotional turmoil that marks the teen years. Recent polling of teens shows that over 50 percent of kids who enter chat rooms—where the conversation can all too often turn raunchy and racy—say they have given out personal information to complete strangers, including their phone numbers, their home addresses, and where they go to school.

And the risks associated with innocent Internet surfing are all too real. Statistics reveal, for example, that children as young as five are now regularly being exposed to porn online. Pornography is more than a thirteen-billion-dollar-a-year industry, working 24-7 to make porn addicts out of our kids—and too often succeeding. It's a devastating problem that destroys the innocence of our children and threatens their emotional, moral, social, and spiritual development.

Here are a few alarming facts every parent should know, as reported on the terrific site InternetSafety101.com:

- Social media is the most popular use of the web.
- Twenty-nine percent of Internet sex crimes were initiated on social networking sites.
- Eighty-five percent of parents with teenage children ages thirteen to seventeen report that their child uses a social networking site.
- Nearly 50 percent of teens have an online public profile that anyone can view.
- Teens often include the following information on their social networking profiles:
    o Real age
    o Photos of themselves
    o City they live in
    o School name/location
    o Their cell phone number
    o Places they typically go

Another problem for kids who go online is cyberbullying. The World Wide Web has taken old-fashioned playground taunts to a new and disturbing level. Bullies can reach a much wider audience now, at all hours of the day, tormenting kids who have been socially ostracized. According to *Internet Safety 101*, 33 percent of social media–using teens have been victims of cyberbullying. Some of this bullying is done anonymously through apps such as Yik Yak.

In many ways, cyberbullying is worse than the "in person" kind. The Internet seems like a virtual world not only to kids but to adults—a place where some people say and do cruel things that they might never say or do in person. That's the focus, in fact, of a series of ads that was launched in 2008 by the Ad Council. The ads feature a young girl who suddenly starts saying horrible things about a classmate right in front of a group of shocked students that includes the girl she's targeting. "If you wouldn't say it in person," the narrator asks, "why say it online?" The words *delete cyberbullying* are then typed onto the screen—and erased.

You are the protector: it's up to you to leave your comfort zone and learn about this brave new world of technology. We must teach our children that the time-honored advice of "don't talk to strangers" applies to the Internet too.

Here are a few more tips:

**Set clear rules about computer usage (including smartphones and tablets).** Explain how much nonschool time your children can spend on the computer and when they can do so—after their schoolwork is completed, for example. Make sure your kids understand that they need to use the privacy settings to keep predators from seeing their Facebook pages or searching their names. There's even a Timeline Review setting that doesn't allow anything to be posted to their timeline without approval.

**Make sure computers are located in a family area and give smartphones only to kids who demonstrate the maturity necessary to be safe online.** Some 25 percent of teens say their parents know little or nothing about what they do online. This is a problem primarily for parents who make the mistake of letting their children have a computer in their rooms. Always locate home computers in an open room so they can be easily monitored. It's a very bad idea to put televisions or computers in kids' bedrooms. You never know who or what they might come across or how much time they might spend blankly staring at the screen. Until you are certain that your children are responsible, block the Internet access on their smartphones. And even when they do have access, check periodically for what is coming across their screens. It also benefits the entire family if you lay down a hard-and-fast rule that the home Wi-Fi access will be turned off at a specific time each evening. If family members access the web directly from their smartphones or tablets instead of through a home wireless system, consider collecting all smartphones and tablets in your home at a certain hour each night. This simple move will prevent everyone in the house from staying up late in the night surfing the web and will help ensure that your children sleep instead of chat online or on the phone. I know this is tough, but if you approach them in the tone of wanting to protect them from outside dangers, rather than a tone of your not trusting them, it will go over much better. We've all heard the true, horrible stories of teens committing suicide because they were bullied online. Those tragic stories might have turned out very differently had the parents been aware of the bullying while their children were still alive. Don't forget that you are the first and last protector of your children. Remember that you should have your kids' passwords and check in on their social media frequently!

**Install an Internet filter.** I cannot stress this enough. Parents should never allow their children to use a computer or a smartphone without an Internet filter; the potential for trouble is simply too great. (See chapter 25, "Install a Reliable Internet Filter," for where to locate good filters.)

**Subscribe to MetLifeDefender.com.** I don't think I've ever been as excited about a product as I am about this newest technological help that hit the market in 2014. The protection now available to parents is astounding! This service actually alerts you when your children might be approached via texts and emails by predators, when they are being bullied, and when pornographers are trying to engulf them. It also protects your and their identities in areas not possible before now. Created by the makers of the technology behind LifeLock (but the companies are not affiliated), this protection system covers all personal devices and Internet connections in your home for one monthly fee and digs deep into the underworld of the web where the child pornographers, sex traffickers, and predators live. It is an astounding service—still not 100 percent foolproof, but better than anything on the market to date. It's worth every penny.

**The best solution should be the most obvious: talk to your kids about using the Internet responsibly!** Only about 41 percent of teens report that their parents talk to them a lot about Internet safety; that leaves nearly six out of ten who aren't doing their job. The web is a window to the world for your kids, but it is also a window into their world for others. Be sure they know that they should come to you immediately if anybody online begins asking personal questions or attempting to invade their privacy. Make them understand that it's better to be overcautious than sorry.

Mom, Dad, you should be the ultimate "filter." It's your responsibility to watch for garbage that might slip through, to warn your kids about online predators, and to teach them not to talk to strangers online. When you fail to take such action, it's as if you have given the perverts your permission to stalk your sons and daughters.

# In Your Shoes

For some reason, many parents still think their kids aren't really at risk. Some develop a false sense of security if they live (or think they live) in safe neighborhoods. But because the Internet knows no geographic boundaries, even families in the smallest of towns and best neighborhoods are at risk to predators from all over the world. I grew up in the charming, relaxed southern town of Lakeland, in Polk County, Florida. I was dismayed to see a story by reporter Stephanie Allen in my hometown newspaper, *The Ledger*, on August 5, 2014. Allen was reporting on "a statewide investigation to catch pedophiles" in which a total of 132 men were arrested—thirteen of them in Polk County. The details are ugly, but please read them. You must, must

take the time to be aware that unsupervised Internet usage by your
children comes with grave dangers:

> During the operation, undercover detectives
> answered and posted ads on websites and chat-
> rooms pretending to be children.
>
> The detectives then talked with the men—
> some of whom revealed disturbing details about
> sexual fantasies and past sexual encounters with
> children—until they agreed to meet at an undis-
> closed location, where they were arrested....
>
> The men arrested ranged in ages from their 20s
> through 70s and included a postal worker, pizza
> deliveryman, landscaper, former law enforcement
> officer and theme park employee, the task force
> said.

One of the law enforcement officers who announced the opera-
tion pointed out that there was no special "run on sexual predators"
in Florida. Sadly, such stories are now commonplace in every town
across the country.

# Reflections from a Daughter

Common sense goes a long way on social networks. Basic safety
principles don't change much between social networks and real life.
Don't talk to strangers, don't post your personal information in public places, always be aware, and in general you'll be all right.

But beyond basic safety, online communities are more complicated because they develop their own virtual cultures, which are constantly changing just like real world cultures. For example, the social norms of Facebook are entirely different from those you would have seen on Myspace, and Facebook users today operate in a very different way than they did six years ago. Every social network has a unique culture. And just as in any society, there are also subcultures to take into account.

The constant flux can be confusing for new users, so my biggest piece of advice to concerned parents who want to try to conquer the steep learning curve of social media is this: act as if you were moving to a foreign country. Observe the culture until you are able to assimilate. The better you understand the ins and outs of the social network, the more effectively you will be able to use it as a tool to monitor what's going on in your kids' lives and to keep them safe both on- and offline.

## Act Now

Date _____

Today I started making social networking safer for my children. I pledge to continuously update myself about Internet dangers and to ensure that my children understand how to use the Internet safely.

Signature _____

# More Help

There are many excellent organizations and websites to help parents "web-proof" their home, which also illustrates how widespread and serious the problem of online dangers really is (see the previous chapter, "Install a Reliable Internet Filter").

I would highly recommend you check out **Komando.com**, the site of Kim Komando, a web-savvy mother who hosts a weekly three-hour call-in talk radio show, which you can listen to online. Her "10 Commandments for Kids Online" is something you may want to print out and post in your home.

I already mentioned the *Internet Safety 101* **workbook and DVD** in the last chapter, but I really cannot emphasize this set of materials enough. Ordering and using it will make you the technology master in your home and will equip you to protect your children in ways you didn't even know you needed to! You can use the DVD or workbook alone or together, and they are divided into useful sections that you can use one at a time. The materials teach you about the prevalence, dangers, and harms of pornography usage by kids; what fuels online predators and how to avoid them; the basic tools you need to keep your kids safe; and lists of great resources. *Internet Safety 101* is designed for both individual and group use and can be ordered for around thirty dollars through Enough.org or by calling 888-744-0004.

*Chapter 27*

# Let the Golden Rule
# Rule Your Home

## The Challenge

It's simple: "Do unto others as you would have them do unto you." This biblical wisdom is so self-evident that it is universally admired, even by those who profess no faith in God at all. Yet how constantly we fail to fulfill this ideal.

It's truly the basic tenet for human relations. Imagine the pain the world would be free of if only everyone followed the Golden Rule. Imagine the good that could be accomplished, the human suffering that would be replaced with human achievement, if we each treated others the way we want to be treated. But fat chance, right? I mean, how many of us practice it in our own homes with the people we are supposed to love the most? With divorced and broken families now the norm in American society, who is modeling the Golden Rule for our children?

The solution is obvious, but the practice is hard: begin putting others first. And that includes taking the time and energy to teach your teens and kids to do the same.

Part of this responsibility means teaching good manners. I don't just mean learning which fork to use at a formal dinner but enforcing

310 30 ways in 30 days to strengthen your family

basic consideration for others. That kind of consideration, of looking out for others, doesn't come naturally. It has to be taught by giving our children something good to emulate.

There's a strong correlation between active parenting and teaching the civility and thoughtfulness that make the world go 'round. How else would children learn to avoid quarreling and whining? Where would they learn to offer someone a seat if the bus is full? How would they learn to take pride in their chores? How would they learn to say "please," "thank you," and "you're welcome"? God doesn't put us on earth knowing these things.

Children learn when parents take the time to teach them and to enforce family standards. Part-time parenting that says, "Go to your room, watch television, get on the computer, amuse yourself, because I have neither the time nor the inclination to make you do otherwise" produces children who will, in turn, think of themselves before the needs of even their closest loved ones.

In the competitiveness of the modern culture, it's easy to lose sight of that. As author Dr. V. Gilbert Beers said, "What our children become is infinitely more important than what our children will do."

In other words, it's who they are becoming on the inside that matters most.

The greatest gift we can impart to our children is to teach them to love God with all of their hearts and minds and to love their neighbors as they love themselves. The toxicity of our culture makes it more important than ever for parents to take an active role in developing the character traits that enable our sons and daughters to live their lives in a manner that strengthens and reveals this call to love.

It's an uphill battle, to be sure. In *Something for Nothing: The All-Consuming Desire That Turns the American Dream into a Social Nightmare*, self-help author Brian Tracy described how mankind's inborn nature to be "lazy, greedy, ambitious, selfish, vain, ignorant, and impatient" without regard to others has plunged our nation into crisis.

Of course, the propensity of humans to scheme about how to get something for nothing is certainly not new to the human condition or to Americans. And the devastating effects that such expectations and attitudes have on the individual and his personal character have been well documented throughout history. As Thomas Jefferson once said, "The worst day in a man's life is when he sits down and begins thinking about how he can get something for nothing."

A huge challenge of parenthood is trying to shape our children into young gentlemen and ladies who will spend their lives with a propensity to give and earn rather than to merely receive and take.

As Brian Tracy pointed out, the best efforts of even the most loving and committed parents to raise children of character are often thwarted because we have failed to realize the necessity of channeling children's natural drives into positive behaviors. This is especially difficult when all around us our society rewards and encourages the "me first with no concern for others" attitude that harms both individuals and civil society.

Commit to model the Golden Rule and teach your kids how to do the same. We can't simply blame society and throw up our hands, however tempting that may seem at times. Parents may not be able to control the overall culture (although we certainly should influence it to the best of our ability), but we have the responsibility and privilege to determine the lessons taught within our own homes.

# From My Home to Yours

Here are five easy ways to begin living and teaching the Golden Rule in your home:

**1. Invest time in your kids.** Teaching the Golden Rule starts with investing more time in their lives. As Brian Tracy reminded us: "Many parents want to get something for nothing in child rearing. They want to be seen as excellent parents without paying the price that this requires. How does a child spell 'love'? Answer: 'T-I-M-E!' Something for nothing parents try to get by on the cheap, spending their precious and irreplaceable time in all the wrong places. The solution to the problems of marriage and parenting is simple. Spend more time with the people you care about the most."

Even the busiest parents can make a concerted effort to be around their children. If you want to shape their values, there's no substitute for simply being there.

**2. Be a role model.** Your children will emulate you, so be a good example! I can practically guarantee that if you find a child who is kind and considerate of others, that child has parents who exhibit the same characteristics. If we want children who are patient, for example, we need to be patient, not only with them, but when we feel exasperated about something (especially in their presence). The same goes for other character traits. Let them see you exercising self-control, not interrupting (even them), being honest, doing good work, and putting others first. You can be sure it will rub off.

**3. Share stories of kindness.** One effective way to teach principles to your kids is to share stories of how lives are affected by the deeds of others. Pick up movies that impart good morals, ones that show good triumphing over evil, that don't mock authority figures or show the "good guys" engaging in boorish or immoral behavior. Many seemingly "family friendly" books and shows actually teach some bad lessons. Choose carefully what your family reads and watches, and start collecting a library of both books and videos that teach decency and thoughtfulness.

**4. Practice generosity in front of your kids.** Ours is a selfish culture. You and your family may not be rich, but you can be generous. One of the simple things I do is carry snacks or inspirational reading materials in my car that can be given to others. When we lived near a big city, we often saw homeless people on the street. Sometimes they walked by our car holding signs asking for money. While most people looked the other way and pretended they weren't there, I finally made it a policy to acknowledge them as human beings in need of love and comfort. Regardless of how they got there, I try to remember that if it were my kid who was homeless for any reason, even his own doing, I would pray for God to send someone—anyone—to be kind and generous to him. I decided that, whenever possible, I would answer that prayer of some distant mother I will never know, and I would be that person. This doesn't mean I always give them money, but I do give them something. Sometimes it is a book I believe in, sometimes it is an apple, sometimes it is a profession of faith. I especially tried to do this when my kids were with me, because more than just about anything in the world, I wanted them to grow up to be generous and to genuinely love their fellow man.

**5. Practice random acts of kindness.** I'm not sure who first came up with that phrase, but it is what we should do every day— starting with our own families! Encourage your teens to do simple, kind things for each other, like pitching in and cleaning each other's rooms, remembering to invite their sibling along when going to Starbucks, or just taking the time to talk to each other. Encourage them to offer to cut the neighbor's grass or simply pick up the newspaper off the sidewalk and put it on their doorstep. Sometimes when my kids were grumpy or whining, I would say, "Think of something nice to do for someone else right now—and go do it." Teaching our children to take the focus off of themselves and put that energy into helping others shows them that no matter how bad things are, they can always make life better for someone else. It also shows them just how many blessings they have.

# In Your Shoes

Sometimes a seemingly casual remark, the kind that arises naturally out of time spent together, can have a big impact in a child's life and truly affect his moral outlook and behavior. Consider this story from Dr. Robert Shaw, author of *The Epidemic: Raising Secure, Loving, Happy, and Responsible Children in an Era of Absentee and Permissive Parenting*:

A significant memory from my childhood is of a conversation I had with my father about a friend's family. My father would come home from work early, and we would both head for the den, where we played checkers and talked. It was during World War II, and everyone knew there were people engaging in black market activities. I remember telling my dad about my friend Joey, whose family seemed to be getting richer by the day. They had a new Cadillac, went on impressive vacations, and bought lots of expensive toys. Of course, I was envious, but what I remember most is my father's response: "I wouldn't do that. I prefer to sleep well at night." And I knew exactly what he meant—he wouldn't do anything that would give him a guilty conscience or interfere with his sense of well-being. I saw that my father stood for something. That phrase became a shorthand reminder throughout my life that I, too, wanted to "sleep well."

# Reflections from a Daughter

Jesus summarized the whole law in two commandments: "Love the LORD your God with all your heart, all your soul, all your mind, and all your strength" and "Love your neighbor as yourself" (Mark 12:30–31 NLT). He didn't say, "Be good" or "Be moral." Instead, he simply said, "Love."

How can we expect anyone to know what it means to be in love if she's never encountered a healthy marriage? How can we expect anyone to love his neighbor if he's never seen anyone truly care for the poor? How can we expect anyone to love justice if she's never witnessed right living? And how can we expect anyone to love God if he's never been around someone in love with his Word?

My parents modeled love of God and love of man—not perfectly, but sincerely. And I know I can always look to them as an example of how to live life according to the Golden Rule.

# Act Now

Date _____

Today I began letting the Golden Rule rule my home. I pledged to help my children understand that the two greatest commandments are to love God and to love other people, and I promised to model these for them.

Signature _____

# More Help

**Everyday Graces:** Karen Santorum has produced a full guidebook of the manners children should know. She covers the bases: how to have good manners at home and school; what to say and not say; how to act at the dinner table; how to wash and dress; how to care for the elderly, sick, and disabled; how to get along with others; how to exhibit good sportsmanship; what to do at church, weddings, and funerals; how to write thank-you notes; and how to respect our country. It's commonsense stuff, and other books include this information. But Santorum uses stories one can't forget to illustrate her points and to show that it's not the rules but the underlying principles that matter: It's being thoughtful. It's being helpful, generous, and respectful.

*Something for Nothing: The All-Consuming Desire That Turns the American Dream into a Social Nightmare:* Long a champion of individual freedom, personal liberty, and personal responsibility, Brian Tracy is a much-sought-after speaker and consultant, having served some thousand corporations worldwide. He addresses a quarter of a million people each year in more than forty countries and has spent a lifetime observing, analyzing, and studying the human situation. He has used his experience to create an invaluable 245-page primer on psychology, economics, and sociology.

*The Family Bible Library* is a series authored by Dr. V. Gilbert Beers and is specifically built on what he calls "the thirty-six building blocks of character," such as faith, self-control, sympathy, and courage. The traits are presented in a systematic program that enables parents to teach—and their children to learn—these crucial aspects of proper living. The series is designed to be read with your family in blocks of fifteen to twenty minutes a day. This useful life manual will be one of your greatest practical resources for teaching your kids how to treat their fellow man.

*Chapter 28*

# Help Your Children Connect Privileges and Ownership of Material Things with Work

## The Challenge

We live in a culture that is all about "me, me, me." Take a stroll through the mall on any given day and you will see children whining when they can't have the latest toy or video game, while discouraged parents shrug their shoulders and give in. Hang around any retail store and it may seem like the "Give Me" generation is running the show. You hear an "I want this," and the register replies with a hearty *ching*.

Overindulging children instead of teaching them the value of earning what they receive is a big problem. It creates an unrealistic perception of life. Eventually our children will be adults. They will have to take care of themselves as well as their future families. If they don't learn the meaning of earning through practical and real experience as children, adulthood will hit them like a slap in the face. They will feel thrown into the pool at the proverbial deep end, and they might not be able to swim. Childhood, while a time of great joy and innocence, is also a time to plunk children in the shallow end, with supervision and devices to help them float, and teach them how to swim with small strokes. That way, when they get to the "deep end" of adulthood, they are strong swimmers, able to handle turbulent waters or whatever might float their way in life.

Helping children learn the value of earning provides real life skills and gives them a deep sense of satisfaction. As humans, we are natural worker bees! We love to see the fruits of our labors, whether that is a life accomplishment such as building a company or everyday tasks like finishing folding a load of laundry. We are not created to lie around slothfully. Working toward a goal and feeling pride in our efforts are what drive human action. Children who learn the value of hard work and the satisfaction that comes with completing that work and earning its reward will have a deeper sense of self-worth and capability than children who are merely given the things they desire.

However, we, as parents, should not necessarily look at desire as a bad thing. Our task is to teach our children the link between the privileges and possessions they desire and a good work ethic.

In 2006, *Time* magazine voted "You" as its Person of the Year. Narcissism is deeply embedded in today's culture, and it's creeping into our children's mentality like a poison. Young people spend hours updating their Facebook pages and posting countless pictures of themselves in a million different poses.

Where are today's children learning narcissism? For starters, they may be learning greed and laziness from our own federal spending practices. We are indeed an entitlement society, with approximately 51 percent of all annual federal expenditures going toward entitlement programs such as Social Security, Medicaid, and Medicare and interest on our nation's debt, according to studies by the Heritage Foundation. It's not surprising if our children look at society and expect someone to take care of them if they don't take care of themselves.

Why is entitlement spending relevant, you might ask? Because children who grow up in a home with an attitude of "give me," disconnected from hard work, will only expand that attitude into the public sphere. Children raised with no work ethic will become adult consumers of the entitlement culture. And study after study on child development is proving that those children will be low-performing and unhappy adults.

Psychotherapist and author on child development Dr. Eileen Gallo reported on an eye-opening Harvard study about just how critical work ethic is in a child's life:

> In a 1981 article in the *American Journal of Psychiatry*, George Valliant ... reported that the single biggest predictor of adult mental health was "the capacity to work learned in childhood"—in other words, the development of a work ethic. Men whom Valliant described as "competent and industrious at age 14"—men who had developed a work ethic during the industry stage of development—were twice as likely to have warm relationships (both family and friendships), five times more likely to have well-paying jobs and sixteen times less likely to have suffered significant unemployment.

Christine Conners, in an article titled "Family Housekeeping: Teaching Our Children the Value of Work," reported that "sociologists Scott Coltrane and Michele Adams found that school-aged children who do chores with their fathers get along better with peers and have more friends. They also found that they are less likely to disobey teachers, cause trouble at school and are happier and more outgoing."

In other words, there is a direct, positive correlation between combating an attitude of entitlement in your children's youth and their success later in life.

Dealing with attitudes of entitlement is easy. Identify privileges and material goods your children value and link them to some sort of quantifiable task. You can start the next time your children ask for something. Find ways to teach them about entrepreneurship when they are young, whether it's opening their own lemonade stand, lining up babysitting jobs, or taking on a paper route. These time-honored, classic kids' jobs still teach great skills and give children a sense of accomplishment when done well.

One enterprising mother I know truly understands the importance of teaching the next generation about the value of a dollar and how critical it is to learn business skills early in life. Linda Raasch started long ago by helping her own four kids open a pretty sophisticated lemonade stand. As Linda said on her website, BizKids.com, "This venture helped teach valuable lessons about communicating with customers, promoting merchandise, and basic financial accounting. It wasn't long before all four children had learned that there was a correlation between effort and reward." Enjoying the pleasure of her own kids' success, Linda decided to start a company that allows tweens and teens to open their own online store and become entrepreneurs at a tender age. Lora, a twelve-year-old (and among the thousands of kids who have signed up so far), said, "After having my store on BizKids.com, I have learned that a dollar is very precious and I have learned that not everyone likes what you like so you must change your merchandise in the store often. I have also learned a lot about marketing and advertising. My mom is very involved with me. She thinks it is a great way to learn about running a business."

We all know how much fun it was to earn our first dollars as children. But if no one is there to guide and encourage us to earn honestly, spend wisely, and give to others freely, the culture of "gimme, gimme" soon takes over. But it doesn't have to be this way.

## In Your Shoes

Two young girls each wanted an American Girl doll.

Amy wanted Samantha because she liked her big brown curls and her stylish early-twentieth-century clothes. Karina wanted Felicity for her cute hats and puffy dresses. Both girls asked their mothers in fourth grade if they could have the doll they picked out.

Amy's parents, though they could have easily afforded to buy her every doll, told her they would need to think through a way that she could earn the doll. After a few days, they sat her down and told her that she had been a very good girl, with a good attitude, always completing her chores and homework. She had earned the right to earn the doll of her choice.

They told her that if she could memorize and recite every state capital city in the country, Samantha would be hers. They were very clear that a doll like Samantha was expensive and a very special treat, one that does not come without some work. Interestingly, each American Girl doll has a correlating set of books and stories telling her story. In Samantha's story, she, too, asks her grandmother for a beautiful doll. Samantha's grandmother tells her that if she dutifully does her piano lessons, she could earn the doll.

So Amy, feeling just like Samantha, eagerly memorized her state capitals. On the day she recited them, her parents bought her the doll. Amy treasured the doll, took excellent care of her, and felt deeply appreciative of the opportunity to have her.

When Karina asked her mother for Felicity, on the other hand, her mother immediately bought her the doll. Karina had to do absolutely nothing to earn what she wanted. After a few weeks, she got bored with Felicity. So she asked her mother for Molly, another doll. At first her mother resisted and suggested they just buy some more accessories for Felicity, but Karina persisted and her mother caved. A year later, Karina had every single doll. And she was still not satisfied.

Karina did not have to lift a finger to get five very expensive dolls. Amy, on the other hand, spent countless hours laboring for one and never felt a moment's yearning for anything more than what she had earned. Not only that, but she learned something valuable along the way!

Such is the way with children and possessions. And such is the way with adults and satisfaction. Humans are hard to satisfy. But we feel much more satisfied when we know we have earned what we have. Teaching your children that profound sense of satisfaction is a lesson that cannot be learned too early in life.

There are a few keys to teaching the lesson of the value of earning:

- You must be consistent and true to your word. When you promise your child something if he or she fulfills the assigned task, you must follow through. I cannot emphasize that enough! Being true to your word is key to earning your children's trust and establishing a regular pattern of work followed by just reward. Amy's parents bought her the promised doll on the day she completed the task. As adults, we know that we do not always feel the immediate fruits of our labors. But children have a short attention span, and it is very important to make the connection between work and reward as clear as possible.

- When possible, thematically link the task you give your child to the reward he or she seeks. For example, if your daughter asks for a prom dress that costs one hundred dollars, tell her she can earn it by working ten hours of community service at a center that helps underprivileged women, women who will likely never wear a prom dress. Not only will she gain some perspective and realize what a true privilege it is to dress up in expensive clothes with friends and have fun, but she will also attach a value to something she would have otherwise taken for granted. The dress becomes a reward for her fulfilling, meaningful work. I guarantee you that the girl who volunteers with underprivileged women to earn her shiny new dress is far less likely to take for granted the privilege of wearing it than her friends who are bought one with no effort on their part.

• Finally, make the task straightforward and quantifiable, something with a clear beginning and a concrete conclusion. One young woman I know had to memorize one hundred Bible verses before being able to get her driver's license. Both of my sons had to earn the rank of Eagle Scout before acquiring theirs. And in the process of being rewarded with a driver's license, my sons earned the lifelong honor that comes with being an Eagle. That hard-earned "piece of plastic" comes with a lot of responsibility and the ability to make possible life-and-death decisions. It is important for your children to understand the responsibility they are taking on, along with the increased freedom and "coolness." One option would be to have your kids spend a year volunteering at a nearby hospital, where they will undoubtedly see the cost of reckless driving.

# Reflections from a Daughter

Proverbs 13:4 says, "The soul of the sluggard craves and gets nothing, while the soul of the diligent is richly supplied" (ESV).

One of the traits I admire most in my dad is his work ethic. He is one of the most driven men I have ever met, and there is not a single lazy bone in his body. He has always worked hard to provide for my family's needs and to improve our lives in every way he can come up with. He also shows that he appreciates what he already has by the way he takes care of things. He gives readily and doesn't show a hint of entitlement, yet he is confident because he knows that he and my mother have what it takes to provide for more than their own needs.

I can attribute my dad's incredible work ethic almost entirely to his parents, who decided to teach him how to work hard with his hands and his mind. And I am infinitely grateful that they taught him that lesson so well, because it has blessed me tremendously, and I know it will bless many generations to come.

# Act Now

Date _____

Before the sun goes down, I will think of something my children have asked for recently and will create meaningful tasks they can complete to earn them. I will discuss with them why I'm going to do this from now on and will vow to be the cheerleader, scorekeeper, and the one who rewards.

Signature _____

My children want _____.

They can earn it by _____.

# More Help

There are many great websites full of tips on how to effectively link the concept of hard work with just reward.

One of my favorite writers on the topic of instilling a good work ethic is **Dr. Eileen Gallo**. She, along with her late husband, Jon, coauthored *The Financially Intelligent Parent: 8 Steps to Raising Successful, Generous, Responsible Kids*. They are also the authors of the critically acclaimed book *Silver Spoon Kids: How to Raise a Responsible Child in an Age of Affluence*.

**CafeMom.com** is also an excellent online community and forum where you can find successful tips from other parents and experts on different ways to teach kids the value of hard work.

*Chapter 29*

# Teach Your Children to Be Good Stewards

## The Challenge

Ask ten young people to define capitalism. Chances are that most will talk about it in context of materialism and greed.

Today's teens have been the pupils of a generation that has created America's worst economic crisis in several decades. In general, Americans spend more than they earn and rely too heavily on credit cards and loans. Most are not saving enough (if anything) for their futures. And, when they get in financial trouble, there is a growing mentality that the government will take care of them.

It's no wonder that young people confuse capitalism with consumerism, devaluing the principles of saving, thrift, personal responsibility, and charity. Capitalism, when properly applied, creates a situation where everybody wins—consumers, suppliers, businesses, and the overall economy. But capitalism practiced in a moral vacuum creates greed and fosters an environment where people and their money are squandered and where corruption breeds.

When referring to the passing of wealth and financial skills within families, sociologists often refer to the cycle of "shirtsleeves to shirtsleeves in three generations." *BBC News* reports that this old American saying originated in the late 1800s when there was booming wealth in the United States. The wealthy class "handed [their] money on as a life belt to their sons who then squandered it, so much so that their sons returned to the shirtsleeves in which [their] grandfather had landed in the United States."

In other words, the cycle of wealth and work would begin with someone toiling to build a fortune from almost nothing. Then they, wanting to spare their own children the pain of hard work and to give their children the privileges they never had, spoil them rotten. Those children grow up with little to no understanding of work ethic, squander their fortune, and leave nothing for their own children. Those children, disgusted with their parents, reject the life of laziness and greed and begin rebuilding.

This may be an exaggerated version of what we see today, but it is undeniable that it is critical we teach our children to be good stewards of their money, their talents, and their futures. If we want to help secure our children's financial future, a good first step is teaching our children how to handle their money rather than allowing their money to handle them. Helping them understand how to be wise stewards is a gift that can free them from the emptiness that comes with materialism and the despair that comes with debt and can help them find the joy that comes with financial stability and the fulfillment that comes with philanthropy. Parents who spoil their children and do not teach them about the value of money and property will raise them to be greedy and confused. It is only a matter of time before they destroy themselves, whether it's with home debt, credit card bills, gambling, or some other financial irresponsibility.

Statistics paint a dismal picture:

- According to a 2014 report by the US Department of Education, over half of twenty-seven-year-olds have a credit card debt of ten thousand dollars or more.
- A 2013 survey by Fidelity reveals that the average college student graduates with college-related debt (including student loans) of $35,200.
- Eighty-two percent of college students failed a basic quiz evaluating their knowledge of financial management.

Yet,

- Ninety-four percent of students say their parents are their primary teachers on financial matters.
- Fewer than half of those parents surveyed felt they are good role models for their children regarding saving and spending.
- Only 27 percent of parents surveyed by FleetBoston felt well informed about managing household finances.

When it comes down to it, the overall solution we need to teach our children is actually very simple: live within your means, save and plan for the future, and be generous to others. Imagine what our children's future would be if they, as a generation, started practicing these basic principles.

Fortunately, there is a wealth of sound advice on the issues of money that you and your kids can bank on. The Bible addresses economic issues with surprising frequency. As a matter of fact, as Crown Financial Ministries points out, there are 2,350 verses in the Bible on money and stewardship, making it "second to the subject of love as the most discussed subject in the Bible. In fact, two-thirds of the parables that Jesus taught are about money, possessions, and stewardship." Regardless of your denomination or faith, the wisdom of this all-time bestseller is undeniable and incredibly applicable to our world today. Here are just a few examples:

- "Where your treasure is, there your heart will be also" (Matt. 6:21; Luke 12:34).
- "The wise have wealth and luxury, but fools spend whatever they get" (Prov. 21:20 NLT).
- "The wicked borrow and never repay, but the godly are generous givers" (Ps. 37:21 NLT).
- "The rich rule over the poor, and the borrower is slave to the lender" (Prov. 22:7).
- "A good man leaves an inheritance to his children's children" (Prov. 13:22 ESV).
- "The plans of the diligent lead to profit" (Prov. 21:5).

One of the most telling verses is 1 Timothy 6:10: "For the love of money is the root of all evil: which while some coveted after, they have erred from the faith, and pierced themselves through with many sorrows" (KJV). Notice how it says the love of money is the root of evil—not money itself. And how true it is that those who covet money injure themselves with sorrow! If you've ever felt the burden of financial trouble, you know just how deeply it can affect your very soul and outlook on life. Don't we want to do everything we can to spare our children from such sorrow?

Some of the greatest Americans have also had a thing or two to say about the importance of good financial principles. Benjamin Franklin coined the famous phrase "A penny saved is a penny earned" and others, such as "Buy what thou hast no need of, and e'er long thou shalt sell thy necessaries" and "He that goes a-borrowing goes a-sorrowing."

"One should be a civilized man, saving something, and not a savage, consuming every day all that which he has earned," steel magnate Andrew Carnegie said in his book *The Empire of Business*. According to him, thrift is the "first duty" of those who aspire to wealth.

We should help our children memorize these wise sayings and offer them ongoing practical ways to implement the principles they embody.

# In Your Shoes

Claudia responded to one of my columns and shared her story about teaching her son financial responsibility:

> Even as a very small child, our son Thomas tuned
> in to fashion trends. He wasn't interested in fads

or what they were wearing on TV because we didn't watch TV. As a kindergartener, he decided his Easter Sunday wardrobe before we even talked about shopping. He wanted to wear a white shirt, gray slacks, and a red bow tie. I never knew how he made that decision; perhaps from something he saw in print. We were happy to comply with his request and he looked great that Easter. As he grew older, his fashion sense grew ever stronger. As a stay-at-home mother, it became much harder for me to find a compromise on costly items. Thomas didn't demand outrageous, inappropriate items, but what appealed to him became increasingly expensive. His interest in designer brands threatened our tight budget. After struggling with the issue, my husband and I came up with a solution that worked for all of us. Before we went shopping, we set a dollar amount that we could afford to spend for each item. If Thomas wished to make a purchase exceeding that limit he would be required to make up the difference from his own funds (allowance, odd jobs, birthday or Christmas gift money). This idea worked extremely well. Even though still quite young, Thomas became acutely aware of expenses. He would do his homework and watch the ads, shopping for sale items. He learned to watch prices and make wise decisions in other areas as well. We didn't know it at the time, but we were raising a

financial analyst. Now he is twenty-seven years old,
works for a great Fortune 500 firm, and is on schedule to complete his MBA next spring. Oh—and he
always looks great!

Carol wrote to me about how she keeps financial lessons and
rules simple and linked to everyday actions in her children's lives:

There are only two rules:

1. They have to earn their allowance with a
specific set of household chores. If they slack off the
chores, I dock their allowance. Bonuses and incen-
tives are allowed if they do something remarkable,
i.e., waxing the car rather than just washing it.

2. Allowance is paid weekly, in cash. They get
the allowance on Sunday, before they go to church,
and have been encouraged to share in the offering that morning. If they spend all the money by
5:00 p.m. on Monday, they are out of money for
the rest of the week. When they've come to me on
Wednesday asking for an advance on next week's
allowance I've only had to say once or twice, "No,
because I can't get an advance on my salary."

The only exception is if there is something
really big that they want that they can use to actually earn more money (like a lawn mower they can
use to start a business or a bicycle to get to their
job, etc.). Loan them the money, have them sign

a note for it, and work out a reasonable payment
schedule that leaves them something to spend.

And here's one of my own personal stories: When my son
was entering his preteen years, fashion suddenly became more
important to him. He wanted to go shopping for new clothes, so
I decided it would be a great opportunity to teach him the importance of thrift. We went to a department store and selected new
shirts and pants. We bought three nondesigner shirts at a pretty
hefty price tag. We then drove down the street to a Goodwill
outlet that I knew was very clean, organized, and stocked full of
used clothing in great condition. I let Drew go through the rows
and rows of clothes and pick out as many shirts as he wanted.
Boy, did he find a huge selection! We then added up the price
of the shirts and I said, "Now, you can have the three shirts we
bought at the department store, or you can have all nine of these
and keep the difference." A sparkle flashed across Drew's eyes as
he realized the obvious choice—it was clear to me that he also
discovered the value of thrift that day.

Drew now always goes to thrift and consignment stores first
when he needs or wants new clothes. It was a fabulous lesson that
not only was good for his personal finances but also showed how
much waste there is. All three of our kids grew to love shopping at
consignment stores. We weren't always successful in such trips and
often ended up in the mall. But it was a blessing to me to see the
joy and satisfaction on their faces each time they found something
they loved and realized how much we didn't spend. Not slamming my bank account actually made them feel good, and there

was always a sense of appreciation and accomplishment on both sides—for me and them.

## Reflections from a Daughter

Now that I'm graduated, married, and independent from my parents, I couldn't be more grateful that they taught me not only good financial responsibility but also how to take care of a home. I can't imagine how overwhelming the transition into adult life would be if neither my husband nor I had ever learned how to keep a house clean, fix things that break, save and budget, pay bills, or plan for the future.

We learned the way most kids learn these things: by our parents' example, by working jobs, and by doing chores. Of course, as a kid, all you can really think about is getting the job done. The long-term benefits of doing chores probably never crossed my mind, yet those simple disciplines have helped me navigate through adulthood and have blessed my marriage more than almost anything else.

## Act Now

Date _____

Today I ordered a workbook or course on responsible finance for kids/teens (and one for me too!).

Signature _____

# More Help

In 2004 my husband and I took a class on money management that changed our lives. Our church was offering the **Crown Financial Ministries** course that focuses on the moral underpinnings, basic principles, and practical tools of finances. Crown is "an interdenominational ministry dedicated to equipping people around the world to learn, apply, and teach biblical financial principles. Crown has taught or equipped more than 50 million people in over 40 nations with the life-transforming message of faithfully living by God's financial principles in every area of their lives. The ministry is located in the United States, Canada, Latin America, South America, and Africa, and is expanding into Europe, India, Asia, and Australia." Given that hundreds of churches around the country offer Crown courses, you just might find one near you. Check out their website, Crown.org, for locations. Even if they don't have a class in your neighborhood, you will find just about everything you need to help you get your own financial house in order and teach your children how to build theirs. The site features interactive exercises, daily tips, devotionals, and personal study on finances. They even offer the services of a personal financial coach! They also provide resources to help you teach your teens financial responsibility. If Crown were the only financial resource in the world, you would still have everything you need to teach yourself and your kids how to live well.

And then there is the great **Dave Ramsey**—noted author, speaker, radio host, and all-around genius on finances. Dave has a fabulous website chock-full of great tips at DaveRamsey.com. He also offers one of the most fantastic life-changing programs for teens I've ever seen: Generation Change. Dave created this program because "every day, our youth are bombarded with a million different voices—everything from billboards to Internet ads—telling them who they are and measuring their worth by what they have. The pressure to be accepted in today's stuff-centered world drives them, and perhaps even their parents, to throw money away on things that don't matter—all in an attempt to 'be somebody.' The result? We're raising a generation that spends money they don't have to buy things they don't need to impress people they don't even like! It's time for a change!" The course is taught by video and comes with a leader's guide.

Now for a bit of parting general advice: Don't overwhelm your children by trying to teach them everything there is to know about money at once. Start with simple principles and digestible points.

*Chapter 30*

# Make Your Own List

## The Challenge

As I've stated before, kids don't come from cookie cutters. And neither do families! So although this book contains thirty specific steps to take in order to protect yours, it probably doesn't address all the issues that might be of particular concern to you. My goal was to start you on the path to realizing that there are concrete steps you can take that actually work and to get you to take them—one at a time. But I obviously didn't have the room to cover everything. There's probably a little list already going in your head of other subjects you need help with.

Every family is going to have unique challenges and opportunities, as I like to call them. You may have even been tempted to ignore some of the most difficult problem areas and opportunities in your family because you feel alone or believe you'll never be able to solve them. Don't give up! Hopefully this book has shown you that you can find help for just about every problem you may encounter.

Here are the steps to take in coming up with your own list:

- Identify the challenge (each of my chapters starts by doing this). Writing out the problem will help you focus on just what it is that is bothering you. Think about the harms the problem can cause and any specific facts that back up your sense that there is a problem in the first place.

• Identify the solution. What is the general, obvious solution to the problem at hand? The solution usually isn't rocket science. But it may contain many steps that need to be taken over a long period of time. That's okay. You will be encouraged to know there is a definitive solution that could be available to you. Taking the step of identifying the solution should bring you hope. After all, if you have a problem and know that a solution exists, you can start working toward it! The hardest part is usually coming up with one concrete step you can take to begin solving the problem.

• Identify the action. What is the one concrete action you can take *today* to help you on your way? Don't make it hard or complicated. You are far better off taking baby steps at first. Just make sure you can do what you write down; even writing it down is part of the action.

• Repeat step number three. As you have read in this book, some problems can actually be solved quite easily, such as ending the threat that online pornography poses to your children by getting a reliable Internet filter (though even that one-step solution requires that you follow up to make sure it is still working, that your kids haven't hacked into it, etc.). Other problems need the action repeated several times. One example is the section on becoming your family's movie critic. You can't just do it once. You need to find a useful tool that will help identify harmful and wholesome films each time your children want to go to the movies. So think about whether the action you listed needs to be repeated. If so, word it in a way that you are reminded that it is an ongoing process.

• Talk to others to find out what worked for them. I included personal stories in many chapters to let you know that others have gone before you. On the vast majority of issues parents face, there is another parent somewhere who has had to bear that burden before you. Seek out the wisest people you know and ask them for their success stories.

# From My Home to Yours

As you well know by now, I have used many tips from others throughout this book. We can all benefit from the experiences of others to strengthen our families. I want you to have plenty of information on each subject, so I have also supplied a list of resources in the back of this book.

Although many of the stories from readers of my weekly column made it into a chapter or two, most did not. In closing, I thought it might be helpful to provide a list of tips from readers that aren't included elsewhere. Perhaps some of these relate to the list you are making.

# In Your Shoes

The following points are from a reader named Galen:

- My wife and I are totally committed to each other, and we stand as a parental unit. Yes, there are times we disagree and sometimes don't even "like" one another, but we are committed and love each other even when we don't feel like it.
- Children must be accountable and responsible for their conduct. They also have to be allowed to make mistakes so long as those mistakes will not crush them physically, emotionally, or spiritually. That's when parenting takes over. They have to be allowed to make decisions and choices and live with the consequences. As the decision process becomes better, more liberty and leeway has to be given.
- Education is important. It is their job while they are at home. Work, recreation, etc., is dictated by whether or not their studies are done. When grades fall, so do privileges.

- Where we will be on Sunday morning is not open to debate; we will be in God's house. The rest of the week, God will be in our house.
- Hang on to the scripture that says "bring up a child in the way he should go and when he is old he will not stray from it."

Carol limits the use of video games for her twelve-year-old son, and she shared what she provides for him instead:

That something has turned out to be adventure stories written for boys on CD. Like most twelve-year-old boys, our son struggles with reading for long lengths of time. He is dyslexic, and it is physically hard for him to concentrate on the written word for more than about twenty minutes. But he's more than happy to listen to someone else read. So where we skip spending money on video games, we use the money to buy him books written by G. A. Henty on CD, or a series like *The Hobbit* and *The Lord of the Rings* (unabridged); and I found some excellent stories of famous naval battles, WWII battles, and military weaponry through the ages.

Michael offered many wonderful ideas he had successfully used in his home, including this helpful list of milestones:

Growing up, our children had milestones they could anticipate and prepare for.

Age eight they could have friends sleep over, with parental consent.

Age ten they got their Military Dependent ID card and a later bedtime.

Age twelve they could get their ears pierced, including our son. (He did not get them pierced.) And a later bedtime.

Age fourteen they were allowed to wear some makeup. And a later bedtime.

Age fifteen Dad and Mom taught them to drive a car, and they got their permit. They were allowed to go to school dances. And they were allowed to get a job as long as they kept their grades As and Bs.

Age sixteen they were allowed to date—first two dates to be at our house or their date's house. And a vehicle would be available for them to drive when they had their license. They had a curfew; the city curfew was 11:00 p.m., and that was theirs as well. We treated them as adults and encouraged them to think and act as such.

Age seventeen they set their own curfew, as long as it was reasonable. They had to cover their own expenses for the automobile.

For graduating high school they got a good used vehicle. Age eighteen we took them to register to vote, and we started charging them rent.

Age twenty-five they will get all the rent money back.

Michael also said,

We taught them to give God the first fruits of their labor, a 10 percent tithe. We taught them to then save 20 percent of their earnings for retirement and to save another 10 to 20 percent for car repairs and other emergencies. They do this to this day.

We taught them that school was their primary job and they had to do their best in all areas. As well, they had chores at home in order to learn responsibility and an allowance that they earned by doing them.

My wife of twenty-five years and I taught our children that marriage is to the death. It hasn't all been sunshine and peaches, but most of it was, and still is. Respect for each other has gone a long way toward our happiness. I think we imparted that to our children.

Carolyn described how her family marched to the beat of their own drummer:

I did things pretty much in reverse of what was considered the norm. My only child was born when I was thirty-three. I continued to practice law until

he was five years old and ready to start school, at
which time I closed up shop and went home to
raise my child. We homeschooled for two years in
a neighborhood where most of the children were
homeschooled. It was a wonderful time, and the
children thrived. There were field trips with formal
homeschool groups for science experiments, lessons
of all kinds as well as just for fun.

Then we moved to the country. We slowly
acquired goats, donkeys, chickens, cows, turkeys …
and the list goes on. For several years, I homeschooled another child the same age as my son. We
did every subject every day, and were finished by
noon. There was no nonsense in the classroom.
Although it was relaxed and fun, the kids knew they
were there to learn. In the afternoons, they were
free to be little boys, building forts in the field,
helping with the animals, riding their bikes, or
whatever they wanted to do. It was a wonderful
time, and the kids were terrific.

Jane described a program her school put together for parents:

At our school, the parents would get together at the
beginning of the year and after an introduction,
break into groups of six to eight to compare notes
on curfew times, what entertainment was allowed
in their homes, and limits parents put on their kids'

behaviors. Lo and behold, the parents found out that other kids had strict and earlier curfews and much more restrictive controls than their kids had reported. Kids had told their parents that Timmy or Abdul, say, could stay out until eleven on weeknights, when Timmy's or Abdul's parents really had a strict 8:00 p.m. limit on weeknights and 11:00 p.m. on weekends, and no midnight movies, since nothing good happens after midnight. Right away, parents were empowered and encouraged to set and enforce limits for their kids. A police officer was brought in another time to show parents innocent-looking rave paraphernalia (pacifiers, funny candy) they might not be familiar with, and stats for accidents while driving with friends were also discussed. Perhaps the strictest warning to parents was that if they served their kids and others alcohol—even at a private party—they would be charged for underage drinking. Another theme before Christmas, so it was early, was to NOT allow kids to go on spring break trips. News reports were shown of kids, drunk out of their minds, jumping to their deaths because of their altered state.

And, here is my final tip for keeping your children safe that didn't fit neatly into a chapter but is something you should do *today*: find out where the sex offenders are in your area. Convicted sex offenders are required by law to register with the government and include their current addresses. With just a few clicks you can find out if there are any living in your neighborhood or near your children's school. Just go to NSOPW.gov and use the National Sex Offender quick search and search by location or go to FamilyWatchdog.us. Both websites are free and their information is sourced from the US Department of Justice. The websites provide detailed information on registered sex offenders (for example, those who have already been caught, convicted, and released back into the public—in other words, only those we know about). The results will likely disturb you: you'll see the names and faces of all the sex convicts who live in your town and in your own neighborhood. The numbers are absolutely stunning. But don't stop there. Put your children and teens in the car, drive by the houses where these convicted child molesters live, and tell your kids to stay away.

# Reflections from a Daughter

One of my good friends is particularly gifted with an ability to spark meaningful conversation. Once when we were hanging out in a roomful of friends and new acquaintances, she asked us all, "If you could take one aspect from the family you grew up in and bring it into your own family, and if you could leave one aspect behind, what would they be?"

The answers given were incredibly honest. In turn, each of us spoke candidly about some of the greatest joys and most painful struggles of childhood and adolescence.

The positive qualities we shared related mainly to traditions or the atmospheres of the homes we grew up in. (For example, I talked about how much I loved growing up with an "open door policy." My parents have a heart for hospitality, so they intentionally created space for us and our friends, and our friends knew they didn't need to knock when they came over.) The theme our answers had in common was community. We noticed the efforts our parents made to encourage both family bonding and our own friendships.

The theme of community carried over to our answers to the second part of the question as well. Many in the room came from broken families. Others grew up without ever discussing faith or religion in their homes, and some felt that communication within their families was lacking in some way. All of us longed for deeper conversation and connection with parents or siblings.

As each person spoke, we knew with greater clarity that something powerful was taking place in that room. By reflecting on and being thankful for the good we experienced in our families and by bringing the hard things to light in that safe environment, we were blessing our future families in a very real way. We were identifying strengths and weaknesses and solidifying our intent to pass on only the positive to future generations.

# Act Now

Date _____


Today I began making my own list of family problems and began writing down the solutions and actions I can take to help solve them.


Signature _____

# More Help

**Concerned Families (Fathers, Mothers, and Youth)**, found at ConcernedFamilies.org, is an excellent resource:

- Concerned Fathers Against Crime conducts neighborhood watch programs in conjunction with law enforcement to help keep communities safe.
- Concerned Mothers Alliance for Children writes letters to express concern about the increasingly negative culture and its effect on children.
- Concerned Youth brings children and adults together to serve their communities.

*Bonus Chapter 31*

# Marriage

## Reflections from an Experienced (AKA Older) Bride

Believe me, I know what it's like to be passionately in love.

When I close my eyes, it takes but a moment to see him standing on the boardwalk along the shores of the Mediterranean Sea. I can still feel the heart-pounding, inexplicable attraction that took me by surprise when I met Andy in 1983.

He was the most handsome man I had ever seen, and yet there was something more. When I got within clear view of his sparkling blue eyes, I felt a current run through me, and I knew our meeting was far beyond chance.

I was on the trip of a lifetime to Israel, along with nine other politically active coeds from around the United States. The North American Jewish Students Network sponsored ten college-aged Democrats and Republicans on an all-expenses-paid ten-day trip to the Holy Land.

We met with members of the Knesset, toured Judea and Samaria, traveled through many small biblical towns, and even had a private audience with Prime Minister Menachem Begin. But the most important person I met was a young US naval lieutenant who "just happened" to be on the same stretch of beach as me, during the same five-minute period, in a country halfway around the world.

We spoke briefly. Suddenly embarrassed that I had introduced myself, I said good-bye and ran back to the water's edge. Hoping he was still watching from the boardwalk, I did what any self-respecting young woman in my situation would do: I set a trap.

Still in my sundress from touring throughout the entire hot, dusty July day, I took off my shoes and strolled through the gentle surf. Every so often I would daintily pick up a small pebble and toss it into the waves.

The scene beyond me was majestic. The last sliver of the perfect red-orange ball that was the setting sun had just disappeared on the horizon, and the deep blues and purples of dusk reflected off the sea. In the distance, the silhouette of a ship could be seen. Its lights seemed to twinkle as the last rays of daylight played across the water's surface.

Months later when he came to see me in Washington, DC, Andy said, "I'll never forget the way you looked the first night I saw you. You carried yourself so well. The sun was setting behind you, and there was a ship on the horizon whose lights were just coming on." Bingo! He had taken the bait!

Back in Israel, I couldn't get him out of my mind. How unlike me to be so enamored of someone I didn't know. I was still thinking about him the next evening, when, walking through the pavilion on the beach in Tel Aviv, I heard someone call my name. It was Andy.

Several naval officers and a couple of people from my group ended up going to the movies that night. Afterward, everyone wanted to go barhopping—everyone but us. He suggested we go for a walk on the beach instead.

We ended up walking and talking for several hours, and by the end of the evening I knew he was the man of my dreams. He spoke of faith, his parents and siblings, and his sense of adventure. I learned he was a graduate of the US Naval Academy and that he had always, even as a child, envisioned going to school there. He was a perfect gentleman with a soft laugh and a warm, gentle voice. As we said our good-byes, he asked for my address: "You're a rare woman. I want to keep in touch."

I was smitten.

And keep in touch he did. The lost art of letter writing was not lost for him—he wrote moving, detailed accounts of his days at sea. The most profound letter described the scene from his ship anchored just offshore in the hours following the 1983 terrorist attack on the US Marine barracks in Lebanon. He wrote of how "the stacks of black body bags on nearby USS *Iwo Jima* grow larger every hour."

He returned to the States that Thanksgiving, and we were wed the next year, in 1984, on the Saturday following Thanksgiving. He is my handsome prince, my knight in shining armor, and my best friend. He is a wonderful father to our three children and a very patient and loving husband. I would be desperately in love with this man even if I had met him in line at McDonald's. God blessed me beyond belief when he brought us together in the most romantic setting possible.

After all these years, I'm still smitten. Throughout our thirty years of marriage, whenever there has been a conflict, whenever I have been disappointed, whenever the stresses of life have begun to interfere with my relationship with Andy, I have called on the memory of falling in love with him and have reflected on the fact that succeeding in marriage is one of the most important of all human endeavors.

No matter where and when you first fell in love with your spouse, you should frequently recall that moment. But don't forget that mere passion doesn't make a marriage.

It's all too easy to get caught up in the busyness of everyday life and forget the work that must go into every marriage. Part of this flows from our media-fed notions of romantic love—the idea that a relationship is worth preserving only as long as we're experiencing that pleasant head-over-heels feeling that nearly every couple enjoys when they first start getting to know each other. But those feelings alone won't sustain a marriage; it takes commitment. As Stephen Covey noted in *The 7 Habits of Highly Effective People*, love isn't just a noun; it's a verb.

And it's the most important action word of your marriage. Treat it as such, and you're well on your way to not only protecting your family but also influencing the culture in a manner that will uplift and inspire all those around you, especially your children.

This bonus chapter on marriage was added to the new edition of the book because it was obviously missing from the first! In fact, my good friend and one of my husband's and my chief mentors, Richard Viguerie, let me know in no uncertain terms that I should have included a chapter on marriage in the original edition. And he was right.

Truth be known, one of the chief reasons I didn't write this chapter the first time is because I was afraid to. Just as I admitted in my introduction to this book that I had fears of writing a book on parenting, the fact that I have not been a perfect wife weighed heavily on my mind—so heavy, in fact, that I actually copped out and did not tackle the marriage chapter. Shame on me.

So, I've said it: I have not been a perfect wife. Surprise, surprise! Has there ever been such a thing? Or a perfect husband? Let's see ... Jesus was the only perfect person who ever walked the earth, and he wasn't married, so ... no ... there has never been a perfect spouse! Whew! (Don't you feel relieved too?) But Jesus's love for us—for his church, his bride—is a spiritual model for us in how to live out our earthly marriages. (See Kristin's section that follows.)

You have no doubt noticed by now that this chapter does not follow the format of the previous thirty. And that is by design. After all, one can't possibly tackle the entire subject of marriage in just one chapter! I decided that the best way to discuss marriage for the purposes of this book was to write my thoughts and then have Kristin write hers. I've been married for over thirty years, and Kristin is a newlywed. We are two different women, from two different generations, with two different perspectives. But we share a common bond: we believe in biblical principles, and we know that God's design for marriage is best. So, whether you have been married for decades, years, or are just starting out, we pray this chapter has something for you.

What a blessing it has been to grow as a person, a woman, and a wife as I have experienced life with the wonderful man I met on that beach so long ago. Like all couples, we have had our ups and downs, our days of ecstasy and our days of dumb arguments. When we went through trials brought on by nothing more than selfishness on the part of one or the other of us; when we faced heartache caused by life circumstances; when we weathered trials of worry over our children; when we were tired from working too hard, stressed over finances, or just plain aggravated for no real reason at all, the main thing that kept our marriage together boils down to another very important action word: commitment.

*Divorce* is not a part of our vocabulary. The word is not allowed, and it has never been entertained, not even for a moment. When it was obvious that Andy and I were falling in love, we had a conversation about how, if we were to marry, that word would not be part of our lexicon. Remove the option from the table and, well, you remove the option from the table.

Not that I would have ever had a reason to think about divorce through these years. I am head over heels in love with Andy Hagelin. Sometimes I'm just giddy with love, like a young schoolgirl in the midst of her first crush! Other times I marvel in the peaceful, fulfilling pleasure of simply holding his hand. Then there are the times when I want to throw a pie in his face! (Or worse.) Thankfully, those moments don't usually last too long anymore because I've learned the incredible importance of letting go of anger over nothing (and even anger over something). I wonder about other husbands and wives who pledged their lives to each other but then go through a hard time and quickly move into divorce. I wonder if they would have weathered the storms had they decided early on that the "D word" did not exist and if they had, instead, always had commitment on their minds.

Please know I am not by any means condemning those who have divorced due to infidelity on the part of their spouse. I would never do so. In fact, the Bible makes it very clear that although God hates divorce, he hates adultery even more and even allows divorce for such betrayal.

And I do not condemn marriages that end because of continued abuse either. In fact, I can't think of a worse betrayal than abusing someone who loves you. God knows the pain of those who suffer. Jesus understands what it is like to be betrayed—to be broken both physically and emotionally. And it is not my place to ever, ever pass judgment on those who leave a marriage marred by such betrayal. If you are in a situation where you or your children are being abused by your spouse, grab them and run like the wind. Do it now! Find a safe place and seek professional help immediately. You must be their protector; you must not be manipulated by your spouse into keeping them in harm's way.

But current statistics show that most marriages that end in divorce end simply because husbands or wives give up on each other. And that is one of the saddest things in the world.

One of the most remarkable traits of Andy Hagelin is that I know, I know, I know that I can fully trust him. I am married to someone who watches my back. Who has my best interests at heart. Who will love me till my dying day.

But that is not the best part of our marriage.

The best part for me is how I have grown as a person. The best part is knowing that I have become someone Andy can fully trust. That he is married to someone who watches his back. Who has his best interests at heart. Who will love him till his dying day.

And it is my faith in Christ that has taught me how to become that type of person. When I see Jesus's patience with me, I am ashamed at the times I have been impatient with my husband. When I accept Christ's immense daily dose of love for me, I am reminded to love my husband to greater depths; and when I feel how quickly Jesus forgives my bad attitudes and selfish actions, I am inspired to quickly forgive (okay, maybe not always so quickly) my husband's faults.

And so, in short, the secrets of a happy marriage that I want to share with you are the following: have a commitment so strong that there is no room for exit, a faith so sure that you know whom to turn to for help, and a spirit meek enough to know that when your mate is happy and can rest in your love for him, then your greatest happiness will also be realized.

There are volumes of books, seminars, courses, and videos by experts on marriage. Read the books, take the courses, watch the videos! If you and your spouse took even one-tenth of the time that you spend at work, on sports, or on hobbies and spent it truly working on your marriage, my guess is that your marriage would be a tremendous success. So why not do it? If you were sick, you would go to a doctor. So if you need a marriage counselor, get a marriage counselor! In the "More Help" section at the end of this chapter, I have listed organizations that I personally know of that have been instrumental in saving and strengthening thousands upon thousands of marriages just like yours. Please use them today. Start this very day.

It has been said that the greatest gift parents can give their children is to love each other. I believe that with all my heart. If you truly want to raise children who will tower above the culture, who will be marked by integrity and strong character, and who will be generous and kind and loving, then start by loving your spouse. The foundation of a happy home is a happy marriage. So, in many ways, this chapter should be first. But I have saved it for last so that it will be what you remember first when you lay this book aside. I pray that you will make strengthening your marriage your first priority. And that God will bless you in your efforts.

To help you better grasp the true beauty of marriage and why it is so very powerful and sacred, Kristin now shares what she has learned through endless hours of studying why God created marriage on earth in the first place. I know it will inspire and bless you, as it does me.

# Reflections from a New Bride

As a newlywed, my experience as a wife doesn't extend very far past my wedding day. By no means do I consider myself any sort of authority on the subject of marriage.

What I do have is some twenty years of experience as a growing Christian. And as my husband and I were planning our wedding, we discovered some remarkable parallels between the ceremony we were about to partake in and the incredible story that is the gospel. Both the process of preparing for the wedding and our adjustment to marriage have deepened our love, our faith, and our joy in Christ and in each other.

The series of thoughts I share are not as much about marriage itself as they are about how preparing for it brought me to a deeper understanding of God's infinite nature.

# A New Life

It took a few months of being married for me to realize that my whole life had changed. Of course, I knew everything would be different, and people had warned me there would be some shock involved, but it took awhile for the reality to sink in. What followed can best be described as an identity crisis.

Rewind a few years and I would have told you, "I know who I am." I was independent with a fierce love of life, and I had some ideas about what the future would hold. My faith was strong, but there were plenty of other things involved in my identity. I also had my friends, my family, my hobbies, and plenty of plans.

Then he entered the picture. As we dated and fell more deeply in love, that same identity remained largely intact. A few things changed, of course. I was in an exclusive relationship, and I was spending my time differently so we could be together. I even changed a few of my opinions. I couldn't wait to marry him, but for the time being we still had our individual lives, and I was in charge of my own.

We married a month after I turned twenty-two. After our wedding, I moved to be with him. I left close friends behind and let go of any dreams I had ever had that didn't include him. I gave up my independence. I gave up my whole identity. I don't mean to sound like a martyr in any way—it's exactly what I wanted to do. I loved him so overwhelmingly that I no longer desired anything from my former way of life. And, of course, he gave up just as much as I did: living with his best friends his senior year of college, his independence, so many of his preferences. But there was still some pain, some struggle involved in my own letting go.

Eventually I came to understand that my old self, the only self I had ever known, was gone. I had a new job, a new home, and a new community—and I was *somebody's wife*. My prayers had been answered and my dream had come true, yet I mourned the loss of who I had known myself to be.

Then I felt guilty about it. I wanted to be the wife who had it all together, but I didn't even know who I was. I wanted to make my husband happy, but how could I when I was in mourning over the life I had lived before him? My pride and sin reared their ugly heads, and I couldn't hide any of it from the man I loved.

I was a mess, but God was at work in the midst of my mess. I didn't know how hard the adjustment would be because I didn't know how much of my identity rested in the life I had created for myself. Through my marriage, God tore a hundred little comforts right out of my heart. But he did it to make room for something bigger and better.

The way to conversion is similar. We "date" Jesus; we make a little room for him in our lives, perhaps even change a few opinions. But at some point, we have to make a decision: keep living separate lives or commit. We gladly commit and are convinced we will be very good Christians, but it isn't long before we discover how much of our old lives we must give up and how bad we are at being good Christians. God tears our little idols right out of our hearts.

Then he fills the void with nothing less than himself:

> Come, let us return to the LORD.
> He has torn us to pieces
>  but he will heal us;

> he has injured us
>> but he will bind up our wounds.
> After two days he will revive us;
>> on the third day he will restore us,
>> that we may live in his presence.
> Let us acknowledge the LORD;
>> let us press on to acknowledge him.
> As surely as the sun rises,
>> he will appear;
> he will come to us like the winter rains,
>> like the spring rains that water the earth.
> (Hos. 6:1–3)

# The Ceremony

The Christian wedding ceremony is beautiful and valuable in its own merit, but it also represents something bigger. Like the Jewish Tabernacle, it is only a copy, a shadow of something better to come. The day is meant to remind us of what we hope for in Christ. Every detail of a wedding is a symbol, and every participant plays a role. Almost like a play, it tells the story of heaven and earth.

**She Wears White:** When I was a teenager, I thought brides wore white to declare their virginity—a purity they were born with, one they had maintained by their wills in order to give it to their husbands. Though on some level that may be true, as I searched through Scripture before our wedding, I came to a different, perhaps more honest, understanding:

"She has been given the finest of pure white linen to wear"
(Rev. 19:8 NLT).

Given. She has been given.

"I am overwhelmed with joy in the LORD my God! For he
has dressed me with the clothing of salvation.... I am like a
bridegroom dressed for his wedding or a bride with her jewels"
(Isa. 61:10 NLT).

He has dressed me. It has nothing to do with me. My white dress
has nothing to do with my personal purity. It says nothing about my
history or my self-discipline. Heaven knows I am far from pure.

"Though your sins are like scarlet, I will make them as white as
snow. Though they are red like crimson, I will make them as white
as wool" (Isa. 1:18 NLT).

My white dress is not meant to fool my husband into believing
I am perfect but to remind us both that we are sinners forgiven
by God, that we are sinners who will need to be forgiven by one
another.

"For husbands, this means love your wives, just as Christ loved
the church. He gave up his life for her to make her holy and clean,
washed by the cleansing of God's word. He did this to present
her to himself as a glorious church without a spot or wrinkle or
any other blemish. Instead, she will be holy and without fault"
(Eph. 5:25–27 NLT).

That white dress has everything to do with the blood of Jesus.
He knows my weaknesses. He knows my past. He still gave everything for me. His love covers a multitude of sins. His love makes me
beautiful.

**Father of the Bride:** A proud, misty-eyed father walks his little girl down the aisle toward the only other man on earth who just might love her as much as he does. He pauses before he lifts away her veil. A kiss on the cheek. He joins his daughter's hand to her groom's. And he steps away.

In your parents' house, you live under their rules. As you grow, those rules frustrate you and humble you, teach you and shape you. There is discipline for bad behavior and reward for doing right. When you move out, you leave those rules behind. There are no parents to discipline you, yet, somehow, you find those rules ingrained upon your soul. You see the reason behind the rules come to life and, with a new understanding, you find yourself thankful for them.

"I will put my laws in their minds and write them on their hearts" (Heb. 8:10).

No parents want to discipline their children forever. They want them to grow up and leave the nest knowing how to live life in a spirit of freedom, not in fear of punishment. The system of rules was never meant to last.

"The old system under the law of Moses was only a shadow, a dim preview of the good things to come, not the good things them-selves" (Heb. 10:1 NLT).

Our parents teach us which way to go by laying down the law. In the same way, our heavenly Father draws us toward Christ by giving us commandments. He knew full well we wouldn't follow them perfectly. Following them wasn't the point. The point was to teach us that there is a right way and a wrong way. The point was to show us that there is something inside of us that wanders away from the path of goodness.

"It was the law that showed me my sin. I would never have known that coveting is wrong if the law had not said, 'You must not covet'" (Rom. 7:7 NLT).

When we recognize that we are sinful, that we are bent toward wandering, we realize that we are in need of help. We cannot choose the path of goodness on our own.

"So the trouble is not with the law, for it is spiritual and good. The trouble is with me, for I am all too human, a slave to sin. I don't really understand myself, for I want to do what is right, but I don't do it.... So I am not the one doing wrong; it is sin living in me that does it.... Who will free me from this life that is dominated by sin and death? Thank God! The answer is in Christ Jesus our Lord" (Rom. 7:14–15, 17, 24–25 NLT).

Our parents lead us into maturity. They lovingly teach us to recognize right and wrong so that when we leave their home, we will no longer need their rules to guide us. It is in this mind-set that a father gives his daughter away in marriage. He transfers her care into the hands of another, giving her over to freedom.

Though the process is painful, our heavenly Father teaches us to recognize right and wrong, bringing us face-to-face with the reality of the sin that controls us. He shows us our need for a Savior. Then he leads us down the aisle toward Christ.

"No one can come to me unless the Father who sent me draws them, and I will raise them up at the last day" (John 6:44).

**The Veil:** Moses climbed a fiery mountain to meet with God. There on Mount Sinai, the Lord etched his law on tablets of stone and gave Moses instructions for building the Tabernacle.

"When Moses came down from Mount Sinai with the two tablets of the covenant law in his hands, he was not aware that his face was radiant because he had spoken with the LORD" (Exod. 34:29).

Moses didn't even see the Lord's face. But his own was so radiant from speaking with God that the people were afraid. He had to cover himself with a veil to hide the glory.

According to God's instructions, the Most Holy Place inside the Tabernacle is where the Lord would dwell. And a thick curtain, called the veil, would prevent sinful people from entering into God's Most Holy Place. If they were to enter in, the power of his presence would overwhelm them, and their weak, sinful spirits would be crushed.

Both in the Tabernacle and with Moses, the veil prevented weak people from seeing God's glory. When we are weak from sin, we can't handle the weight of glory.

Jesus nailed our sins, our weaknesses, to the cross.

"And Jesus cried out with a loud voice, and breathed His last. Then the veil of the temple was torn in two from top to bottom" (Mark 15:37–38 NKJV).

The only thing left standing between us and God's presence is our unbelief.

"The same veil covers their minds so they cannot understand the truth. And this veil can be removed only by believing in Christ. Yes, even today when they read Moses' writings, their hearts are covered with that veil, and they do not understand. But whenever someone turns to the Lord, the veil is taken away" (2 Cor. 3:14–16 NLT).

Christ's righteousness, his purity, and his strength are given to us. The veil is torn in two. We have the freedom to see and reflect God's glory.

"Wherever the Spirit of the Lord is, there is freedom. So all of us who have had that veil removed can see and reflect the glory of the Lord" (2 Cor. 3:17–18 NLT).

A bride's father lifts away her veil and she stands there, beaming on her wedding day, as she gazes upon the face of her beloved.

**A New Name:**

> I cannot remain silent.
> I will not stop praying for her
>> until her righteousness shines like the dawn,
>> and her salvation blazes like a burning torch.
> The nations will see your righteousness.
>> World leaders will be blinded by your glory.
> And you will be given a new name
>> by the LORD's own mouth.
> The LORD will hold you in his hand for all to
>> see—
> a splendid crown in the hand of God.
> Never again will you be called "The Forsaken City"
>> or "The Desolate Land."
> Your new name will be "The City of God's
>> Delight"
>> and "The Bride of God,"
> for the LORD delights in you
>> and will claim you as his bride.
>> (Isa. 62:1–4 NLT)

He saw that I was hurting, broken, sinful, and ashamed, but he didn't turn his face from me. Instead, he fought my demons. He fought in spirit and in truth, offering up his body like the prayer that drew blood from his pores.

Then he draped his God-glory over me. A white dress. But he didn't stop there. How could he possibly do more?

All of who he is—the perfect Son of God, the Risen Lamb, the Eternal King, the Prince of Peace—is wrapped up in his wonderful name. The name by which blind men see and the dead are raised to life. The name that brought heaven to earth. God with us. His whole identity.

He gave me his name, identifying himself with me for all eternity. "I no longer live, but Christ lives in me" (Gal. 2:20).

**Divine Love:** It's easy to put the gospel on display in a wedding ceremony. My husband and I have watched many of our friends get married, and at every single service, we heard the salvation message as loud and clear as the joy of the bride and groom.

Though it is admittedly more challenging to see the beauty of the gospel in the day in and day out of marriage—when it feels like laying down your pride to ask for forgiveness or letting go of your anger to offer it—it is also much more meaningful. Because that's when it counts most: when our spouses and onlookers see weak and vulnerable human love infused, strengthened, and repeatedly redeemed by dependence on the love of the divine; when love in marriage isn't just a fairy tale that falls apart in reality but a living, breathing, broken thing that heals and grows and points to a Healer who understands our weakness.

# More Help

The following are some marriage-building resources—please use them! Although there are many terrific resources and books to help you get through marriage challenges and strengthen your bond with your spouse on a daily basis, these are three terrific places to start. Please explore these websites as soon as possible, no matter the current state of your marriage. They will bless you!

**Visit Family Talk (drjamesdobson.org)** for wisdom, encouragement, and real help from the world's most beloved doctor and expert on families and marriages, Dr. James Dobson. I am so very humbled and grateful to serve on the board of Family Talk. I can tell you from many hours of interaction with Jim and Shirley Dobson that they are the real deal, and they have much to share with you that will heal and strengthen your marriage. Dr. Dobson's team even has phone counselors who are ready to speak with you and connect you with more personalized help. You can find articles, books, podcasts, DVDs, loads of inspiration, and, as I mentioned, real help at the website of Family Talk.

**FamilyLife.com,** the website of FamilyLife, is also an excellent source for marriage help. The FamilyLife organization offers marriage seminars across the country that you and your spouse can attend to help you identify and work through issues on a very personal level. There are books, CDs, podcasts, and many articles available on their site. They can also connect you to marriage counselors in your area who can help guide you to a strong, fulfilling marriage (and help you and your spouse fall in love all over again).

**MarriageEncounter.org** is the website for a powerful weekend marriage getaway that has helped repair and solidify hundreds of thousands of marriages over several decades. You can find weekend retreats near you and be connected to resources and real people who can help you prepare for a successful weekend session.

# Even More Help

In this section I have compiled additional great resources, along with some of the ones mentioned in the book, with contact information for your convenience. In most cases, I have quoted the organizations' own descriptions of their work. But in other places I added my thoughts too. *Please use these resources*! I believe God has had a hand in creating them in order to help your family in many ways. You don't have to go through life alone—these groups can be your allies!

**4EveryGirl**
213-403-1325
4everygirl.com
"For our mothers, our daughters, our sisters: Campaigning for media images that value, respect, empower and promote the true value of every girl!"

Note from Rebecca: What a beautiful purpose for a much-needed and valuable nonprofit organization.

## Abstinence Clearinghouse

801 East 41st Street

Sioux Falls, SD 57105

605-335-3643 or 888-577-2966

abstinence.net

"The Abstinence Clearinghouse serves as an affiliation network for the abstinence community. The Clearinghouse is a non-profit educational organization that promotes the appreciation for and practice of sexual abstinence through distribution of age-appropriate, factual and medically-accurate materials."

## Alliance Defending Freedom

15100 N. 90th Street

Scottsdale, AZ 85260

480-444-0020 or 800-835-5233

alliancedefendingfreedom.org

Alliance Defending Freedom is a legal organization that advocates for the right of people to freely live out their faith. More than thirty prominent Christian leaders launched Alliance Defending Freedom in 1994 because they recognized the need for a strong, coordinated legal defense against growing attacks on religious freedom. This unique organization has brought together thousands of Christian attorneys and like-minded groups that work tirelessly to advocate for the right of people to freely live out their faith.

## American Center for Law and Justice

PO Box 90555

Washington, DC 20090-0555

800-342-2255

aclj.org

"Founded in 1990 with the mandate to protect religious and constitutional freedoms, the American Center for Law and Justice (ACLJ) engages legal, legislative, and cultural issues by implementing an effective strategy of advocacy, education, and litigation that includes representing clients before the Supreme Court of the United States and international tribunals around the globe."

## American Family Association

PO Drawer 2440

Tupelo, MS 38803

662-844-5036

afa.net

"AFA spurs activism directed to:

- Preservation of Marriage and the Family
- Decency and Morality
- Sanctity of Human Life
- Stewardship
- Media Integrity

We believe in holding accountable companies that sponsor programs attacking traditional family values. We also believe in commending those companies that act responsibly regarding programs they support.

AFA has been on the frontlines of America's culture war. The original name of the ministry was National Federation for Decency but was changed to American Family Association in 1988. Today, AFA is led by AFA President Tim Wildmon, and it continues as one of the largest and most effective pro-family organizations in the country with hundreds of thousands of supporters."

**American Heritage Girls**
175 Tri-County Parkway, Suite 100
Cincinnati, OH 45246
513-771-2025
ahgonline.org
"American Heritage Girls is the premier national character development organization for young women that embraces Christian values and encourages family involvement." It is a nonprofit organization dedicated to the mission of "building women of integrity through service to God, family, community, and country."

**The Becket Fund for Religious Liberty**
1200 New Hampshire Ave., NW, Suite 700
Washington, DC 20036
202-955-0095
becketfund.org
"The Becket Fund for Religious Liberty is a non-profit, public-interest legal and educational institute with a mission to protect the free expression of all faiths. The Becket Fund exists to vindicate a simple but frequently neglected principle: that because the religious impulse is natural to human beings, religious expression is natural to human

culture. We advance that principle in three arenas—the courts of law, the court of public opinion, and the academy—both in the United States and abroad."

**Center for Innovative Public Health Research**
555 N. El Camino Real #A347
San Clemente, CA 92672-6745
877-302-6858
innovativepublichealth.org
"Our vision is to promote positive human development through the creation and implementation of innovative and unique technology-based research and health education programs. Public health is ever evolving and so are we."

**Citizens for Community Values**
11177 Reading Road
Cincinnati, OH 45241
513-733-5775
ccv.org
"Citizens for Community Values (CCV) exists to promote Judeo-Christian moral values, and to reduce destructive behaviors contrary to those values, through education, active community partnership, and individual empowerment at the local, state, and national levels. CCV is a grassroots organization of citizens who are concerned for the well-being of the community, the strength of its families, and the future of its children. We strive to be a leader in the restoration of those Judeo-Christian moral values upon which this country was founded in hopes of leaving a lasting legacy of

citizens endeavoring to foster and maintain healthy, wholesome, safe, and happy communities."

## ClearPlay

866-788-6992

clearplay.com

"ClearPlay is all about choice. You establish your ClearPlay settings based on your family values, then they'll automatically be applied to anything put in the player from our list of over 4,500 ClearPlay compatible movies and TV shows. So even when you're not around, your family will be protected from the content you don't want them exposed to—and they'll enjoy the best content from the latest releases."

## Concerned Women for America

1015 15th St., NW, Suite 1100

Washington, DC 20005

202-488-7000

cwfa.org

"CWA is a unique blend of policy experts and an activist network of people in small towns and big cities across the country working to address mutually held goals and concerns. CWA works with many other groups around the country. The mission of CWA is to protect and promote Biblical values among all citizens—first through prayer, then education, and finally by influencing our society—thereby reversing the decline in moral values in our nation."

## ControlWithCable.org
This site features information on cable's blocking technology, descriptions of family-friendly cable programming, and resources devoted to media literacy and education.

## Crown Financial Ministries
9 Market Square, Suite 202
Knoxville, TN 37902
770-534-1000 or 800-722-1976
crown.org
Their vision is to "share truth, deliver hope, advance transformation." Their mission is to "equip servant leaders to live by God's design for their finances, work and life … to advance transformation."

## Dave Ramsey
The Lampo Group
1749 Mallory Lane
Brentwood, TN 37027
615-371-8881 or 888-227-3223
daveramsey.com
Dave Ramsey offers life-changing financial advice as host of the nationally syndicated radio program, *The Dave Ramsey Show*, and through his many educational books, speeches, seminars, curricula, online tools, and events. "Ramsey Solutions provides biblically based, common-sense education and empowerment that gives HOPE to everyone in every walk of life."

**The Dove Foundation**

4467 Byron Center SW, #1

Wyoming, MI 49519

616-454-5021

dove.org

The mission of the Dove Foundation is to "encourage and promote the creation, production, distribution and consumption of whole-some family entertainment." The nonprofit organization is "dedicated to advocating for families and moving Hollywood in a more family-friendly direction. The Dove reviews ... are based on traditional Judeo-Christian values. There is a content chart and descriptions that gauge six criteria: Sexuality, Language, Violence, Drug and alcohol use, Nudity, and Other. While Dove's scorecard reviews online are what Dove is probably best known for, the Foundation is making waves behind the scenes, too."


**Emily Post Institute**

444 South Union Street

Burlington, VT 05401

802-860-1814

emilypost.com

The Emily Post Institute, Inc., is an incredibly unique American family business. The name Emily Post has been the premiere source on etiquette for many years. "Spanning five generations, this family business maintains and evolves the standards of etiquette that Emily Post established with her seminal book *Etiquette* in 1922. According to the Posts, though times have changed, the principles of good man-ners remain constant. Above all, manners are a sensitive awareness of the feelings of others. Being considerate, respectful, and honest is more important than knowing which fork to use. Whether it's a handshake or a fist bump, it's the underlying sincerity and good intentions of the action that matter most."

**Enough Is Enough**
PO Box 1532
Great Falls, VA 22066
enough.org
"The Enough Is Enough (EIE) mission is to Make the Internet Safer for Children and Families. We are dedicated to continue raising public awareness about the dangers of Internet pornography and sexual predators, and advance solutions that promote equality, fairness and respect for human dignity with shared responsibility between the public, technology, and the law. We stand for freedom of speech as defined by the Constitution of the United States; for a culture where all people are respected and valued; for a childhood with a protected period of innocence; for healthy sexuality; and for a society free from sexual exploitation."

Note from Rebecca: It was my honor to help launch Enough Is Enough many years ago—in fact, when I was pregnant with Kristin. I now serve on the advisory board because I believe that Enough Is Enough is still the most powerful resource for helping parents protect their children from pornography.

**FamilyFacts.org**

214 Massachusetts Ave. NE

Washington, DC 20002

The Heritage Foundation's "FamilyFacts.org provides data on family and religious practice and analysis of their role in maintaining civil society in America. Charts, Briefs, Reports, and Videos are organized in eight major topics, from Marriage & Family to Economic Well-Being to Community Involvement."

**FamilyLife**

1-800-FL-TODAY

familylife.com

The mission of FamilyLife is "to effectively develop godly families who change the world one home at a time." Their website goes on to say, "Your family is important. No matter what your current circumstances are, or what your family history has been, we still believe in a God that works miracles. And we're here to help *you* transform *your* marriage and family with resources and events that outline God's blueprints for the family.... For decades now we have been *ministering to* couples and families with our radio broadcasts, events, and our resources. Recently though our attention has shifted to *minister with* you by focusing on adding resources that you can use to reach your friends, neighbors, co-workers, and community. The Art of Marriage®, Stepping Up™, and the SmallGroups are just a few. Need a bit more help to get started? Contact one of our advisors who will guide you to the right resource. Rome wasn't built in a day and a journey of a thousand miles begins with a step. We may not be able to transform every family all at the same time, but we can start with one family. Perhaps that's your family, or maybe there's someone else you're thinking about that could use one of the tools that FamilyLife has to offer."

## Family Talk

540 Elkton Drive

Suite 201

Colorado Springs, CO 80907

877-732-6825

drjamesdobson.org

Family Talk's mission is "to help preserve and promote the institution of the family and the biblical principles on which it is based, and to seek to introduce as many people as possible to the gospel of Jesus Christ. Specifically, the focus of the ministry is on marriage, parenthood, evangelism, the sanctity of human life and encouraging righteousness in the culture."

Note from Rebecca: It is my honor to serve as a volunteer board member of Family Talk. I hope you will visit drjamesdobson.org and explore Dr. Dobson's years of teaching, counseling, and informing families around the world on how to improve our relationships with God and each other! Noted pediatrician and bestselling author Dr. Meg Meeker cohosts the radio show with Dr. Dobson, and all her great resources are also available through drjamesdobson.org. In addition, you can find the inspiring work of Ryan Dobson, who addresses family issues from the perspective of the younger generation of parents. Together, these three provide everything you need to strengthen your family.

**FamilyTime**

101 Merritt Blvd.

Trumbull, CT 06611

familytime.com

"FamilyTime provides you with online household organization, menu planning, and money-saving applications, as well as advice from home organization and cooking experts on how you can best run your household."

**Focus on the Family**

8605 Explorer Drive

Colorado Springs, CO 80920

719-268-4811 or 1-800-A-FAMILY

focusonthefamily.com

Focus on the Family's mission is "to cooperate with the Holy Spirit in sharing the Gospel of Jesus Christ with as many people as possible by nurturing and defending the God-ordained institution of the family and promoting biblical truths worldwide."

**Grace Marriage**

270-570-1479

gracemarriage.com

We cannot win the cultural battle and the battle in our own families with a defensive approach that simply tries to fight off attacks. We have to go to war and make our own marriages so awesome, pleasurable, and grace filled that the world has to take note. "Grace Marriage's *Book on…* coaching is a grace-based, wellness, protection and enrichment model. The day to day issues of this world are so dominating that we rarely have time to stop, think and talk 'big picture' about our marriage and families. Marriage coaching is an opportunity to come together one day every three months, enjoy each other and seek the wisdom of God and others to spark growth and protect our marriages. As we have an enemy who is trying to destroy our marriages, proactive efforts to strengthen and protect are a must. Marriage coaching is for all marriages, as each one of us have room for growth. My prayer is that God will bless our marriages beyond what we could ever expect or imagine. (Ephesians 3:20)."

## Grow Together

866-786-6483

growtogether.org

Age-based apartheid keeps the church from realizing its epic potential. Young adults are walking away from the faith. But there is good news. A new resource developed by Dr. Jeff Myers, president of Summit Ministries, helps churches reconcile the generations through learning to break down generational barriers and develop meaningful lifelong relationships. This resource includes a discussion-starter film and book called *Grow Together: The Forgotten Story of How Uniting the Generations Unleashes Epic Spiritual Potential.* The content is deeply compelling and divided into simple, manageable steps. Help your church grow its influence by harnessing the wisdom of the older generation and the energy of the younger generation.

## Home School Legal Defense Association

PO Box 3000

Purcellville, VA 20134

540-338-5600

hslda.org

"Home School Legal Defense Association is a nonprofit advocacy organization established to defend and advance the constitutional right of parents to direct the education of their children and to protect family freedoms."

## Internet Solutions for Kids

isolutions4kids.org

"Our mission is to promote new and innovative methods that improve the health and safety of young people."

## Liberty Counsel

PO Box 540774

Orlando, FL 32854

800-671-1776

libertycounsel.org

"Liberty Counsel® is an international nonprofit litigation, education, and policy organization dedicated to advancing religious freedom, the sanctity of life, and the family since 1989, by providing pro bono assistance and representation on these and related topics. With offices in California, Florida, Virginia and Washington, DC, and an outreach in Israel, Liberty Counsel has hundreds of advocates around the world."

## MetLifeDefender.com

855-693-3637

"MetLife Defender combines real-time digital technology, highly trained cyber security experts and a four-pillar approach to offer comprehensive identity theft protection that can help stop threats before they occur." One of those four pillars is Online Child Protection. It's child safety features include:

- Highly specialized systems and software to detect cyberbullying activity on your children's social media pages including Facebook, Twitter and Instagram
- Cyber security experts who understand the difference between kids just being kids and a serious threat
- Time-sensitive alerts to notify you of any cyberbullies or predators
- Protection of your children's Social Security Numbers and notifications on any fraudulent activity or risks.

## Movieguide

4073 Mission Oaks Blvd.

Camarillo, CA 93012

805-383-2000

movieguide.org

"Located just outside of Los Angeles CA., MOVIEGUIDE®'s mission is to redeem the values of the entertainment industry, according to biblical principles, by influencing industry executives and artists.

MOVIEGUIDE® reviews all movies from a Christian perspective and how movies affect children at different stages of cognitive development."

**National Law Center for Children and Families**
501 West Broadway, Suite 1310
San Diego, CA 92101
703-548-5522
nationallawcenter.org
"The National Law Center for Children and Families (NLC) was formed in 1991 and has since served as an agent of change and education in the areas of child sexual exploitation. The NLC is proud to continue this service today in seminars and through its website, www.nationallawcenter.org. The NLC PROTECTS Seminar Series is an effort to train prosecutors, investigators and local government attorneys on the challenges involved in child sexual exploitation. The seminars feature experts on topics including child pornography investigation and prosecution, Internet forensics, on-line enticement investigation, human trafficking, sex offender management at the local level, the Adam Walsh Child Protection & Safety Act of 2006, and other child sexual exploitation issues. A seasonal newsletter, *The Enforcer*, and a law enforcement-only website are additional components of the Seminar Series."

## National Organization for Marriage

2029 K Street NW

Suite 300

Washington, DC 20006

888-894-3604

nationformarriage.org

"The National Organization for Marriage (NOM) is a nonprofit organization with a mission to protect marriage and the faith communities that sustain it. Founded in response to the growing need for an organized opposition to same-sex marriage in state legislatures, NOM serves as a national resource for marriage-related initiatives at the state and local level."

## Parents Television Council

707 Wilshire Blvd. #2075

Los Angeles, CA 90017

213-403-1300 or 800-882-6868

parentstv.org

"To protect children and families from graphic sex, violence and profanity in the media, because of their proven long-term harmful effects."

Note from Rebecca: This organization of some 1.3 million members is the most effective group I know of that is advocating for family-friendly entertainment. You can log on to their website to join a local chapter and receive free email updates about how to make a difference.

## Plugged In

8605 Explorer Dr.

Colorado Springs, CO 80920

800-A-FAMILY

pluggedinonline.com

A website offering reviews of a wide variety of movies, music, and
television shows to help parents make a more informed decision
about what their children should or shouldn't be watching and listening to. "Each month, Plugged In is visited more than 1 million
times by people looking for detailed information about what's really
in popular movies, videos, television episodes, songs and games.
Entertainment industry ratings only tell you so much. We go deeper,
diving into specific content and the meaning behind it. Our award-
winning website also offers news and blogs."

## Promise Keepers

866-PROMISE

promisekeepers.org

"Promise Keepers is a catalytic event for men, challenging them to
embrace their calling to lead their families, churches and communities in worship of, and in obedience to Jesus the Messiah. Through
powerful worship and anointed preaching, men are called out to
become everything that God has called them to be, and then to
return to their families, churches and communities with a commitment to hear and obey God's Word in the power of the Holy Spirit.

**The Rutherford Institute**

PO Box 7482

Charlottesville, VA 22906

434-978-3888

rutherford.org

"Founded in 1982 by constitutional attorney and author John W. Whitehead, The Rutherford Institute is a civil liberties organization that provides free legal services to people whose constitutional and human rights have been threatened or violated."

*Salvo*

4125 West Newport Ave.

Chicago, IL 60641

773-481-1090

salvomag.com

"*Salvo* is dedicated to debunking the cultural myths that have undercut human dignity, all but destroyed the notions of virtue and morality, and slowly eroded our appetite for transcendence. It also seeks to promote the Christian worldview."

Note from Rebecca: The reason I volunteer my time as a senior editor for *Salvo* is because my heart is breaking for young adults whose happiness is being robbed by cultural lies. *Salvo* shares truth in a bold, no-nonsense way—truth that will have an impact on their lives for the better, for all who will listen.

## Summit Ministries

PO Box 207

Manitou Springs, CO 80829

866-786-6483

summit.org

For more than fifty years Summit Ministries has been cultivating young leaders to transform culture with a biblical worldview. With more than forty thousand trained through its life-changing twelve-day programs in Colorado, Tennessee, and California, Summit graduates have risen to prominence in business, the military, politics, medicine, science, the arts, and academia. What makes Summit so powerful is the combination of world-class experts in worldview, apologetics, economics, ethics, and culture and a dynamic community that readies young adults to live out a fearless yet compassionate faith. Summit also features trusted resources for churches, Christian schools, and homeschools. You absolutely must get every young adult you know involved sometime between the ages of sixteen and twenty-one.

## Trail Life USA

10612 Augusta Rd.

Belton, SC 29627

321-247-7761

traillifeusa.com

Trail Life USA is a Christian adventure, character, and leadership program for young men. The K–12 program centers on outdoor experiences that build a young man's skills and allow him to grow on a personal level and as a role model and leader for his peers.

Participation in Trail Life USA is a journey established on timeless values derived from the Bible. Trail Life USA's vision is "to be the premier national character development organization for young men which produces Godly and responsible husbands, fathers, and citizens." Their mission is "to guide generations of courageous young men to honor God, lead with integrity, serve others, and experience outdoor adventure."

**United States Justice Foundation**
932 D Street, Suite 2
Ramona, CA 92065
760-788-6624
usjf.net
"The United States Justice Foundation is a nonprofit public interest, legal action organization dedicated to instruct, inform and educate the public on, and to litigate, significant legal issues confronting America."

**Women of Faith**
888-493-2484
womenoffaith.com
"Women of Faith has been encouraging women since 1996 with compelling stories, laugh-out-loud humor, heart-tugging music, rejuvenating worship, and more! Women of Faith events are produced by the world's largest producer of inspirational events for women, based in Plano, Texas. Through authentic connection with audiences, humor, and an atmosphere of encouragement and acceptance, world-class communicators deliver life-changing messages through high-quality programs in cities across North America."

**Worldview Academy**
PO Box 2918
Midland, TX 79702
432-618-0950 or 800-241-1123
worldview.org
"Worldview Academy is a non-denominational organization dedicated to helping Christians to think and to live in accord with a biblical worldview so that they will serve Christ and lead the culture."

**Young Life**
PO Box 520
Colorado Springs, CO 80901
877-438-9572
younglife.org
Young Life's mission is to introduce adolescents to Jesus Christ and help them grow in their faith by building relationships. Their amazing outreach, Capernaum, offers faith and relationship building for teens and young adults with disabilities.